DIVORCE CORP.

By

Joseph Sorge, with James Scurlock

Divorce (noun): the action or an instance of
legally dissolving a marriage

Corp. (noun) (abbreviation): a group of merchants or
traders united in a trade guild

ISBN: 978-0-9912831-0-1

Library of Congress Control Number: 2013958435

Printed in the United States of America.

DC Book LLC
PO Box 11480
Jackson, WY 83002
Tel: 307-739-8990
Fax: 307-739-8992
www.DivorceCorp.com

To the victims of the family courts who have lost precious time away from their children.

Table of Contents

Foreword

No, I'm not divorced. Married, happily, would best describe my wife and me. So when I was approached with a documentary on divorce, I began thinking about those in my life who had been through divorce and all of the accompanying stress they sometimes dealt with for years. At the same time, divorce seemed like familiar territory. I've spent three decades listening to people in a variety of personal crises. I know a lot about addiction and toxic relationships, as well as what it takes for people to heal and move on with their lives. Very little shocks me. But when I was asked to narrate the movie *Divorce Corp.*, I popped it into my DVD player, and was simply blown away.

If a hospital routinely made its patients sicker, it would be shut down. The doctors and nurses would be sued for malpractice and maybe even lose their licenses. Even the patients who seemed fine would have recourse—their own bill of rights, for starters, and hopefully the common sense to get a second opinion and see what previous patients had to say about their experiences, good or bad.

Family courts were envisioned in the late 1960s as hospitals for sick marriages. Each court was supposed to provide its own kind of rehab, making it easier for families to heal. These courts were even stocked with an ample supply of psychologists and psychiatrists who would diagnose their "patients" and deliver their "scientific" opinions as to the best course of action. Aside from these noble intentions, family courts are, in every other sense, the opposite of their medical counterparts. They and their practitioners, armies of lawyers, judges and "friends of the court," routinely leave families in more conflict than when they started. They also bankrupt moms and dads at an astonishing rate and engender an increasing amount of violence. Whatever the end result, the court's practitioners wash their hands and assure us that everything they do is automatically in the "best interests of the child," a catch-all phrase that allows them to quash criticism, oversight, and most of the constitutional rights we assume, like the rights to an attorney, an appeal, a fair and speedy trial, and even free speech. For the record, I believed this last right was absolute. But it is not available in family court.

I was also blown away by how much money is wasted on a ritual that might have seemed exotic a century ago but is now more common than not. Indeed, $50 billion a year is lost on divorce. A lot of good could be accomplished with that. At a time when most families cannot even afford to save a dollar, how could wiping out this much money possibly be in the best interest of their children, I wondered? And where could it all possibly go? Spoiler alert: while the top divorce lawyers make upwards of $1,000 an hour, they're just the beginning. The court can order a whole raft of complementary services, including five-figure psychological tests and "evaluations," which are all billed to the parents, who have no choice but to comply if they want to continue seeing their kids. Good parents probably consider any ransom a bargain, no matter how ruinous. Little wonder that some attorneys call children of divorced parents "little bags of money."

To borrow a clinical term, this may sound histrionic. If only that were true. Although, it's not that no one is talking about divorce, most people have no idea how broken the system really is until they go through it. And because half of marriages end up in family court, plenty of people are venting their nightmares in private. But the public mostly hears about celebrity divorces, exposed affairs, contested fortunes, private jets, plastic surgery, and who gets what vacation home. TMZ and *People Magazine* and the countless blogs love to show rich and attractive people acting their worst. What they tend not to do is examine the system that so often causes these people—and the less glossy average good person—to behave that way.

This book is about the family court system. The topic itself can be complex, especially its legal code, which has grown so convoluted that average citizens cannot hope to make sense of it all. What tend to be obvious are the conflicts of interest, involving a great deal of money changing hands, often between lawyers and judges. Family law is an industry whose clients often describe it as a racket. Its practitioners are rewarded (and sometimes punished) based on a carrot-and-stick code, enforced by coziness and nods and winks and *quid pro quos*. And, of course, money. After you finish this book, you may swear to never consider divorce (like I have), run to share this with your spouse (like I did), and you will certainly understand its title: *Divorce Corp.*

If you are considering divorce, put down whatever you're doing and read this book now. Happily married? Remember that divorce is not a mutual decision. Once one party initiates the process, both enter the system, as do any minor children, whose lives become subject to a judge-knows-best standard. From that point forward, what happens to you and your family is outside of your control. Where your kids go to school, what they eat, where they vacation, who they live with and when, what medications they should take, may all be decided by the court. Of course it's wonderful to have a pre-nup, but judges can (and do) toss them aside. And it's great to agree to behave like adults and swear off conflict and acrimony. But mediation only works if both parties—and the judge—can all agree. Keep in mind that Divorce Corp. is not fueled by peace, but by fighting: $50 billion worth, more or less.

I ended up recording the narration for the *Divorce Corp.* documentary, and I feel privileged to be part of this book. Humbled, also, by the many courageous people who have contributed their stories: the parents who questioned the court's competency or motives and lost their children, the mothers and fathers whose children are still under the court's thumb and risk retribution every time they step into court, and the husbands and wives who have everything to lose by angering a judge in a black robe who can always claim to know what is in the best interest of them and their children. These folks believe, as I do, that exposing the truth is the only way to shed light on the system, generate a public dialogue, and maybe even begin to heal the system.

I've always been concerned with what happens to American families. Every one of us should be. The simple truth is that some of our families are not well in this country and the family courts are not making them any better. We need healing and we're not getting it, even at $1,000 an hour and $50 billion a year. So, unless you want to move to another country, please don't consider yourself immune.

If you want to learn more, and maybe even join the discussion about how we can help make this work the way it was supposed to, please visit www.divorcecorp.com.

Dr. Drew Pinsky

Preface

*In criminal court, you see bad people on their best behavior;
in family court, you see good people at their worst.*
—*Anonymous*

IN THE FALL OF 2011, WE BEGAN PRODUCTION ON A DOCUMENTARY FILM
with the working title *Divorce Corp*. We were certainly aware that divorce
was more than an unpleasant fact of life for about half of American
families. We knew that family law, which had barely existed for most
of our country's history, had morphed into a gigantic industry over the
past several decades. We knew that some divorce lawyers had become
tabloid celebrities and that the custody battles of the rich and famous
were selling millions of magazines and fueling much of the blogosphere
(the *Huffington Post* even created a spinoff devoted to divorce). We knew
that the breakdown of the family unit had spawned dozens of cottage
industries, from "revenge surgery" to divorce insurance to $500 per
hour private judges.

In short, we did not consider ourselves naïve. One of us, in fact,
had suffered through a divorce and custody battle. The other had
just finished a book on a case known as the World Cup of Probate.
Nevertheless, what we would discover over the coming months—
largely from the mouths of divorce attorneys, judges, and litigants
themselves—shocked us. What we found was the last vestige of law-
lessness in America. A dark corner of the judicial system where fiefdoms and tyrants still thrive, where the supreme law of the land is
routinely ignored, where children are taken hostage for profit, and
where lives are destroyed as a matter of course.

Even more disturbing was the realization that none of this was
necessary, that there are places elsewhere in the civilized world where
adults are trusted with dissolving their relationships and moving on

with their lives, cultures where men and women and fathers and moth-ers are treated as equals and miraculously manage to get divorced with-out attorneys or judges. In these cultures, we discovered, none of the ills of the American family court system exist. And yet, everywhere we traveled, we heard the same chorus from those who ply their trade in family court: yes, the system is punishing and draconian and sometimes horrific, but that's because people just refuse to get along. However, we found the opposite to be true.

So this is, at heart, an indictment of the American family court sys-tem, a system that we have now studied at length. We are not academics or attorneys, but we have interviewed the top practitioners, examined the most influential cases, and spoken to many of those who have tried, often at unfathomable harm to themselves and their families, to speak out and somehow make a difference. Anyone who has endured a family court case knows that the codes are mind-bogglingly complex, and we are well-aware that defenders of the system will hide behind the web that they and others before them have spun in order to claim that out-siders simply cannot understand what these insiders do and why they must do it. What these defenders of the system may fail to appreciate is that the litigants, who are seldom—if ever—listened to in family court, know far more than the insiders do about the court's shortcomings. The litigants may not know the Latin terms or be able to quote paragraphs of the code from memory, but they know something far more impor-tant: *they know what it all means because they deal with the consequences of the court's dysfunction every day.* Sadly, the same level of understanding cannot be claimed by many of the judges and attorneys who practice family law five days a week.

That we had opened a Pandora's box became clear during our first few interviews. There would be far too many important subjects to be addressed in a 90-minute film. We therefore decided to write a book. Still, distilling a subject as vast and as disparate as family law—each state legislature writes its own family code and each court within that state may establish its own rules—into a substantial book was a daunting task. We decided at the start not to go down the rabbit hole of any particular case or to concern ourselves with the typical "he said/she said" issues that are part and parcel of every divorce case. Instead, we set out to show how the *system itself* behaved. What we found was a system that encourages battle, festers acrimony, and prolongs the process far longer than necessary. The result is a $50 billion windfall for members of what we refer to as Divorce Corp.— a vast and decentralized network of judges, courts, lawyers, psychologists, consultants, private investigators, and others who make their living from the family code.

So here is that Pandora's box presented in stories, interviews, and finally, solutions. Nothing in this book should be interpreted as legal advice. Instead, we provide an expose of an industry that allegedly provides sound legal advice. We conducted interviews in more than a dozen states, although a substantial portion of our subjects live in California, where no-fault divorce began and where nearly five decades later the State Auditor is battling an out-of-control family court system. Although each state adopted its own system, the California family law system was the model and thus its complexity and absurdity are apparent in every family court of every state in the union. But sometimes the most complex diseases are blessed with the simplest cures. Such, we believe, is the case with Divorce Corp. A better path awaits us, if we would only pivot and choose it rather than the familiar one. But before we present that path, we offer something rarely seen in family court itself: the evidence.

Prologue:
Five Perspectives

This is the Court of Chancery, which has its decaying houses and its blighted lands in every shire, which has its worn-out lunatic in every madhouse and its dead in every churchyard, which has its ruined suitor with his slipshod heels and threadbare dress borrowing and begging through the round of every man's acquaintance, which gives to monied might the means abundantly of wearying out the right, which so exhausts finances, patience, courage, hope, so overthrows the brain and breaks the heart, that there is not an honourable man among its practitioners who would not give—who does not often give—the warning, "Suffer any wrong that can be done you rather than come here!"
—Charles Dickens, Bleak House

THE WHISTLEBLOWER

Emily Gallup's eyes light up when she talks about her former life. A small-town girl from a devoutly Christian family in Northern California, Gallup's red curls, freckles, and deep dimples still cause her to get carded when she orders a glass of wine at a restaurant. But the veneer of cuteness belies both a determination and intellect that earned her a scholarship to Stanford, where she first studied psychology and fell in love with the idea of making a living by helping people conquer their most personal problems. After Stanford, it was Chico State, two hours' drive from her hometown of Grass Valley, for her master's degree, then back home to Nevada County, a bucolic patch of Northern California dotted with old silver mining towns. That's where she settled into the practice of psychology in an office nestled among tall pine trees. Like most psychologists, Gallup ended up doing some work for the local family court in Nevada City, the town next door and the county seat. It didn't take long for the court's director of mediation to realize Gallup's passion and talent. An older man looking for someone to carry the torch, he soon hired her full-time at the court as one of a handful of child custody mediators.

Gallup was thrilled. Her energy and idealism, once channeled into evangelical purposes, could now be used in a distinctly practical and non-ideological way. Her work would be inherently meaningful—what could be more important than fostering a healthy environment for children in the midst of crisis? And if she could persuade parents to reach a child sharing agreement without litigating, a positive outcome could be achieved in hours.

Nevada County is one of a handful of "recommending" counties in California, meaning that the custody mediator not only tries to bring the parents to agree on a custody schedule for sharing time with the children, but if the mediation fails, makes a recommendation to the judge, who then makes the final decision as to custody. The "recommending" part of mediation has raised eyebrows in the legal community because mediation is supposed to be confidential. In exchange for leaving their attorneys at the door, the parties can trust that whatever they say in the session cannot be used against them later on. Otherwise, they might use mediation to jockey for position in court or to convince the mediator to make a favorable recommendation to the judge, rather than as a means to compromise.

Gallup was the perfect sales woman, the kind of person others tend to trust immediately. Despite her youthful, almost girlish looks, she has an intensity that informs people that they matter. According to several of her former clients, she was the first person they encountered in the divorce process—including their own lawyers—who seemed to listen before taking sides. Gallup tended to earn their respect quickly, even if they didn't get exactly what they wanted out of the mediation. On one occasion, a father whose visitation request she denied later thanked her for taking the time to explain her reasoning. She made it a point to make sure that her "clients," as she called them, understood why she felt the way she did. And even though the form they'd signed made it unnecessary, Gallup would tell them what she planned to recommend to the judge. Gallup was so effective and so qualified that the director of the mediation department publicly announced that she would become the next director of mediation in Nevada County Family Court as soon as he retired.

But Gallup never got the job. Instead, she was passed up without explanation in favor of a much older woman who lived hundreds of miles away and was known for falling asleep during mediations. When Gallup expressed her disappointment, the director made a vague comment about her not being ready and promised that the appointment of the older woman was temporary. Why such an important job would be doled out on a temporary basis to someone who only worked in the court part time, and why the process had to be so opaque, was never explained. Gallup was, however, told that she was not fast enough.

Although Gallup dug into statistics compiled by California's court administrator and discovered that she was above average in both speed and effectiveness, the Court insisted that she was throwing a wrench in a well-oiled machine. In Nevada County, mediators were allotted barely 15 minutes to talk with parents before deciding what should be done with them and their children. In spite of her overall above-average speed, when Gallup tried to spend more time on challenging cases, she was scolded for being too slow. When she attempted to verify the violent backgrounds of fathers and the veracity of mothers, she was accused of being obsessive and biased. Her boss even admonished her for looking into a parent's conviction for sex crimes, calling it "irrelevant" to the custody determination.

Gallup butted heads with the court on other issues as well. The court instructed its mediators to urge parents to sign a form that allowed the judge to decide custody matters without the parents present. Most of the parents, even attorneys, would sign the form with nothing more than a glance. They assumed that signing was a prerequisite to mandatory mediation. They assumed they didn't have a choice. Gallup watched as the form was used to share confidential information with the judge and to make decisions about custody essentially in the judge's chambers. She witnessed a judge make clinical diagnoses of parents and children in the courtroom, while Gallup's boss made custody decisions for the judge. And when parents resisted, Gallup held her tongue as the same judge, whom Gallup and colleagues suspected of drug and alcohol abuse as well as borderline personality disorder, held the specter of hugely expensive private psychological evaluations over their heads or threatened to send their children to foster care if the parents failed to tow the line.

The Nevada County court had coined a name for their way of doing things: the "emergency room" (ER) model. The ER model was a way to move a lot of people through the court very quickly, Gallup says, of meeting benchmarks and quotas for processing cases and out-sourcing work to friends of the court. Like in an emergency room, only the immediate, urgent problem was handled (refusal to allow visitation, support payment not made, etc.), but there was no time to explore the root causes for these emergencies and structure a more meaningful family plan. Indeed, both Gallup's boss and the judge felt that their ER model should be the model for family courts in the entire state, but she felt otherwise. "I didn't understand it," Gallup says. "If a patient goes to the hospital with a broken arm and they merely put a Band-Aid on some skin scrapes and tell them to come back in a couple of weeks, that patient is just going to come back sicker and sicker." Gallup was being ordered to apply Band-Aids that required families to return over and over again rather than facilitate agreements that would stick. But within the confines of the ER model, she wasn't given enough time to do more.

Had Gallup been able to leave her professional problems at the office, she might have waited out her new boss's retirement; but Gallup, who had lived in Nevada County, where everyone knows everyone else, all her life, was confronted by the ripples of the court's behavior on a daily basis. The breaking point came when she read about a wife who had been murdered by her ex-husband with a nail gun. Gallup knew the case. The wife had come to their courthouse less than a week before, begging for protection and describing her husband's threats in vivid detail. But Gallup's boss had dismissed the woman as hysterical and con-vinced her to go home without a protective order. Having witnessed, but not challenged, the court's dismissing of serious charges based on whims and hunches, Gallup felt personally culpable when she read the news of the woman's murder.

She soon came to realize that her superiors had long used a lie to absolve themselves of any responsibility: there will always be unhappy parents because family court always resulted in at least one "loser," and the losers always complain that they are victims. So instead of the court working with families, the judges and lawyers and even the mediators had created an "us versus them" system. The court knew what was best and it was their job to shove it down "their" throats. And if "they" complained, "they" were obstructionists or whiny or vexatious or all three. But Gallup now began to realize that the opposite was true. Most parents didn't want to be obstructions any more than they wanted to be victims. They expected a judicious decision that would allow all parties to move on with their lives.

Things got even worse for those in family court in Nevada County. "Us versus them" had institutionalized false assumptions and bad decisions. For example, with their children and life savings in the balance, parents rarely complained for fear of the court's retribution. But Gallup's superiors misconstrued this fear as respect for their superhuman powers of perception, and because they assumed that the parents had such respect for their decisions, evidence was irrelevant. Why verify anything if its only purpose would be to slow down the revolving door of litigants in and out of the courtroom?

"The director of mediation and the judge believed that they had this intuitive ability to assess what was going on with a family," Gallup says, the corners of her mouth sinking downward. "My boss told me that a good mediator could size up any family in less than 15 minutes. She bragged that she herself didn't even have to read the files. Now I like to think I'm pretty intuitive, but that's just a recipe for introducing your own biases into a case."

With the aid of an experienced commissioner in the adjoining court, Gallup began challenging the emergency room model. Her first target was her new boss's rule that mediators not run criminal background checks on parents. Gallup considered this a direct violation of the California family code, which stated that mediators "shall" run the checks when allegations of criminal activity are made. When the commissioner provided Gallup with the section of the family code that mandated the checks, Gallup's boss found out and was incensed, admonishing Gallup for going "outside the chain of command"—a remarkably thin-skinned response considering the court's stated open-door policy. Suddenly, Gallup's once-stellar performance reviews began to take on a negative tone. She heard criticism that she was abrasive and acrimonious—not a "team" player. When these reviews were used to deny her a raise, Gallup filed a grievance, a move that required the court to investigate whether she had been the victim of retaliation for asking the advice of a commissioner who worked in the very same courthouse. The matter was handed over to the court's CEO, a former marine with no legal background named Sean Metroka, who, after what appeared to be a cursory investigation, quickly determined that her complaint had no merit.

Gallup smelled a setup. "He didn't interview one person on my list of character witnesses," she recalls. "He interviewed the bailiff instead." Gallup appealed for arbitration and dug in her heels. The court hired a former partner at a big corporate law firm in San Francisco to hear Gallup's arbitration case. But in the middle of arbitration, Metroka fired her, ostensibly for showing her attorney some notes that her boss had written about her job performance. The stakes were now raised higher than Gallup could have imagined. She was not only accused of being irascible but of breaching confidentiality! Her reputation was on the line.

Once arbitration began, Gallup's character witnesses and co-workers were interviewed. They testified that Gallup had wanted to do her job too well, that she had insisted on following the law rather than the ER model. She was resented for gumming up her bosses' machine. More unforgivably, perhaps, she was advising parents of their rights and thus threatening the court's previously unbridled control. She was, to use a popular term, being transparent.

The last time Gallup stepped through the door of the county courthouse, an imposing, six-story art deco building that dwarfs Nevada City's quaint downtown, she was threatened with arrest by the same bailiffs who used to greet her every morning with warm smiles. Metroka, the CEO, claimed that Gallup was trespassing, even though the courthouse is a public building. Gallup countered that she was protecting parents' constitutional rights by warning them not to sign the form that allowed mediators to make recommendations to the judge without the parents being present—a clear violation of their due process rights since there was no way that parents could either know what the mediator was recommending or challenge the information upon which it was based. Metroka was unmoved. Fortunately, Gallup had brought along a reporter from the local newspaper, *The Union*. When Metroka ill-advisedly also evicted the reporter from the courthouse, Gallup's cause began to receive statewide attention.

Over the past three years Gallup has exhausted herself and her family's financial resources trying to get her reputation back. In several depositions and interviews, she has described how the Nevada County court resembled the Court of Chancery detailed in Charles Dickens' *Bleak House*, a place so Byzantine and inscrutable that one prominent journalist has termed it "American jurisprudence through the looking glass," a parallel universe where normal assumptions rarely apply. In the process of pursuing justice for herself, Gallup has pulled back the curtain on a small court from which the results of bad policy and presumptions of infallibility have rippled out among thousands of families.

Not long after being fired, Gallup founded a court reform group to reach out to those whom the court had hurt. But it was when a member of the local family-law bar association reached out to *her* that Gallup experienced the most disturbing revelation of her ordeal. Despite the court routinely dismissing her complaints as entirely without basis, and despite being told repeatedly by the administration that as a non-lawyer she had no idea what she was talking about, the county's own family bar association had raised almost the exact same concerns in a letter to the court several years earlier. When she saw their list of concerns, Gallup was shocked. She might have written it herself. It was almost identical to her list of complaints. But equally shocking was the court's cavalier response to the bar's letter, a few terse paragraphs from a presiding judge that treated violations of due process and the destruction of families as technicalities and intimated that those who dared bring them to the attention of the court were violating the chain of command.

Gallup has learned the hard way that everyone, even the lawyers and judges, seem well aware that something is very, very wrong with family courts; but she has also learned that even to set forth a modest proposal like her own results in being treated as the enemy. In reaction to criticism, the wagons circle around the judge, around the absolute power that has gone unchecked for nearly four decades. And virtually no one, certainly not the lowly employees whose livelihood depends on the court or the litigants whose children and bank account can be plundered at will, dare stand up to question it.

THE INSIDER

Sorrell Trope cracks a grin as he recalls starting his namesake law firm with his older brother nearly seven decades ago. The nonagenarian super-lawyer is dressed in a dark tailored suit and a silk tie. Eight floors below, tucked in a prime parking space seen by every visitor to this office building on L.A.'s Westside, is his polished Bentley sedan that's worth many times more than the average American family's yearly income. Trope has been at the divorce game longer than any lawyer in the country. His clients stretch from Cary Grant to Britney Spears. His fee has grown to $950 an hour ("I think I'm worth it," he deadpans), and it's a fee that clients like Frank McCourt, owner of the Los Angeles Dodgers, seem happy to pay. McCourt's divorce from his wife Jamie cost an estimated $30 million in legal fees, but thanks in part to Trope's negotiating, he held on to the Dodgers, which he recently sold for more than $2 billion. McCourt's wife hired the most expensive attorney in Hollywood to challenge the settlement, but a judge promptly dismissed her suit.

"I used to drive by a wedding and think, 'That's inventory!'" Trope says of his early years in the business. Among his peers, Trope is known for his razor-sharp mind and command of every detail of a case. He was perhaps the first attorney to recognize that divorce was a business, and with more money flowing through family courts now than all other courts combined, his decision to get into family law has proven prescient. But while plying his trade in family court has made Trope a very wealthy man, introduced him to countless celebrities, and even handed him a leading role in deciding the ownership of professional sports' most storied franchise, he can barely hide his disgust at how divorce has evolved (from a relatively straightforward affair where mom got the kids, the house, and alimony—at least until she remarried—and dad kept the business) into a battle royal over money—including a perverse outcome whereby the less you see of your children the more you pay in child support.

Trope is not a fan of so-called guideline child support, which directly links the percentage of child time that a parent is awarded to the amount of money they pay or receive. From his oversized corner decorated with Franklin Delano Roosevelt memorabilia, the old man can peer over the 405 Freeway to the Holmby Hills, Beverly Hills, Bel Air, and the Hollywood Hills, where wealthy residents and their marital troubles have provided a steady stream of income for Trope & Trope. He has an equally impressive view of Century City, home to several of his prominent adversaries, including Dennis Wasser, lawyer to Steven Spielberg and Tom Cruise, and Wasser's daughter, Laura. The entertainment press has dubbed Laura Wasser the "Disso-Queen," a reference to dissolution, the softer term family courts began using instead of divorce beginning in the early 1970s. Laura represents both Maria Shriver, the wife of action-star-turned-governor-and-back-to-action-star Arnold Schwarzenegger and reality sensation Kim Kardashian. The Wassers reportedly each charge even more than Trope. Trope and the Wassers were recently featured in *Vanity Fair* Magazine as Hollywood's top family lawyers, a distinction that Trope does not seem eager to share with anyone.

In the past year, Trope has represented everyone from the world's number-one pop princess to an aspiring Russian musician who also happened to be Mel Gibson's mistress and "baby mama." He is an equal opportunity lawyer and he doesn't mind taking the Bentley for a spin downtown to the courthouse. "If you pay our rate," Trope says dryly, "we'll show up." How to fix the system? "Go back to the way it was," he replies immediately. Other suggestions are met with succinct rebuttals: "Ridiculous!"; "Are you kidding me?"; "I don't know how else to explain it to you!"; "If you give people an arena, they'll fight, won't they?"

Trope does admit that some of his clients become so entrenched in their positions, especially when it comes to the big money custody battles, that they lose sight of what they are actually fighting over. "I don't even think they know that they're doing it," he says with a shrug, and he must be referring to the damage they do their children because surely they notice his bills. What he doesn't mention is that, notwithstanding the mailing of those six and seven-figure bills, none of their trusted legal advisors and no one from the court ever seems to discourage those poor souls from fighting. And why should they? The fighting fuels a multi-billion dollar industry that has defied several recessions, a drop in the number of divorces, and even the rise of the double-earner and gender-neutral household.

Indeed, family court seems less like a place where justice is dispensed amid the blinding, sanitizing light of truth than it does a casino: a hermetically sealed environment where customers stream in, sit down in the dusky light and feed money into the machines until they've spent it all, and then borrow even more and gamble that away too. A place where the only rule is that the house always wins.

After speaking for an hour, Trope, the man who has argued thousands of cases, whose gift of persuasion has made him a legend, apologizes for his ineloquence when trying to describe the place where he does business. "I wish I could explain it more clearly," he says. "It just sounds like words coming out of my mouth."

THE BEREFT

Danielle Malmquist, a petite and pretty Asian woman in her early thirties, is a minor celebrity in Memphis, Tennessee. She and ex-husband Shem, an executive pilot for FedEx, are engaged in the city's most bitter and longest custody battle over their two sons. The fees for three psychological evaluations alone topped $50,000, and attorneys have cost both sides more than ten times that amount. Once solidly upper-middle class, both Malmquists have seriously considered filing for bankruptcy—and the battle is far from over. Though the marriage lasted only four months, the divorce is now nearing its fifth anniversary with no end in sight. Ironically, there has recently been a respite of sorts, but only after the judge labeled Danielle Malmquist, who has been forced to represent herself due to lack of funds, a "vexatious" litigant. This is a favored tactic of judges who become tired of reading motions penned by amateurs. There is no equivalent term for members of the legal profession, which means that Danielle can resume filing as many motions as she chooses as long as she hires another lawyer. But she can no longer afford to do so.

Yet this is not what makes Malmquist unique, at least not in the parallel universe of high-conflict custody battles. Sitting at the dining table of a family friend's home south of San Francisco, she describes how her ordeal began while she was still laid up in a Memphis hospital recovering from the birth of her second child. According to Danielle, her infant son was taken from her by her husband and never returned.

Shortly thereafter, she learned that her husband had filed for divorce and that he wanted her to sign a custody agreement in order to see her infant son. A short while later, she received a cold call from a random (or so it seemed) attorney offering her services. How this lawyer knew that her husband had just filed for divorce remains a mystery. Malmquist now believes that the attorney had access to the courthouse filings on a daily or even an hourly basis to pursue for leads.

Malmquist's new attorney convinced her to sign a temporary custody order that allowed her to get back the infant, who needed to be breastfed, but to give up custody of the older son. The deal had a Solomon-esque logic, but rather than divide the babies in half, the lawyers had simply given one to the mom and one to dad with liberal visitation for both parents to see the other child. The temporary arrangement worked for eight months until, according to Malmquist, days before their first divorce hearing, her ex-husband's attorney joined the judge's re-election campaign committee. Although campaign contributions by a lawyer or a litigant to a judge do not disqualify a judge from hearing a case, joining the election campaign committee of a judge will typically require the judge to recuse (disqualify) him or herself. Malmquist's judge did in fact disqualify herself, and a second judge was assigned to the case.

According to Malmquist, she then learned that the second judge had once worked as a lawyer in the same law firm as her ex-husband's lawyer. Malmquist also learned that the same law firm was making campaign contributions to the second judge. She became concerned this was all a setup.

Malmquist wrote to the Tennessee Ethics Commission about the potential conflict of interest, but nothing happened beyond her second judge becoming curt towards her in court. She worried that the ethics committee might have sent him a copy of her letter, which, in fact, they had. She filed a motion for the judge to recuse himself. But, strange as it may seem, in many states judges themselves decide whether they believe they are biased or not. He refused to recuse himself.

Sensing that the odds against her were growing, Malmquist went to the media regarding conflicts of interest between judges and the lawyers appearing before them in court. The story was broadcast on Fox TV news in Memphis, publicity that further infuriated her judge. Her judge responded to an extreme: he took her two sons away from her.

Malmquist filed an appeal, which was unsuccessful. She filed additional motions asking her judge to reconsider his rulings, but he became annoyed by her repeated requests and issued a court order banning Malmquist from filing any more papers with the court. In short, not only could she not see her two boys, but she was no longer allowed to even *ask* the court if she could see them.

Eighteen agonizing months passed, her boys growing up without her. She had lost the two most precious people in her life, and out of desperation and in defiance of the court order, she filed another motion asking to see her boys. In response, her judge ordered her sent to jail. Malmquist was shocked. She had had no lawyer and there had been no jury, no witnesses, no cross-examination, and no evidence.

But the cycle has since repeated itself three times: Malmquist gets out of jail, files another motion with the court, and the judge sends her back to jail. Without her boys, she says, her life has little meaning or purpose, and so what more can she lose? Malmquist does not regret her decision to fight, but the vortex of judicial indifference that has consumed her once promising life inspires a surreal bitterness, as though she still cannot believe what is happening. "I've not committed a crime," she says, wiping away tears. "I've not broken any laws. But I've been to jail three times now, just for wanting to see my boys."

THE PEACEMAKER

A few blocks down Wilshire Boulevard from Trope's office, in an older building with fewer floors and a modest courtyard, are the offices of another legendary figure in family court: Forrest "Woody" Mosten. Mosten, a gentle man maybe 20 years younger than Trope, sports a simple blue blazer and does not wear a tie. He smiles often. His office is a desk and a round table with four chairs. There is no conference room, only a children's playroom, and his secretary leaves before he does. He does not charge retainers, which is unheard of in the family law business where lawyers who represent the middle class mostly complain about unpaid bills. Mosten says that he smiles on his way to the office, also unheard of in the world of divorce professionals.

As a UCLA law school student in the early 1970s, Mosten helped found the nation's first storefront law firm, which advertised divorce services on television for low fees. Now Mosten, whose high-conflict mediation practice has counted Roy Disney as a client, refuses to enter a courtroom. He even objects to family court verbiage. "Custody," he says, "is for prisoners. Not children." It's the kind of one-liner that gets clients to pay attention. Mosten estimates that of the 250 or so issues faced by divorcing couples, 90-95% are never really in dispute. "Most people are not conflictual when they walk into court," he says. The system goads them into a fight because that's how courts work. Then, he says, it punishes them financially, emotionally and spiritually—more than they could have ever imagined when they first walked through those heavy doors.

Unlike Emily Gallup in family court mediation in Nevada County, Mosten is free to take as much time at his work as necessary. Breaks for the clients during the mediation process are critical, he says, but more important is that his clients know that *they*, and not he or any government authority figure, are in control of their lives and their families. Mosten has been known to lay a gentle hand on clients who have become visibly agitated and remind parents constantly that, although their children will in fact judge them, they will judge them not by how much money they win but by how they handle this conflict. His services do not come cheap, and he knows that most families cannot afford them. So his latest innovation is called "unbundling"—mothers and fathers (he does not use the term "litigants" and certainly not "petitioners and respondents") can hire a lawyer for a specific hearing rather than keep an expensive law firm on retainer. But those fees, too, must be paid, and they start in the hundreds per hour. When he represents clients in "Collaborative Law", Mosten and the opposing divorce lawyer sign a contract disqualifying them from ever going to court for their clients. This means that if litigation starts, the lawyers are fired. With no incentive to fight in court, 85% of families who use Collaborative Law never step foot into the courtroom

Ultimately, whatever agreement that Mosten or any private mediator is able to broker between ex-husbands and ex-wives will be subject to approval by a family court judge. And if that agreement involves custody or child support, it may be re-opened and re-argued and re-adjudicated (or "modified" as the court puts it) at any time, no matter what the agreement states and no matter if one party objects to the lack of closure. In family court, it only takes one to tango. So, even within a non-confrontational, mediated divorce, the "shadow of the law," as one of Mosten's friends in the business puts it, looms large.

The egregiousness of dealing with the family court system is in fact a selling point for mediators. Mosten's most effective weapon in getting his clients to *yes* is the threat that he will wash his hands of them and send them off to a place as unharmonious as family court. And, he says, he is unabashed in using the tactic. "The threat of a family court battle," Mosten says, his voice suddenly grave, "is like Armageddon."

THE HOUSE OF FRANKENSTEIN

This book is about vicious cycles and the pall that family law has cast over our country. It is about rich and poor, black and white, young and old, liberal and conservative, and now in some states, gay and straight. It is about celebrities in Hollywood forced to pay their wives child support even though the wives have no custody of the children, and it is about a poor father in the Midwest who sits in jail for daring to criticize the judge who took his young daughters away from him (and their father away from them). It is about a Los Angeles businesswoman forced to pay thousands of dollars for a psychiatric evaluation by a controversial psychiatrist in order to determine whether or not she is a fit parent for her own child, and about a housewife in Dallas ordered to pay her wealthy husband hundreds of dollars every month when she can barely afford to provide shelter for their children. It is about a second wife in Boston who must work two jobs in order to keep her husband out of jail and to keep his first wife in the lifestyle to which she became accustomed. It is about a former NFLer in Wyoming forced to pay a half million dollars to his ex-wife's attorneys after she reopened their divorce case, one that was supposedly final in the 1970s. It is about a system run amok, one of the last fiefdoms left in our culture, a place so corrupted by power and money that Charles Dickens himself would be hard pressed to find adjectives bleak enough to adequately convey the current state of affairs. And it is about a system that affects every one of us every day, whether we come from a broken home or an intact one, whether we are single or coupled, male or female, and whether we plan to be married some day or not.

Roughly half of all marriages now end in divorce. How those families are dissolved ripples outward and leaves an impression on the culture as a whole. The statistics on children raised by single parents are stark, and it seems a given that any child thrown in the middle of a legal dispute between warring parents would suffer all kinds of damage. We now know that divorce is the third most-cited cause of bankruptcy, and we surmise that the threat of ruinous and unpredictable litigation is a major reason that both the marriage rate and the birth rate are sinking. We also know that a system that consumes its own, like a house divided against itself, cannot stand. But in order to understand why the family courts must be dismantled, how to accomplish that and what to replace them with requires a journey in time, from an equally unjust past to the present. Although we may think that the family courts were always there, in reality they are just a modern legal invention, a four decades-old experiment that may have begun with the best intentions but whose design, as we will see, was fatally flawed.

Armageddon, indeed.

Part I

Birth of an Industry

Divorce has rather suddenly become big business. In a great many cities the number of divorce cases filed annually exceeds the number of all other civil actions combined.
—Judge Paul W. Alexander, 1952

There's an old saying that, 'You get as much justice as you can afford.' And most people can't afford any justice at all.
—Gloria Allred, attorney

1 | The Legal Landscape

We're gonna fight you. And even if you win, you're gonna think that you lost.
—Gerald Nissenbaum, attorney

COST/BENEFIT

During his long and occasionally controversial tenure as the presiding judge in a New Jersey family court, Thomas Zampino managed thousands of attorneys arguing everything from who should pay for a child's private education to who got the family dog. Zampino is a big, jovial man with a peach-colored tan and a boyish grin that belies the inestimable conflict and heartbreak he's witnessed over the years. He recalls one day when, looking over the courtroom from the bench, he totaled up the cost of the legal representation before him at $27,000 per hour—for a single case. He once tried, he says, to limit the attorney's fees in a particular case to $50,000 on each side in order to save the child's college fund, but to no avail. The lawyers sued for four times that amount and an appeals court let them have it.

"I tell people," Zampino says, "You are spending the money that you would use for your children's college education for the college education of your lawyers' children." But in the United States, judges are not allowed to dispense legal advice and rarely mediate as they used to. They are supposed to be referees, not peacemakers. So husbands and wives do not receive their legal counsel from an impartial observer in a black robe but from an advocate who is being paid by the hour to press their case as aggressively and for as long as they can.

Zampino recalls a divorce trial in which he sat listening to an expert witness testifying to the value of a marital asset. When the witness estimated the asset at $60,000, Zampino raised an eyebrow and interrupted. He had previously been informed that the witness was being paid approximately $70,000 for his testimony. "Why on earth would you charge $70,000," he asked the man from the bench, "when you know that the most your client could possibly get from this asset is half of $60,000—less than half of your fee?"

The expert witness shrugged and pointed to his client at the lawyer's table. "Because she wanted me to," he said.

BLANK CHECKS

Divorce attorneys are accountable to their clients, at least in theory. Each party has the right to inspect the bills issued by their attorney and to terminate the services of that attorney if they feel underrepresented or overcharged. If the client is sophisticated enough to know the limits of what their attorney must do to accomplish the core objectives versus over-working the case and billing excessively, the client can try to limit the attorney's activities. But most divorce clients have never been involved in litigation and so place their trust in their attorney's view of what needs to be done rather than plotting strategy and tactics. Attorneys can be sued in most types of courts for over-working a case with the intent to harass the opponent—a cause of action known as malicious prosecution.[1] But they cannot be sued for malicious prosecution in the family courts of certain states, even if they pursue a frivolous or fraudulent claim with the sole purpose of harassing or intimidating the opponent.[2] In California, the malicious prosecution cause of action has been eliminated entirely, allegedly to "reduce the amount of litigation" that can result from family law cases.

---

1 An action for damages brought by one against whom a civil suit or criminal proceeding has been unsuccessfully commenced without probable cause and for a purpose other than that of bringing the alleged offender to justice.

2 See Bidna v. Rosen (1993) 19 Cal. App. 4th.

But attorneys *can* be sued for not being aggressive enough (ironically, considered malpractice). So with no penalty for over-litigating and a potential penalty for under-litigating, the attorney's financial interests are not always aligned with their client's financial interests.

If this were the only disconnect between a client's interests and the attorney's, the lack of financial controls might not be so problematic. At least the expense would be borne by the party who was too unsophisticated or too selfish to delineate their interests from their lawyer's. But unlike all other forms of litigation, the billings of both parties' attorneys are viewed together by the court and are usually paid from the joint marital assets. Consider the hypothetical case of Martin and Alison, who own a house, two cars, and some personal property with a combined worth of $100,000 after their debts are paid off. This $100,000 will be used to pay both of their attorneys. If Alison's attorney billed $20,000 and Martin's attorney billed $50,000, the family court judge will add the two bills together and subtract the $70,000 from the $100,000, leaving them $30,000 to split down the middle.

Why wouldn't a family court judge split the $100,000 into two $50,000 amounts and then subtract each side's legal fees from their respective $50,000? Martin's attorney might claim that representing Martin's interests required more investigation than required by Alison's attorney. Alison might have owned a small business that required Martin's attorney to do more investigative work, for example, whereas Alison's attorney might only have needed to review Martin's pay stubs and credit card statements. Or Martin's attorney might claim, accurately or inaccurately, that Alison and her attorney were difficult to work with, perhaps by withholding information or waiting until special motions needed to be filed before cooperating, necessitating more work. Thus family court judges tend to view the combined legal work as a joint debt, and so they subtract the cost of this debt from the marital assets before splitting the remainder.

But under many circumstances, there is no remainder. The joint marital assets are not sufficient to pay both parties' legal bills. In that event, the family court judge can look for separate (non-marital) assets and invade those separate assets to pay the attorneys. For example, if one party received a gift or an inheritance from a relative, those assets are considered separate property. Or if one party had a significant amount of savings prior to the marriage, those savings would be considered separate property. What if, for example, our hypothetical couple's $100,000 of joint marital assets was not sufficient to pay both parties' attorneys because Martin's attorney billed $120,000 and Alison's attorney billed $30,000? If Alison had entered the marriage with some savings, let's say $150,000—money that by all rights should be hers alone—the family court judge could use Alison's separate property to pay the remaining legal bills. The judge could order the sale of real estate, investment securities, or any asset that Alison owns separately. Even if Alison had been trying to keep her legal bills to a minimum, she has no power to limit what Martin's attorney does. And once Martin realizes that the $100,000 of joint marital assets has been used up to pay legal bills, Martin has no incentive to stop his attorney from consuming Alison's separate property. If Martin is feeling particularly hurt or vindictive for some reason, he might even encourage his attorney to over-work the case to leave Alison with nothing after the divorce: the scorched earth approach. Ironically, the financial interests of these two people, once fused upon marriage, are now totally undermined by the court's willingness to invade separate property. The system itself instigates a financial conflict of interest, not so ironically resulting in a financial gain for the attorneys.

There is another reason it might make economic sense for one party to consume the marital assets in order to repeatedly go back to court to see what else a judge might award. Marital assets are only one part of the equation in family court, and quite possibly the smaller part since they are distributed only once. Not so for alimony or child support, which could be paid for 20 or more years, or even a lifetime. If the payer party makes a substantial income, the value of the alimony and child support payments over time could easily surpass one half the value of the joint marital assets. Many couples, especially younger ones, have not saved much and the value of the joint marital assets is modest. One could accuse the recipient spouse of being greedy or even resentful, but to call that person irrational would be inaccurate. The law and the court conveniently provide a financial incentive to spend the modest marital assets on legal fees in an effort to achieve the largest alimony and child support award possible. And if the provider spouse has separate property that would not otherwise be split upon divorce, but that the court can invade to pay the recipient spouse's legal fees, why not go to extreme measures to convince the court that the provider has substantial future earning potential, in hopes of winning the largest potential alimony and/or child support award?

On the surface, one might think that any rational observer with the power to do so, which in this case is the court and only the court, would penalize a litigant for being vindictive or for squandering the martial assets. After all, the marital assets will be needed to create two households where there was once just one. But in fact family court judges do not prevent the marital assets from being depleted. More often than not, it is quite the opposite.

It might seem obvious that there is something fundamentally wrong with making divorce a far more convoluted and expensive process than marriage, but neither issue is addressed by any family code nor is trying to make the length or cost of a divorce proportional to the underlying marriage ever a consideration in court. While those who write the laws have promoted the institution of marriage, by making it fast, easy, and inexpensive, there has been no corresponding legislation to allow those who realize they have made a mistake to unwind a marriage. Instead, the legislatures have created a bottleneck that the court and its legions of professionals exploit.

ZEALOUS ADVOCACY – TO A FAULT

"I know one attorney," says David Hoffman, a Boston divorce lawyer who lectures at Harvard, "who won't even consider settling until he has conducted discovery." Discovery is the legal term for investigation, an extremely involved and expensive process used in corporate litigation that has become commonplace in divorce proceedings. It might seem obvious that a tool designed for cases involving millions—or even billions—of dollars would be disproportionately expensive for cases involving small amounts of money where the litigants are sharing limited resources. "The adversarial system," he says, "is uniquely ill-suited for divorce. It pits mother against father."

But Hoffman and Zampino are unique in calling out their own for, as Hoffman calls it, "throwing fuel onto the fire". Ask most divorce attorneys to name who is responsible for the increasing nastiness, expense, and duration of divorce battles and they will, like the expert witness, usually point the finger at their clients. "Some people just have to have a judge declare that they're right," says "Disso-Queen" Laura Wasser, echoing Sorrell Trope's portrait of clients who become so lost in their personal warfare that they fail to see the scorched earth smoldering beneath their feet.

While blaming the litigants may be popular within the profession, the notion that attorneys are merely doing their clients' bidding seems farfetched, however. Considering the complexity of the family code and courtroom procedures, the average litigant has no idea what to expect in a courtroom let alone whether their attorney is doing necessary work or expensive busywork. That they are paid what Wasser acknowledges are "incredible fees," not for their adversarial-unto-pugilistic abilities but for their knowledge of something that most of us could not possibly hope to understand, dispels the notion that the clients are driving the bus alone.

And a random sampling of family law firm television ads reveals lawyers who are largely playing to their clients' worst instincts. In these spots, attorneys strike aggressive poses, warn of the damage the other side will do, and occasionally speak of the opposing parent/husband/wife as a "jerk," a "loser," or a "psycho." Several years ago, five California attorneys got together to film a DVD titled "Brutal Divorce Tactics" that featured, among other sections, "Ex parte the bitch!" (Ex parte is the tactic of one party going directly to the court without the other party necessarily being present, usually over an allegation that is considered so disturbing and/or time-sensitive that it cannot follow the normal protocol.) Although the judges before whom these attorneys appear, as well as the California Bar, possess the ability to discipline such incendiary behavior, it's nearly impossible to find a case of a divorce attorney cited for unnecessarily fanning the flames of a family conflict. Indeed, Hoffman, the Harvard lecturer, doubts whether it's even possible considering the laws surrounding malicious prosecution and malpractice. In California the law has been written so that only litigants themselves can be financially penalized and not the professional who represented them. In other states, the law goes even further in protecting the officers of the court, providing a legal force field for lawyers and judges typically reserved for whistleblowers, elected officials, and high-level government informants: immunity.

IMMUNITY

It was in the discovery phase of his battle with his first wife that Bob Simms' judge came to a shocking realization, that the woman suing her ex-husband for more money had herself hidden a major trust fund of which she was the beneficiary. Even more shocking, her attorneys had been well aware of the trust fund when they appealed for more support. In fact, they had gone to some lengths to help her hide those assets, ostensibly because that trust income would not only have reduced the amount of additional support to which she would have been entitled but probably would have convinced her to drop the suit altogether.

In a dramatic twist, the judge informed Simms that she believed both his ex-wife and her attorneys were defrauding him. But rather than refer the fraud to the district attorney or a grand jury, the judge promptly washed her hands of it, which meant that Simms would be forced to take up the issue himself by suing the opposing attorneys in order to recover some of the money he had spent defending himself. When Simms did exactly that, however, he learned something even more absurd. The courts had decided to grant his ex-wife's attorneys "absolute immunity" from the fraud they had perpetrated against him. Why? According to the appellate court, were they *not* to give divorce attorneys a career-long hall pass on the truth and an exemption from the court's own code of conduct, they might be less likely to be "zealous advocates" for their clients.

In most settings, zealots are looked upon as illogical, irrational, one-sided individuals incapable of having reasonable discussions. They stand on street corners with megaphones, warning us that the world is going to end. But under the adversarial family law system, zealotry is revered as a quintessential trait of a great litigator. Perhaps zealous advocacy might have a role when defending the accused in criminal court, but in family court? On the one hand, family courts are supposed to be kinder, gentler courts where family issues are resolved with compassion. But at the same time the judicial system allows, if not encourages, lawyers to say and do anything they please, no matter how untruthful, inflammatory, or deceptive.

Simms carries a copy of the decision with him in the inside pocket of his blazer and shows it to any journalist who cares to see it. He has spent $5,000 filing a complaint with the state's judicial grievance committee—two-thirds of the group lawyers and all members appointed by the State Superior Court. Simms says that the committee has already informed him that he will not be able to recover any damages, but he's pushing to the bitter end anyway (maybe because $5,000 seems like a drop in the bucket compared to what his wife's litigation has cost him to date, or maybe because he has already endured 200 hearings and three trips to the State Supreme Court).

Simms has lately succeeded in drawing the attention of some national press and exposing what he considers the absurdity of the immunity decision, but the coverage has been fleeting and the reaction muted. Perhaps it's not easy for people to sympathize with someone who can afford huge legal bills; or perhaps there is a bias left over from the paternalistic days that he, the provider, should pay no matter what. Or maybe many people regard divorce as a failure deserving of punishment, and however fair or unfair that turns out to be, Simms is guilty of bringing it upon himself (even though his ex-wife filed for divorce).

Ultimately, the judge who discovered the fraud meted out her own justice and reduced Simms' ex-wife's alimony from $75,000 a year to $10,000. The judge also denied her recovery of legal fees, meaning, Simms notes, that she will not live nearly long enough for her future alimony to pay off her legal debts. "She's broke," the aging ex-linebacker with a mop of silver hair and broad shoulders says with a sigh. Why the system allowed such an outcome is a question he's pondered a lot. "The legislators are the lawyers and vice-versa," Simms says. They are just protecting each other, he thinks, and the gold mine that the family code has created off the backs of people like him is far too lucrative to shut down, no matter the price paid by the general public.

THE RISE OF THE *PRO PERS*

While it would be a stretch to claim that the thousands of legislators and attorneys working on 50 family codes over the past half-century were secretly executing a vast conspiracy to increase the fees that their friends could charge, the family code has often been a product of opposing goals. Some politicians have wanted to make the family code simpler and more predictable, but instead the legislatures have made it more complex. Some legislators have wanted to give courts less discretion to judges, but the legislatures have often written broad and impossibly vague mandates that give each court an excuse to establish its own local rules, which, in turn, give each court almost limitless authority. The impossible complexity of the new family codes has confused litigants, leaving them with no reliable expectations or much of a clue as to how to approach the process. The result of all of this tinkering has been an exponential increase in the cost of a contested divorce—from around $1,500 when Judge Zampino began practicing law to 30 times that today.

As the system became more complex, millions of families were priced out of a basic right to justice. The laws became too complex to navigate on their own while lawyers became too expensive. Compounding the problem, family courts do not need to provide certain protections spelled out in the Constitution pertaining to criminal trials. Family courts do not need to provide lawyers to people who cannot afford them, for example. Therefore, many people have no choice but to blindly fend for themselves in the family courts. These litigants are known by a nickname among the attorneys and judges, an abridgement of the Latin term they are taught in law school: *pro pers*, short for *in propria persona*.

Like many *pro pers*, Andrew Karres' mien is that of a reluctant warrior. A second-generation Greek-American of middle age, he now runs an Internet car brokerage from a run-down building on the outskirts of Sacramento. He works the phone and Internet surrounded by boxes full of documents from his two year-old divorce, a conflict that has consumed the vast majority of his time and energy and exhausted all of his financial resources. To tell the tale succinctly would be impossible. Where does one start, after all? With the marriage? The engagement? The arguments? The day of reckoning? The moment that he entered the courtroom for the first time? The process has become a blur infested with Latin and a thousand three- and four-digit numbers—references to sections of California's voluminous Family Code. The only thing that Karres is fighting for these days, he says, is joint custody of his young daughter, who clearly adores her father and her paternal grandparents. But he is fighting an adversary with more or less unlimited resources, an ex-wife whose family owns several auto dealerships in the area. Worse, as someone who represents himself, he is considered a nuisance, a male version of Danielle Malmquist in Tennessee. In the parlance of family court, a "vexatious litigant." California keeps a list of such litigants, found at http://www.courts.ca.gov/12272.htm. Like Malmquist, these Californians are not allowed to file motions or suits with any court in the state unless they first obtain permission from a judge. This is one way in which the courts try to keep persistent *pro pers* out of their courtrooms. The other is to ensure that the process remains too Byzantine for them to navigate successfully.

"The judge will recite a civil procedure code or a family local rule code or whatever," Karres says. "You'll ask for a clarification, but the judge won't give you the clarification. It always comes back as, 'Well, you should know.'" While the code is written in English, family court has kept up the tradition of referring to legal principles by their Latin names, further handicapping his arguments. Litigants are expected to be conversant with terms such as: *ad litem, affidavit, amicus, ex parte, fiduciary, gravamen, in camera, in limine, inter alia, interlocutory, mandamus, pendent lite, pro per, per se, prima facie, res judicata, subpoena duces tecum, vide infra, vide supra* . . .

A situation like Karres' is not supposed to exist. Indeed, there has been much added to the family code that, in principle at least, might ensure a fairer fight. This typically means that the wealthier spouse, the earning spouse, pays the legal fees for the less wealthy. But Karres fell through a giant loophole. His wife's family controlled his income because they employed him at one of their dealerships. When the marriage went sour, the job disappeared. When that happened, the judge could have ordered Karres' ex-wife to pony up an equivalent amount to what she was spending in legal fees for his representation, but the judge declined. Karres believes that part of the reason for the judge's apathy is that he is a man, and the assumption in many family courts is still that men should be able to pay, regardless of their status in the marriage. In Karres' case, several experts were hired, at his expense, to determine what his income "should" have been. And even though his actual income was much lower than their calculations, hardly surprising since he was going from being the boss's son-in-law at a major car dealership to hanging his own shingle, the judge accepted the highest estimate. Karres the used car dealer, the judge decided, should be making more than $100,000 a year.

Karres had no choice but to tap another resource: his own immigrant parents. He settled upon a divorce attorney that he thought he and his parents could afford, which is when he learned how the process works. "The first thing you do," he remembers, "is fill out a financial form listing all of your assets and debts." When he asked the lawyer about this, Karres received an amazingly candid answer. "He told me that it was just like the car business," Karres says, breaking into a smile. "He said, 'We find out how much money you have and then we take it from you.'"

At least Karres was warned. Things got much worse when his wife hired a well-connected attorney known for a particularly effective strategy when dealing with an opponent of limited means like himself. "She will paper you to death," the friend warned, meaning that the attorney would file so many pleadings and motions with the court that there would be virtually no way for Karres to respond to them all without quickly exhausting his resources. Which is exactly what happened. The retainer his parents funded dried up within a month and Karres found himself in a law library trying to make sense of a thick, dog-eared paperback tome: *The California Family Code.* Ironically, the hundreds of hours he has spent studying to be his own lawyer has taken even more time away from his daughter, but his judge has shown remarkably little patience or sympathy with his predicament, and he has not sanctioned Karres' wife's attorney for her voluminous filings.

Of all the zombie-like creatures that populate family court, *pro pers* like Karres are both the saddest and least understood. They may spend hours and hours responding to motions from real attorneys or even preparing their own at Kinko's or, if they are lucky, from home offices, only to show up in court and be informed by a terse judge that they have not done it quite correctly or that the filing is late and will not be admitted into the case at all. If they do this too many times, they risk being labeled vexatious and getting frozen out of the process that will determine the minimum level of income that the court will "deem" they are able to earn (or else go to jail falling behind on support payments), and often their right to see their own children. So they must keep trying, like Sisyphus pushing his rock up a hill eternally, and accept the rejection and abuse with utter humility. If they dare to argue in court, they get into it directly with the judge, who can signal dissatisfaction by refusing to look at them or by ruling against them time after time after time. And if the litigant fails to get the hint, the judge can find them in contempt of court and send them off to jail.

Karres has endured all of these punishments. He says that Greeks are known for their tempers, and he has verbally quarreled with his judge on more than one occasion. Not long ago, the judge ordered Karres to attend anger management classes, at his own expense, run by another divorce attorney in the county. Karres refused on principle, noting that the counseling firm was not licensed to do business with the court and that his credit report would then reflect the fact he had attended anger management classes, hurting his ability to get credit for his business as well as insurance and even utilities for himself—all things that are fairly necessary to be both an entrepreneur and a parent. So off to jail he was sent.

Karres tried to see the positive side, that being in jail would at least allow him time to work on his motions to regain shared custody of his daughter. But when the judge held an impromptu discussion with his ex-wife's lawyer in open court regarding withholding the "carrot" of time with his daughter as an incentive since the "stick" of jail time had not worked, any hope that Karres would be given a fair hearing and an equal parenting role was crushed.

At least Karres is not alone. In 2012, the same year that he was sent to jail for not attending an anger management course, the Administrative Office of the Courts—the organization that oversees all court systems in California—announced that for the first time in history more than half of all litigants in family court were representing themselves. Not all, however, were being treated equally in court. Judges seem to have far more patience with the uneducated and destitute, either because it was easier to understand why they had no counsel or because they tended to be more submissive out of long habit.

But those whom the court thought *should* retain counsel—those who had some money or the ability to borrow some money for a retainer—were treated with disdain and sometimes outright hostility. When Elena Haskins, a middle-aged actress and writer in Nevada County, showed up to divorce court representing herself, her judge announced that he would order her home sold in order to pay for an attorney if she continued to come to court making grandiose pronouncements about due process and her first amendment rights. This might sound like a clear violation of due process—Haskins certainly thought so—but family law codes give attorneys and judges special powers to create what is known as a "real property lien." Unlike most liens, which require the lienholder to wait until a property is sold in order to recoup their judgment, a real property lien gives the lienholder an immediate equity stake in the asset—the marital residence or an investment property, for example. For divorce attorneys, the real property lien is not only a guarantee of payment but puts them in the front of the line of creditors should the parties declare bankruptcy—something that attorneys know is a likely outcome during divorce. Once the attorney's name is on the title, all that's required for payment is to file a motion for the court to order the property sold as part of the divorce settlement. As Haskins found out, a judge can market the services of attorneys and then seize the marital assets to which the attorney has attached his or her name in order to pay them. Although the family code dictates that the attorneys' fees be "reasonable," it seems a contradiction to litigants that "reasonable" fees would result in the loss of their homes. Worse, the real property lien eliminates any incentive for the attorneys to keep their fees down. Instead, it has become a preemptive solution to a foregone conclusion: that divorce will consume every asset and leave the litigants in a ruinous amount of debt.

No wonder, then, that Jeffrey Elkins, a telecom consultant in Northern California, decided to forego attorneys and represent himself—not because he could not afford an attorney *per se* but because he did not intend to have a court spend his life savings on attorneys. With no minor children, Elkins expected the proceedings to be straightforward. California law is a community property state, meaning that anything accumulated during the marriage, with a few clear exceptions, is split 50/50. If the couple were to hire any type of expert, an accountant would have made more sense than a lawyer, he reasoned.

When the divorce went to trial, Elkins presented a list of the exhibits he planned to introduce in order to value the marital assets, a requirement of his court. But, in the interest of processing more divorce cases, the court had established a local rule (one that does not even appear in the published Family Codes) that forbade testimony or exhibits being introduced at the time of trial. Such exhibits needed to be filed with the court ahead of time, using special procedures. Rather than inform Elkins of the local rule and reschedule the hearing for a future date, the judge rejected Elkins' exhibits on this technicality, which meant that only Elkins' wife, who had hired an attorney, was allowed to present her case. The judge then ruled in her favor and against Elkins on every count. Elkins' divorce seemed less an equitable dissolution of a marriage than a warning from the judge to other middle-class folks who might try to represent themselves: hire a lawyer and pay the crony tax, regardless of whether or not this will wipe you out financially, or else.

Elkins appealed, but even with an excellent appellate lawyer, his odds were terrible. Appeals courts don't typically second-guess judges, particularly family court judges, and the fact that family courts often establish their own rules has been tolerated as long as the court claimed it was necessary to keep the cases flowing and costs down. It is also true that appellate courts generally focus on other matters of "higher significance" than those heard in family courts. But, citing the sheer number of citizens who had turned to representing themselves in family court, the California Supreme Court found that Elkins' due process rights had been violated, and the Court not only ordered a new trial but established a commission to study how the laws could be made simpler and more transparent and how *pro pers* could get a fair shake in court.

Elkins passed away from a brain tumor before the Supreme Court decision. His attorney, Garrett Dailey, says that he would have been thrilled with it. But the commission ordered by the court, comprised of judges and lawyers and which bears Elkins' name, would probably not have evoked much celebration. Its first two recommendations were not to make the family code smaller or simpler for the average citizen, or to make the local rules more transparent or even provide an attorney for those not able to afford one. Instead, the commission's first major recommendations were to encourage more law school graduates to become divorce lawyers and to encourage judges to order earner spouses to pay the legal fees of dependent spouses at an earlier stage in divorce cases, neither of which would have applied to Elkins or the millions of other *pro pers* who could not afford a lawyer.

That same year, the issue of *pro pers* in family court came to the attention of the Texas Supreme Court—not because of a grievance from a well-educated litigant like Elkins but because attorneys and judges were complaining that *pro pers* were clogging up the system by wasting too much of the courts' time. The Texas Supreme Court concluded that the divorce process should be streamlined, that plain-English forms should be made available on-line, and that do-it-yourself litigants should have a direct route to the court. But the Texas Bar Association blocked the recommendations. They said amateurs should not be dallying in family law to begin with, since only a lawyer was capable of understanding the process. If litigants could not afford to play, why should the Texas courts make it easier for them?

OFF THE RECORD

The journalist arrives at the Stanley Mosk County Building in downtown Los Angeles at the appointed hour, makes his way past security and over to the public relations office on the first floor. He is asked to wait in a cubicle littered with calendars, which he does, until a nervous woman, the court's chief publicist, arrives to collect him. She reminds him that today's meeting is strictly off the record. The judges have agreed to meet him as a courtesy. He must not record their conversation.

He agrees.

She leads him down a hallway, into a cavernous room that resembles a college lecture hall, circa 1965. The 20-odd rows of wooden chairs are empty. The only human being in the room is a clerk who toils under a desk overrun with stacks of paper to the left of the judge's pedestal. The publicist glides past her, into the judge's chambers, also cavernous, where several more clerks toil away at desks similarly overrun with stacks of double-spaced pleadings. Finally, they enter the office of the presiding judge, which is pristine, like its current occupant, a thin, handsome woman, a corporate attorney by trade, who stands by her desk in anticipation. Sitting near her is a middle-aged man, a family court judge, a maverick who decorates his courtroom with sunny surfing photos but is known for his aloof judicial demeanor.

The conversation begins after the publicist has once again laid down the rules: no recording, the judges' names must be kept off the record, and they cannot be quoted. The presiding judge says little anyway, but the maverick judge, peppered by caveats and qualifications from the chief publicist, takes a decidedly upbeat tone. The court, he says, wants people to know that, while there are a lot of problems, things have gotten much, much better. Family courts are on the cutting edge of the law. They are creating the law, not just following it, on a daily basis.

As for those denied justice, the pro pers, *the maverick judge says that things are not nearly as bad for them as the* Elkins Report—*and the press—like to suggest. The journalist would not believe, the maverick says, how many attorneys give of their time, how many* pro bono *hours of work they do on behalf of those poor souls. Plus the court has a Family Services Center on the fifth floor, where attorneys help those who cannot afford representation manage their cases—find the right forms, check the correct boxes, etc., etc. After an hour, the meeting is adjourned. The reporter finds it is hard to imagine what, exactly, might have worried the publicist or the judges. Everything discussed could have been gleaned from one of the court's glowing press releases. Both the presiding judge and the maverick judge have shown far more candor in public speeches than in this "off-the-record" conversation.*

The next day, the journalist enters another office, this one less than two miles from the courthouse. It's a small, ugly building on an ugly street on the cusp of where Los Angeles becomes Little Mexico. It houses one of the two legal aid firms that deal with family law in all of Los Angeles.

The journalist is buzzed in and led into a small conference room, where he is greeted by a middle-aged woman in casual clothes. This meeting too is off the record. The legal aid lawyers fear the wrath of the court and their budget is almost entirely funded by the big family law firms. But when told of the judges' rosy portrait of family court, the woman can't help laughing out loud. The Family Services Center is run by law school students, she says, and her lawyers spend a lot of time correcting their mistakes. As for the vast hours of pro bono *work cited* by the judges, she shakes her head. *The journalist has been bamboozled by the court, she intimates. Even if the* pro pers *manage to get a legal aid attorney to take their case, which only a small fraction can, most cannot afford the fees that the court itself charges for translators and paperwork and transcripts and even hearings. And to get a waiver of these fees is difficult, sometimes impossible, even for those unfortunate enough to be poor and handicapped.*

A few weeks later, in a hotel in Beverly Hills, the presiding judge will give a speech to a collection of lawyers and family law professionals. No journalists are invited. Of course, it too must be off the record. At least this time there is a reason: here, in an audience of her peers, she will describe family court as a house on fire . . . before changing her mind.

Actually, she will say, the house has already burned to the ground.

2 | Patriarchy

*An honorable man and his equally honorable wife come
to realize and have to admit that their marriage is not
working out well, that the relationship is unhealthy for
them and is producing an atmosphere of tension in their
home. They respect each other and love their children.
After serious reflection they agree that their own health
and the happiness of the children will be promoted by
divorce. They agree to petition for a divorce and they
agree on custody and financial support.*

*From beginning to end, everything is clean and
straightforward. They appear in court and tell the truth.
They are accustomed to talking truth. And having sworn on
the Bible in open court, surely they must tell the judge how
they feel and why they have agreed. They start to do so.*

*At that point, the judge must dismiss the case. A
divorce is legally impossible. The man and the woman are
guilty of a crime they may never have heard of. It is the
crime of "collusion."*
　　—*Reginald Heber Smith, "Dishonest Divorce,"*
　　　　　　　　　　　　Atlantic Monthly, 1947

*Marriage is a wonderful institution,
but who wants to live in an institution?*
　　　　　　　　　　　—*Groucho Marx*

A BRIEF HISTORY OF DIVORCE (AND MONOGAMY)

Tucked away in a secret archive deep inside of the Vatican, banished to an underground room so secure that it has been designed to withstand an atomic blast, rests what some historians consider the

Western world's most important historical document: a scroll, five pounds in weight and two feet wide by three feet long, hand-penned in Latin and notarized with 81 wax seals. It is a letter from Henry VIII, King of England and commander of the world's most powerful empire, to the Pope. The letter contains a single request: the granting of a royal divorce.

As students of history are well aware, the divorce was not granted. King Henry subsequently made himself head of the Church of England, abandoning Catholicism for the Reformation, a movement that had begun in Germany but never really caught on in Great Britain. For the simple right to exit an unhappy marriage—his queen had repeatedly failed to deliver Henry a male heir—the faith of an entire nation was thus transformed, a revolution that would soon travel across the Atlantic to a nascent America and around the world. After granting himself an annulment, Henry married his ex-wife's most charismatic lady-in-waiting, her sister, Anne Boleyn. When she, too, failed to deliver a male heir, he decided to move on once again. But this time, rather than attempt to jump over the bureaucratic hurdles of divorce all over again, the king chose a much more direct route. He ordered Boleyn's head chopped off. This pattern would repeat itself more than once in King Henry's reign. The resultant rift between the United Kingdom and the rest of Europe, most of which remained beholden to the Vatican, echoes in England's present-day refusal to use the Euro as currency, as well as in family courts, where the process can seem oddly—and disturbingly—similar to the process in the United States.

Every divorce, whether that of a medieval king or an average person in 21st century America, obviously begins with a marriage. While most modern couples, just as the Vatican's ruling indicated all those years ago, still like to think of marriage as a perfect union blessed by a higher power, the truth is that marriage has changed a great deal over time, both in terms of mechanics and purpose. In Henry VIII's time, for example, most marriages were probably arranged based on financial and social considerations, or to produce children, who were expected to work at a young age. While there is no record of the first marriage, it is safe to assume that unions made before that time were similarly based on practical concerns: coupling a hunter and a gatherer, for example. Moreover, wives and children were usually considered the property of their husbands, a standard that prevailed in the United States until the 1930s.

Although adultery would become by far the most popular grounds for divorce, an exclusive sexual arrangement was not always the norm for humans. The mathematics alone would have made monogamy impossible for most of human history. Mitochondrial genetic evidence suggests that there were substantially more women than men in the human population 80,000 years ago. The genetic record shows that the ratio of men to women became roughly equal only upon the advent of agriculture, a bit over 10,000 years ago, which is when scientists speculate monogamy, and thus marriage, as we know it, became more common. Still, evolutionary scientists estimate that only 17% of human cultures are strictly monogamous.[3]

Nor is monogamy a given in the animal kingdom. According to a 2013 study published in *Evolutionary Anthropology*, only 3% of mammals and 15% of primates are monogamous. The males of herd animals (e.g., horses, sheep, deer) compete to win the right to mate with a plurality of females. Other animal species live in polygynous families (one male mates with several females, e.g., gorillas, lions); and other animal species live in polyandrous groups (one female mates with a plurality of males, e.g., honey bees). Though we tend to associate monogamy (and marriage) with religious convictions and traditional values, in nature it tends to have more to do with gender size than social mores. That is, monogamy is more common in animal species wherein the males and females are of roughly equal size and weight and the presence of both parents increases the chances that the children will survive (95% of birds are socially monogamous, although genetic tests show that about 30% of baby birds in any given nest were fathered by a different male). As it happens, polygyny is more common when the males are larger and stronger than females, and polyandry is more common when the females are larger and stronger than males.

---

3 "Monogamy, Strongly Bonded Groups, and the Evolution of Human Social Structure," Bernard Chapais, *Evolutionary Anthropology*, April, 2013

Human males tend to be taller and heavier than women, which would suggest that humans might be inclined to polygyny. But children tend to have a greater chance of survival and success when both parents are involved in their care and upbringing, which would suggest that humans might be inclined toward monogamy. The answer: we humans love to have our cake and eat it too. Humans have practiced both monogamy and polygyny over recoded history, and often at the same time—which is when divorce usually enters the picture.

Although there are references in the Old Testament to polygyny, most Judeo-Christian teachings require young adults to marry prior to having sexual intercourse and to remain both socially monogamous and sexually exclusive. There are many theories as to why these traditions developed, ranging from the containment of sexually transmissible diseases, to the reduction in social tension, to the maintenance of social class structure, to the higher survival rate of children coming from families with monogamous parents, to the belief that marriage for life is simply God's will—as is often quoted from the Bible: "What God has joined together, let no man cast asunder!" This may very well have been the Pope's justification for rejecting Henry VIII's entreaty, but marriages, including the King's, tend to be less monogamous than assumed.

Social behavior usually parallels mating behavior, but not always. Species with larger males tend to be patriarchal, a male-dominated social structure. Species with larger females tend to be matriarchal, a female-dominated social structure. Most human populations are organized under a patriarchal structure although women today have more influence in certain countries than others and most Westerners would agree that we are moving towards a gender-neutral model.

Like marriage, divorce is steeped in both practicality and in dogma. Under Old Testament Law, only the man could dissolve a marriage. Although fault, usually adultery on the part of the wife back then, could precipitate a divorce, fault was not a necessary prerequisite. It was, however, a consideration in the financial settlement. If there was no fault on the part of the wife, a husband was typically expected to provide for her after divorce, which seemed only fair in an era where the lack of virginity made re-marriage unthinkable and patriarchal customs prohibited women from earning their own income. In certain societies, the obligation to support an ex-wife was even memorialized in a document called a Ketubah, a pre-marriage contract. Funding of the Ketubah came either from the bride's father, in the form of a dowry, or from the husband's assets. Christians modified some of these customs and laws, as documented in the New Testament, forbidding divorce except under circumstances of infertility, adultery, or abandonment. But Christian law perpetuated the one-sidedness of divorce. For example, physical abuse, presumably almost always perpetrated by a husband on his wife in historical societies, was not considered grounds for a divorce. Husbands could theoretically do to their wives whatever they pleased. The authorities simply did not invade the home.

American divorce laws largely followed the New Testament until the 1930s, when domestic violence became a crime and divorce required either party to prove in court that the other was at fault. The intent was to keep marriages intact, which was considered a prerequisite for a productive, moral country, but unhappy husbands and wives proved as determined as Henry VIII. Forced to show cause, they flooded courtrooms with photographs from staged affairs, complete with actresses portraying mistresses (one Los Angeles actress testified that she had "played" the other woman in more than 100 divorces), while abused women who lacked the cooperation of their husbands were forced to beg their husbands for permission to divorce, sometimes negotiating themselves into destitution just to get out. Judges were given absolute discretion to divide the assets. If they felt that the husband and wife were guilty of collusion, conspiring to prove fault in order to obtain the divorce, the judge could deny the petition. Far more likely, however, the judge would determine who was at fault for the marital breakdown and punish the guilty party. The punishment of choice, the original "stick," was a large financial award from the guilty to the innocent. While men could recover from such a penalty, in an era when women rarely worked outside the home, women thus punished for being unfaithful could find themselves on the street, their children in tow.

In the early 1950s, an interstate gathering of attorneys calling itself the Special Committee on Divorce and Marriage Laws & Family Courts was formed by the American Bar Association. Its mission was to address the issue of making divorce a right rather than a crime. Lawyers, judges, psychologists, and religious authorities all weighed in, warning of the dire consequences of everything from making divorce too easy to giving lawyers too much power in the courtroom. A consensus emerged that, if leaving a marriage was to become a right, then the court's role should be one of reluctant healer, not enabler. Social workers, psychologists, ministers, and mediators would first try to salvage a marriage. If that proved impossible, the officers of the court would help facilitate an amicable settlement of funds and child custody, which was now to be shared more equally between husband and wife. And everything was to be done with a nod first and foremost to the interests of the children, provided there were any.

Feminists sensed a monumental opportunity in redefining divorce, maybe because it implied the redefinition of marriage itself. In her 1963 book *The Feminine Mystique*, which has been credited with launching the contemporary feminist movement, Betty Friedan characterized marriage as a "comfortable concentration camp." Millions of women were then entering the workforce to attain some semblance of economic independence. Friedan thought this indicated that they wanted out of the marriage camp. Feminists eager for equality wanted the right to file for divorce without having to prove fault or obtain permission from their husbands. California was the first to draft so-called "no-fault" divorce legislation. Its then-governor, Ronald Reagan, signed it into law in 1969. Forty-six states quickly followed. Then, as its critics feared, came the deluge.

Freedom was in the air. From 1969 to 1980, women and men were taking advantage of the new law, and the divorce rate tripled. As the family courts struggled to keep up with the surge, feminists and other activists lobbied for more and more changes to the family code. Legislatures obliged, increasing the size of the family code 100-fold and sometimes more (the codes differed by state, but all grew exponentially). With so many families being processed through family courtrooms, judges could no longer serve the role they once had, keeping lawyers in check and bringing husband and wife to terms. Laws were enacted pertaining to the computation of child support and alimony, the definition of income, children's entitlement to a certain lifestyle, an ex-spouse's

entitlement to a certain lifestyle, the power of judges to impute a minimum level of income to the working spouse, law enforcement responses
to allegations of domestic violence or abuse, the division of assets, the
definition of paternity and parental rights, the right to move children
out of state, and on and on. Substantive differences in no-fault divorce
laws began to emerge among states, the most important of which was
the difference between equal and equitable division of assets. In some
states, marital assets were automatically divided 50/50. In others, they
were divided "equitably, meaning that the judge decided based upon
what he thought the parties deserved, a throwback to the days of fault.
Furthermore, some states set limits on child support and alimony. Others did not. In some states, the wealthier parent paid for everything; in
others, a housewife might pay her millionaire ex-husband child support
if he was awarded custody.

And on and on.

As family codes ballooned from a few pages of basic code buried
in a state law book to a 2000-page volume of fine print, the ideal that
family courts could be kinder, gentler courts began to crack under the
weight of something else: money. Home values and household wealth
were going up every year, meaning there was a lot more money to divide and potentially to fight over. Pretty soon, aggressive and expensive
litigation tactics like discovery were introduced into family courts, and
divorce litigation began to resemble the rough and tumble of business
litigation rather than the gentleness and compassion implied by the very
term "family court" and envisioned by the architects of no-fault laws.
Large corporate law firms opened up divorce practices. Corporate
lawyers, who might have handled the divorce of a client as a personal
favor and assessed a modest fee after it was settled, now started advertising their services and charging by the hour, payment guaranteed by a
five-figure advance. Law school graduates who might have opted for
careers at big law firms could now envision making their fortune in
family court.

As some of the original framers of "no-fault" divorce had feared,
Divorce Corp. was becoming a self-fulfilling prophecy. Over the coming decades, the number of divorce lawyers would increase by more
than 2000% in California alone as dissolving the family unit morphed

from a discreet sideshow into a $50-billion industry. Under the auspices of a kinder, gentler system, Divorce Corp. would explode into a litigation machine dwarfing every other legal specialty.

THE CELEBRITY DIVORCE

While the drafting of the family code grinded on outside of public view, and while divorce remained a taboo subject in polite company, a handful of marital break-ups captured the public imagination: celebrity divorces. When Marilyn Monroe divorced Joe DiMaggio, she held a tearful press conference outside of the court. When Eddie Fisher dumped Debbie Reynolds, formerly "America's Sweethearts," the news was blasted across the tabloids for weeks. And when Patricia Loud of Santa Barbara, the mother of the country's first reality-show family, decided that her marriage of 30-odd years had become irretrievably broken, millions watched on television as she calmly informed her husband that she was moving out.

These famous divorces collectively served a greater purpose: visibility. While no American could keep track of the jostling for power going on between the legislature, which seemed to want to limit judicial discretion by imposing standard guidelines on things like alimony and child support, and the courts, which were becoming expert at using vague terms like "in the best interest of the child" and "in the lifestyle to which they have become accustomed" in order to exercise even more discretion over what happened to the families before them, the tabloids kept the average person abreast of how the other half dissolved their marriages. From the pages of the *National Enquirer* or *People Magazine* they learned that divorce court was a real-life soap opera, a battle royal for money whereby one could become set for life or bankrupt and which consumed some of the most beloved public figures of the day: talk-show host Johnny Carson, pop mega-star Neil Diamond, and actress Elizabeth Taylor, to name a few. While a handful of popular Hollywood films like *Kramer versus Kramer* and *E.T.* attempted to portray divorce as it was for the typical American family, it was these celebrity feuds, replete with bombastic attorneys and oversized fortunes, that really captured the public imagination.

WRESTLING THE HULK

When it comes to sheer publicity and metaphor, few divorces can match the 2012 split between pro-wrestling mega star Hulk Hogan and his wife Linda Bollea. Bollea, a platinum blonde in her mid-fifties fond of revealing clothes and very expensive automobiles, tells her side of the story in the living room of her Tuscan-style mansion overlooking a 200-acre avocado farm named Sunny Girl, after herself, that borders the Ronald Reagan Presidential Library in Southern California's Simi Valley. The reality-show-star-turned-agricultural-magnate was once a young Valley girl who had just opened her own nail salon. Hogan was a rising star in the pro wrestling world who had just been cast in *Rocky II* opposite Sylvester Stallone. On their first date, according to her, he led her to a crappy apartment—not his own—in the San Fernando Valley where he introduced her to the bed and had his way. Then he invited her to one of his matches. The sex was wild, she recalls, but infrequent because he was always on the road. She convinced him to settle down long enough to start a family just as Hulkamania was taking off. Before long, they had a million dollars in their bank account and two kids. As his celebrity entered the stratosphere, their wealth increased exponentially and she settled the family into a Florida mansion. She opened an antiques store, and he was voted father of the year. When his behavior turned aloof, she hired a private investigator who confirmed her suspicions that he was cheating. He asked her to sign a mid-nuptial agreement, essentially a division of assets without a divorce, and she refused. Then came the war and, soon after, the rewriting of family history.

According to Bollea, Hogan was not a model father and husband but a bully who had physically threatened her. He retaliated, trash-talking her on a radio show and alleging that she had an alcohol problem. She hit back on national television, accusing him of beating her, insinuating that he was gay, and equating him with accused killer O.J. Simpson. He shot back, telling the paparazzi that she'd taken every possession they owned, including the toilet seats. She accused him of sabotaging their daughter's recording career and enlisting his friends to hide assets from her. She catalogued her side of the dispute in a book titled *Wrestling the*

Hulk. The cover is a photograph of Bollea dressed in a sequined gown and jewels and leaning back on the ropes of a wrestling ring. The drama continued. He tussled with her attorney outside the courtroom. She bought a yacht and christened it "Alimoney." They both paraded much younger lovers in front of the cameras at every opportunity.

Bollea says that she decided to file for divorce rather than accept a mid-nuptial agreement, which would have divided the assets but kept the marriage intact, because she wanted closure. She blames her lawyers for firing her up. She blames herself for serving divorce papers to her husband on the set for a television show on a day that she knew their son was visiting to see his dad perform a big stunt.

But now, Bollea admits, she's finally grown tired of it all. "I'm tempted to just tell him, 'take it!'" she says, sipping a glass of white wine. "But the lawyers don't want me to stop. They're making a ton of money." At the time of this writing, her lawyers were sparring over the value of her husband's alter ego, including the phrase "Hulkamania," his signature and the trademark ripped t-shirts that she claims to have invented. In the middle of explaining it all, she breaks down in tears. "What happened to that family?" she asks, gesticulating into the air, eyes darting into the ether. "Where did that family go?"

THE ERA OF ENTITLEMENT

Under a different system of divorce, Bollea and Hogan could have gone their separate ways. They could have started fresh with someone new, perhaps with more knowledge and experience. But under the U.S. system they have neither disentangled nor experienced closure. Instead, they have become inextricably attached, 'til death do they part, by the system. Indeed, they are more bonded to one another than ever, mainly because the family courts have replaced the concept of fault with a battle over long-term, ever-modifiable entitlement payments. The spouses no longer fight for the divorce itself, but fight for money. Someone kept moving the goalpost, and the game became fiercer and the rules more complex as they played along.

What Bollea really needed to prove was an entitlement to the goods that the court had been empowered to distribute: support payments (including the future income of one party or another) and an appropriate share of the marital assets. However, although the family codes were supposed to be progressive, their basic conception of a family proved to be steeped in the past, wherein a marriage consisted of a provider spouse and a supported spouse. Moreover, the codes expected that relationship to continue long past the life of the marriage itself. By virtue of earning more money, an income earner, in the eyes of the law and the court, had created an ongoing obligation to provide for the other. Conversely, by earning less money—or none at all—the supported spouse had become entitled to be supported by the other, often for life. And not just be supported in the sense of having basic needs taken care of, nor be supported in the marital lifestyle, nor in, as was often read in the media, "the lifestyle to which they had become accustomed." The standard was to be supported in the lifestyle to which the court determined they had been able to afford during the marriage.

The flaws in these assumptions might have been obvious. For one, the era of an earner husband and stay-at-home wife incapable of a career and stigmatized by divorce was long gone by the late 1970s. Secondly, as bankruptcy expert and law professor Katherine Porter points out, unless the court was dealing with a very wealthy family, there was simply no way of supporting two households in the same lifestyle on the same income that previously only supported one household. The math just didn't work.

But the notion of a family court was built on ideals rather than mathematical reality, and no fantasy was more enduring, nor more appealing politically, than that of the supported spouse continuing as though nothing had happened. By the 1990s, the fantasy had become so pervasive that the chairman of the New Jersey Family Bar, Frank A. Louis, decided to write a blunt article titled "The Marital Lifestyle: To Whom Does It Belong?"

"There are very few legal principles with which the average layperson is familiar," Louis began. "Yet I would guess that everyone has heard and is familiar with the concept that the husband is 'obligated' to maintain the wife in the 'standard of living to which she had become accustomed.' Clients raise it at initial conferences and comedians joke about it. Is it, however, the present law? Should it be?"

Louis declined to answer these questions *per se*. He did, however, point out that the "lifestyle" standard was never intended to rise above a host of other considerations in determining support payments and become *the* law. He also warned of the slippery slope created by making spouses, who presumably already did not like one another very much, fight for the previous lifestyle for the rest of their lives. Louis pondered: Who was entitled to vacations? To savings? To spare time? To the freedom of changing careers or moving to less (or more) expensive locales?

Politicians jumped on the bandwagon and won votes with certain crowd-pleasing platitudes: No one, especially not someone who had grown used to being supported, should be penalized just because they're getting divorced. So while the individual filing for divorce was seeking a profound change in their life, the family court system was demanding that the status quo be maintained. Forever.

Thus, rather than go their separate ways, Bollea and the Hulkster, like other husbands and wives, were forever tied together and made to fight over who was entitled to how much of the prior marital lifestyle.

Six years after filing for divorce from her famous husband, and two years after wrapping up a national book tour in which she leveled new accusations against him—more variations on homosexuality, domestic violence, and tax fraud—Linda Bollea is still "wrestling the Hulk." Bloggers will either crucify her as greedy and entitled or cheer on the wife and mother whose husband cheated and should be made to suffer. But there's another argument: none of it is her fault *or* his.

That's because the family court has created a vortex that she and her ex-husband may never escape, a place where every seemingly straightforward question has spawned another, more incendiary question. The Hogans have agreed to divide the value of their marriage, so why can't the court determine what belongs to him and what belongs to her? Clearly she feels entitled to a certain lifestyle—and the law backs up her claim—but why is a woman of such obvious wealth, a woman who has started three businesses in her lifetime, entitled to a life pension from a man whose professional career is clearly in its twilight? What entitles a spouse to publicly destroy the very brand whose value they are demanding half of? Why is a "no-fault" divorce loaded with recriminations and character assassination? If the legislature has granted them the right to dissolve their relationship, to terminate their family, and allow everyone involved to move on with their lives, why is the court simultaneously enabling a battle with no conceivable end and whereby an objectively fair, equitable, and final settlement is impossible? Why are her attorneys leading the fight onward rather than stopping it?

The Hogans were fortunate in at least one respect. Both of their children were of majority age at the time of the divorce, meaning that there was no child support or custody to argue over, just alimony (although Florida, where the divorce was initially filed, is a lifetime alimony state, meaning that alimony awards are generally for life or until remarriage). So it is not inconceivable that the Bollea/Hogan divorce will go on for years as lawyers continue to hunt down assets and accountants argue over their value.

The Hogans' experience is not uncommon. Not long ago, the ex-wife of another celebrity filed suit more than a decade after their divorce was made final in order to grab a share of a film sequel, the original of which he'd made while they were still married. The wife of Jon Cryer, a star of the show *Two and a Half Men*, was stripped of custody after endangering their son, and yet he has been ordered to continue paying child support to her anyway. Kirk Kerkorian was duped by a phony DNA test and has been shelling out more than $100,000 a month in child support for a child he never conceived. His ex-wife, the one who swapped the DNA of his biological daughter with her infant by another man, has just filed papers demanding that his assets be put in a conservatorship for the benefit of the child, ostensibly because it is in the child's best interest to have a relationship with her non-biological father whom her mother has been deceiving since before her first birthday. In every case, the laws allow, and the lawyers promote, this type of behavior.

While the examples that appear in the tabloids each week represent a small subset of American society, they have helped form a popular narrative: family courts empower and reward the greedy, or at least one greedy member of a couple. No matter how rich, certain people will air their dirty laundry in public and fight a demeaning battle in order to pile sinful amounts of money on top of sinful amounts of money. And the courts and their cronies love it.

If family court can be this punishing for the rich and famous who can hire the most expensive lawyers and the best advisers and walk away with something left over, how do the courts treat the average American family? The hint of an answer can be gleaned by taking a walk down the halls of any family court in the United States. Without even entering a courtroom, the observer can discern a great deal: from the chatter of divorce attorneys in the elevators to the zombie-like litigants trolling the hallways waiting for their turn and the voluminous docket sheets posted outside each courtroom. The latter reveal a shocking trend. Modern divorce proceedings last longer, sometimes far longer, than the marriages themselves.

3 | Alimony without End

Our government puts two people in this arena with the money in the middle and says, "Now go fight for this!" And then when people do fight, they point at them and go, "Isn't it terrible that they're fighting!" What else can you say but that the entire [family court] system is just completely insane?

—Mike Newdow, activist

ONE WAY COSTS

Bob Simms was a young rookie in the NFL when he met his future wife on a flight from Buffalo to New York City more than four decades ago. After the NFL, Simms became a Wall Street banker. Now sporting a mop of silver hair over a leathery face often punctuated by a pair of reading glasses, the only remnant of the athleticism of his youth are his broad shoulders, now covered by a navy blue Brooks Brothers blazer. Over lunch at a Manhattan restaurant, he can no longer remember what compelled him to marry his first wife. But when they divorced in the late 1970s, he says he made a generous offer that she accepted. The package included a large home, half of the marital assets, enough money to complete her education, a car, a country club membership, and alimony for life, which would be adjusted upward at 5% every year to account for inflation. The monetary arrangement was the kind of pension that disappeared from corporate America long ago because not even large corporations could commit to guaranteed payouts decades into the future. But Simms somehow made it work.

However, after several years, the monthly checks were no longer enough. Simms' ex-wife filed for an increase and was denied. Then

Simms remarried and his ex-wife sued him again. Because of the way the family code is written, the addition of another person's income to Simms' income tax return upped his ability to pay the woman he had divorced long ago. That the first wife had nothing to do with the new wife, and that their greater combined income was earned by and supported two people rather than one, was not considered relevant by a family court judge. The bottom line was that the after-tax income on his tax return had increased.

But things got worse for Simms. Not only could his original divorce settlement be re-opened for what the court calls a "modification," but under the law his first wife could try to make him pay for suing him—a double insult.

Over the next several decades, his ex-wife sued him four times for modifications. Each time filings were submitted, e-mails were sent between attorneys (at $90 a pop), and the parties were summoned to a courthouse in Stamford, Connecticut to wait in a security line that Simms now terms the "parade of broken dreams." After being scanned for weapons, they would simmer for hours at a time in a small courtroom, squeezed next to their attorneys who were billing them $600 an hour for waiting.

In 2005, the last time she filed for a modification, Simms' first wife demanded an extra $15,000 a year, which could amount to several hundreds of thousands of dollars over a lifetime. But Simms' legal bills were already approaching half a million dollars. He says that she has gone through 37 attorneys and estimates she has spent at least that herself. The bill from her last attorney alone was $142,000, an amount that would eat up 10 years of the modification she sought. "At no point," he says, shaking his head in disgust, "did anyone—a lawyer, the judge, anyone—ever tell me that fighting the modification wouldn't be worth it, to just give her the bump and be done with it." As in most cases, Simms' lawyer had not communicated any estimate of the likely costs nor did the judge make any effort to control the activities or the billings of the lawyers on either side.

Where Simms had once signed the alimony check with a sense of resignation, now his hand shook so much that the numbers were barely legible. The battle began to take its toll not only on his new marriage but also on Bob's mental health. He became despondent, a feeling expressed by many litigants in family court, as the trial became an endless tunnel without exits.

Family law trials are often heard in "pieces," meaning that the court schedules an hour or two here or there, sometimes scattered over months or even years, until the trial is completed. Every "piece" requires the litigant to take time off from work or family obligations, travel to the courthouse, and stand in line in what the court refers to as a "cattle call." Because Bob had retired to Wyoming, each time the court heard a "piece" he would have to fly to Connecticut to appear for just a small segment of the case. And each time the judge and the attorneys would have to get back up to speed, requiring extra time and money. Who paid for it all? "*Moi!*" Simms says with a shrug.

Just as "no-fault" divorce has failed to stop litigants from lobbing accusations of marital and paternal infidelity, the laws written over the past few decades have failed to remove incentives for continuing the fighting past the date of settlement. Because the guidelines for support—read alimony and child support—are based upon complex calculations of household income, any change in the guidelines or in the composition of a household or its resources can spark a fresh fight.

And here the incentives create a perfect storm for continuous conflict. The notion of Simms being the provider spouse, which was memorialized in his divorce settlement, entitles his ex-wife to share in his standard of living for life. When this standard improves—or even the presumption that this standard has improved as in the case of his re-marriage—that entitlement dictates that his first wife can fight for more. Further, the family code states that he should pay the legal fees for determining how much more his first wife is entitled to receive. Having tapped into its fuel tank, the court re-opens the case and the litigation machine grinds forward. Maybe Simms can be blamed for not just capitulating, for not understanding how quickly his legal bills would eclipse the increase that his first wife sought, or maybe he can be forgiven for fighting what he considers extortion. What bothers him most is that his second wife, "a wonderful woman," has been dragged into a mess he neither contemplated could exist nor understands.

THE JUSTIFICATION

Lynn Toler, the feisty Harvard graduate and former municipal judge who has hosted television's *Divorce Court* since 1999, replies to a question about the effectiveness of family courts: "If you're looking for fair," she says, "family court is not the place." Like Bob Simms, she has coined another name for divorce: "Balance the Books Boulevard." And Toler should know. As a municipal judge in Cleveland she oversaw thousands of family law cases. In her current job alone she has decided in excess of 1,200 contentious issues, all between divorcing or divorced spouses.

Toler muses on the origins of the one-earner/one-dependent family unit as she sits in the well-appointed living room of her home outside of Phoenix. Her camera-ready smile eases the impact of controversial statements as she offers up fast answers to tough questions about alimony and child support: "All of that was based on the model that the woman stays home and takes care of the children and the man was the primary and sole breadwinner." She says that family courts remain stuck in the 1950s-model of one worker bee and one nest builder. "It is going to be less and less relevant as time goes on because women are less and less likely to be solely housewives," Toler concludes, a freeze passing through her face as she realizes she has touched upon, on camera, what remains a somewhat taboo subject in the United States: the elimination of the paternalistic mindset.

The reality is that there are now more women in the U.S. workforce than men, and although the wages paid to women have not quite caught up to those paid to men, the income gap has been closing, and is almost equal if one compares men and women with equal education and equal job duties. In 1990, men were earning an extra 30% of total income. In 2009, that differential had been cut in half, and was primarily due to women gravitating toward certain occupations where both men and women were paid a lower wage. In March of 2012, *Time Magazine* featured a cover showing the image of a woman fabricated out of a dollar bill over the title: "The Richer Sex: Women are overtaking men as America's breadwinners."

Still, the legal concept that a marriage is a partnership between a provider spouse and a dependent spouse lingers amongst the practitioners of family law and inside family law courts. Although there is less need for dependent support payments today, the amount of cash

flowing from spouses deemed the provider to those deemed the dependent (and also to their attorneys) has increased far faster than inflation
would dictate. Consider the fact that, since 1980, there has been a significant decline in both the divorce rate,[4] down 33%, and the absolute
number of divorces, down 16%. Yet the total amount of dependent support awarded by family courts has skyrocketed, from $16 billion in 1980
to $44 billion at the time of the 2010 Census.[5]

Dependent support payments primarily come in two forms: alimony (spousal support) and child support. Alimony comprises payments made by the earner spouse to the dependent spouse, irrespective
of whether the couple has had children or not. The original purpose
was both noble and necessary—to provide a safety net for a divorced
woman in an era when women were not accepted in the workforce nor
trained with skills sufficient to support themselves. However, in the 20th
century, legislatures transformed alimony from a safety net to a stream of
equalization payments intended to keep the divorced so-called dependent spouse in the lifestyle they had in the marriage, sometimes forever.
If that was mathematically impossible, the goal was then to equalize
the difference in monthly income between the ex-spouses, "to spread
the pain" as a retired Los Angeles judge puts it. Instead of providing a
mechanism to keep dependent ex-spouses out of poverty, alimony was
thus transformed into a lifestyle entitlement fund.

THE GENDER ENIGMA

In the 1970s, men's rights groups challenged certain state alimony laws
that provided alimony only to women, not to men. The U.S. Supreme
Court found these laws unconstitutional and stated that alimony laws

---

4 The divorce rate is measured as the number of divorces per one thousand
   marriages.

5 In 1993, 415,000 U.S. alimony recipients reported $4.2 billion in alimony
   payments on their federal tax returns. When adjusted for inflation, that
   equates to $6.22 billion in 2009 dollars, or about $15,000 per recipient per
   year. In 2009, 438,000 alimony recipients reported $8.8 billion in alimony
   payments. That amounts to about $20,000 per recipient per year. That's a
   33% increase in alimony received compared to 20 years ago after adjusting
   for inflation.

must be gender-neutral.[6] As Justice Harry Blackmun pointed out in the 1975 majority opinion of *Stanton v. Stanton*, "No longer is the female destined solely for the home and the rearing of the family, and only the male for the marketplace and the world of ideas."

Since that time, family courts were supposed to grant alimony on a gender-neutral basis. But the bias has remained. The Internal Revenue Service does not break out the total amount of alimony paid and received each year by gender, but various reports cite the percentage of alimony paid to men at 4% as of 2006, which of course means 96% goes to women.

But why are family courts awarding more alimony in an era when the income gap has shrunk and the number of divorces is down anyway? Part of the answer may be that divorce lawyers have become very good at getting courts to award support payments. There are no rules restricting how much alimony a family court judge can award, after all, only recommended guidelines. So judges are free to determine whatever they believe is "equitable." However, in 2007, the American Academy of Matrimonial Lawyers (AAML) laid out a list of suggested guidelines for judges:

> . . . 30 percent of the payer's gross income minus 20 percent of the payee's gross income. That amount, when added to the gross income of the payee, should not exceed 40 percent of the combined gross incomes of the parties.[7]

Were it only this complicated, judicial awards might be predictable and constant over time. But the AAML went further and complicated the guidelines with factors that are meant to determine the degree to

---

6 A sampling of United States Supreme Court decisions establishing that dependency may not be assumed based upon gender include Reed v. Reed (1971), Frontiero v. Richardson (1973), Stanton v. Stanton (1975), Weinberger v. Wiesenfeld (1975), and Craig v. Boren (1976).

7 Take our hypothetical divorce case of Martin and Alison again. If Martin is earning $100,000 per year at his job and Alison's small business is earning only $20,000 per year in profit, then Martin would need to pay Alison $26,000 per year (30% x $100,000 = $30,000 - 20% of $20,000 or $4,000). Alison's $20,000 of earnings plus alimony of $26,000 (total $46,000) does not exceed 40% of the combined $120,000 in gross income ($48,000).

which one spouse might be more or less dependent and in need of support. The factors, other than income differential, are:

1. length of marriage
2. education of claimant
3. age of claimant
4. number of children born to the couple
5. if children are grown, the role of the claimant as a child caretaker

The Kaufman Alimony Guidelines impose some weighting of factors and the case score is a combination of weighted sub-scores. Without adjustments, the weighting is:

1. duration 30% of the score
2. income 35% of the score
3. education 15% of the score
4. age 10% of the score
5. children 10% of the score

It is interesting to note that factors such as the length of the marriage and the number of children born are still relevant—as if both being married and producing children are considered occupations that deserve financial compensation rather than lifestyle choices that men and women are both free to make in an equal society. For Andrew Karres, the used car dealer who has been labeled a vexatious litigant, his judge justified shifting the balance of payments by saddling Andrew with a "deemed income," an imaginary stream of paychecks that Andrew only wishes he had. So not only are the guidelines malleable and non-binding on judges, they can be used to achieve the judge's social, religious, or cultural agenda—regardless of what the Supreme Court says!

To the delight of those getting rich working for the divorce industry, the fact that the recommended alimony factors are soft, debatable, require exhaustive investigation and data collection, and require experts to interpret and then issue extensive opinions allows divorce professionals to bill their clients for an unquantifiable number of hours. It doesn't matter whether Martin and Alison had adopted a traditional earner/

dependent relationship or a modern two-earner relationship. The expensive investigation and data collection, aka discovery, will take place in either case. If the end result of the investigation is that both our hypothetical couple, Martin and Alison, are considered potential breadwinners and deemed to have equal earning capacity going forward, so be it. The parties do not get refunds for the billable hours involved in the investigation. The attorneys were just following what the law dictates and turning over every stone.

THE PUPPETEER

Ulf Carlsson says he was blindsided by his wife's announcement that she wanted a divorce after more than a decade and a half of marriage. He didn't understand why she was unhappy with the marriage, other than perhaps he had spent too many hours at work and not enough time with the family. But since there had been no affair, at least not to his knowledge, he thought that the process would be straightforward based on his understanding of how things worked in Sweden (more on that later).

A first-generation Swedish-American, Carlsson certainly has a better excuse than most for not being aware of how Divorce Corp. works in the United States. "I figured that we would just split everything 50/50," the mild-mannered silver-haired and slight Carlsson says. "I wasn't looking to 'win.'" Carlsson was then a civil engineer who had worked for the State of California for almost two decades. His wife was a dental assistant. Between them, they owned a house, two cars, and a rental property. They had a teenaged daughter, Mackenzie, who was approaching the age when she would not want to spend much time with her parents. A pending-divorce scenario, he reasoned, could not be more straightforward.

Carlsson says that he initially reached a verbal agreement with his wife to divide their modest assets as well as share custody of Mackenzie. Then something strange happened. His wife announced that she had hired a lawyer and that their verbal agreement was no longer good. When Carlsson argued that they would just end up giving the money to lawyers to achieve the same result as they could achieve on their own, she disagreed. Her attorney had advised her otherwise.

A few days later, the divorce papers arrived on his doorstep. The first thing he noticed was that his wife had hired the same attorney that was representing the wife of his friend, Andrew Karres, the lawyer known for flooding her opponents with legal motions. The papers said that his ex-wife expected Carlsson to pay her attorneys' fees—around $40,000 or so. Given the complexity of the documents, he was immediately forced to hire a lawyer of his own just to respond to all of the paper he was now paying his ex-wife's attorney to generate. In his mind, he would now lose double an unnecessary expense. This, however, turned out to be just the first of many rude awakenings. Carlsson says that his soon to be ex-wife began to spend $2,000 per month more than she earned. She claimed that it was the lifestyle to which she had become accustomed during their marriage. And she moved into a house far larger than was needed by a single person.

When Carlsson went attorney shopping, the first few lawyers who interviewed him declined to take his case. "They said they had serious reservations about the relationship between my wife's attorney and the judge assigned to the case," he explains. It seemed like a setup: his wife hires an expensive attorney who immediately voids their verbal agreement and who is rumored to have a personal relationship with the person deciding the case. But there was nothing that Carlsson could do but watch the bills pour in. "It was like dealing with the mob," he says, shaking his head.

INVESTING IN DIVORCE

Even in states like California where lifetime alimony is rare and child support is usually calculated by computer, the amount of money pouring into divorce cases is skyrocketing. Stacey Napp, founder of Balance Point Funding, an investment fund based in Los Angeles that finances contentious divorces, says that her firm is seeing more and more money used to fund divorce battles. What's interesting, she points out, is that while the law does not allow family law attorneys to charge a percentage of the settlement as they do in other big money contingency cases, firms like hers have essentially figured out an end run around the law by separating the financing function (which a law firm does when it takes a contingency case) away from the litigation function. According to the legislatures, allowing contingent-fee divorces would encourage lawyers to fight for larger and larger settlements at the emotional expense of the parties and their children. Yet Napp's firm, which is typically contacted in the middle of the case after the litigant's initial resources have already been exhausted, is allowed to merely sub-contract out the litigation services and sit in the finance seat as though she were a law firm taking a case on contingency. The higher the ultimate awards for alimony and child support, the easier it is for Napp's clients to pay off Napp's financing. In short, it is now possible to invest in someone else's divorce.

In essence, Divorce Corp. has become more adept at squeezing greater and greater amounts from the future incomes of people going through the divorce process. And because neither the use of alimony nor child support is audited in any way, they can be used to pay legal fees. Nor is there anything to stop an attorney from soliciting or re-soliciting a client beyond the divorce—just the opposite. The laws and the professionals foment a vicious cycle that drives up the amount of cash flowing through the system.

While abolishing the assumption that all families follow the provider/dependent model would reduce the number of contested family law disputes, thereby reducing the need for family court lawyers and judges, family court lawyers and judges have clung assiduously to the old norm and to the need for post-divorce income equalization.

SMOKE AND MIRRORS—MASSACHUSETTS

"I'm not saying I'm worth $700 an hour," the attorney Gerald Nissenbaum says with a smirk, "but that's what I charge." He adds: "Some days I leave court and I think, 'I don't know what I'm doing!'"

Nissenbaum, approaching 70, sits at an antique desk in his corner office high above the financial district in downtown Boston. His wife has dressed her slight and irrepressible husband in matching suspenders and a bow tie—his trademark outfit. He got into the divorce business after working as a mob lawyer for several years in a tough neighborhood in South Boston. "Back then," he says, "divorce was considered dirty." It was, however, one of the few areas of law open to Jews like himself. "At the white shoe firms downtown, guys with last names like Nissenbaum need not apply."

A dozen copies of a *Boston Magazine* issue featuring Nissenbaum on the cover under the headline "Super Lawyers" are splayed out in his lobby for the taking. His razor-sharp mind cranks and a mischievous grin flashes every time he discusses one of the cases he's litigated over the past three decades. There was, for example, the wife who suddenly remembered on the stand how her husband, who was refusing to give her half of the assets, had forced her to participate in bestiality. There was the wealthy financial executive who refused to pay for more than half of her child's college, even though her husband was unemployed. There was the obsessive-compulsive husband who scribbled his thoughts on whatever surface was available, providing a detailed account of how he had molested his daughter, and the other husband who crumpled on the stand after being confronted with his son's account of him beating his wife. He says he could go on and on . . .

Nissenbaum's job is to spin these tales into narratives to help increase his client's share of the estate, their percentage of custody and, most important, win them an award of alimony. In states like Massachusetts, alimony can be awarded for life or until the supported party remarries. And while Massachusetts is technically a "no fault" state, there is plenty of leverage to be gained spilling family secrets in open court. "Everybody has secrets," Nissenbaum says with a conspiratorial smile. "We tell our clients, 'Tell us everything you would tell your best friend and then tell us everything you wouldn't tell anyone.' We need that information in case we can use it for them or in case it can be used against them."

The fact that divorce in Massachusetts has remained a dirty business of accusation and innuendo, all wrapped up in a neat package to be traded for a lifetime of financial penance for one party and a lifetime of guaranteed comfort for the other, finally came to the attention of the state assembly a few years ago. Divorce, as it turns out, has not been a popular legislative priority unless it involved going after deadbeat dads for missed child support or alimony payments. But by 2011 a chorus of discontent began to swell within the electorate and it attracted the attention of State Senator Gale Candaras.

Candaras, a small but energetic woman fond of navy blue pantsuits, could be the mother of the Stanford educated mediator, Emily Gallup. And she is just as unlikely a reformer as Gallup. Candaras is herself a lawyer and her husband is a law professor, and she is also a liberal democrat and second-generation feminist like attorney Gloria Allred.

Candaras initially seems nervous to discuss alimony in her tiny, cluttered office in the statehouse overlooking Boston Common. Surprisingly, she wants to frame the discussion of alimony reform as a feminist issue. What if, she says, someone had told her not to get a job, that a man would support her for the rest of her life? Where would she be now? Would she have gone to college? Law school? Headed off to Wall Street or won political office?

When Candaras hosted hearings at the statehouse on the topic of alimony a couple of years ago, it became clear that the floodgates had suddenly opened. "We heard all kinds of horror stories," she says. There were parents who could not afford to drive their children to birthday parties, much less buy presents for their kids. There were men in their 70s and 80s forced to continue working in order to support their ex-wives. There were second wives forced to work in order to support the first wife. But the stories that seem to resonate with Candaras the most were told by the women, many of whom are from her generation, who simply refused to move on with their lives. Terrified that their sole source of support, alimony, would end, they decided not to look for work or remarry. Many of their lives, Candaras says, revolved around "waiting for the check to arrive."

Because of the way the laws had been written in the 1960s and 1970s, judges claimed that they were powerless to change the status quo. The law demanded that they provide support for an ex-spouse in the marital lifestyle until that person remarried. If things were going to change, there would have to be a legislative fix.

On July 20, 2011, Candaras submitted her alimony reform bill to the State Assembly. It would replace permanent alimony with three new tiers: Rehabilitative Alimony, which would be paid to ex-spouses expected to become economically independent; Reimbursement Alimony, which would go to an ex-spouse who, during a marriage of no more than five years, helped put the payer through graduate school or job training; and Transitional Alimony, which would help equalize the payer and payee's lifestyles after marriages of more than five years. Echoing other state guidelines that considered the length of the marriage, Candaras's bill also placed specific time limits on alimony. For marriages of five years or less, alimony could not be ordered for a period of more than half the length of the marriage. For marriages of between six and ten years, alimony would last no more than 60% of the length of the marriage.

The bill, Candaras admitted, was not perfect. But it would be a start.

THE SECOND WIVES' CLUB

The push for alimony reform in Massachusetts was actually started six years earlier by a small-town entrepreneur named Steve Hitner. Hitner, who resembles a small Rob Reiner but with snow-white hair, had gotten divorced in 1998 after a three-day trial. Nearly a year after that, the judge ordered Hitner, who owns a Sir Speedy printing franchise in a suburb of Boston, to pay his wife $45,000 a year in alimony—forever. Hitner thought this was unfair at a number of levels. For one, the Internet was revolutionizing the digital publishing business, and thus the assumption that his business would continue to earn what it had in perpetuity seemed less than a sure thing. Second, the judge did not "impute" income to his wife. Imputing is often used by judges when one party is thought to be unemployed or underemployed by choice. At the end of the day, Hitner was stuck with a dying business while his wife took off to Florida with half of the marital assets and a $45,000 annual pension. She also sued him for half of the stock in his printing company, a case that would later be remanded to probate court and keep the acrimony—and the legal bills—flowing.

As he had predicted could happen, within several years Hitner's circumstances had changed dramatically for the worse. Under the law, he was allowed to go back to court to seek a modification of the alimony award. All he had to do, theoretically, was prove a material change in his circumstances. But by the time his hearing was scheduled in 2005, Hitner was nearly broke. So, armed with tax returns and accounting statements showing that both he and his printing business were in a precarious state, he came to court representing himself. The judge was unsympathetic and declined to change the alimony order. The judge, according to the Hitner, simply told him how much he needed to earn in order to maintain his existing alimony payments and, like an incompetent bureaucrat in an Ayn Rand novel, demanded that he figure out a way to make his printing franchise as profitable as it had been before the rise of the Internet, the technological revolution be damned. A year later, Hitner declared bankruptcy.

Bankruptcy has lately become the legal equivalent of divorce's ugly stepsister. Or perhaps it's the other way around. Roughly the same number of families file for bankruptcy and for divorce every year, and as family courts have awarded higher and higher support awards, the number of bankruptcies is increasing. One might assume, then, that there would be some cooperation and communication between the bankruptcy court and the family court, but this is almost never the case. While bankruptcy courts are tasked with re-setting expenses to a reasonable level, they cannot modify family support awards, which can easily be a household's highest expense. Nor do family courts tend to consider bankruptcy a reason to modify support awards. It is within this vortex that Hitner soon found himself. With no other sources of income to make his court-ordered alimony payments, he took out a home equity loan in order to keep himself out of jail. The irony is that, by borrowing money to pay the award, Hitner was putting himself in an even more precarious financial position and guaranteeing that he would not be able to make his alimony payments in the future. He was living on borrowed time.

Beyond broke but unbowed, the jovial Hitner, whose favorite party trick is cutting off his friends' neckties, convinced a lawyer friend to draft an alimony reform bill. When that died on arrival at the statehouse, he started a website and began accumulating horror stories. The stories included that of an elderly owner of a construction firm who, like Hitner, had been unable to pay his wife's $75,000 alimony after the economy tanked. That guy, however, had been sent to jail. His wife's tart response to a reporter who asked if she regretted the punishment was: "It's his own fault."

As Hitner plodded along with his crusade to bring alimony reform to Massachusetts, he began to wonder if the attorneys in the State Assembly were simply not interested in reforming legislation that gave them and their friends and business partners so much work. The State could have easily drafted guidelines for alimony, but instead legislators had left the amount paid entirely up to the judge. That created a totally unpredictable situation that both earner and supported spouse could not plan for, and it explained the willingness of litigants to pay attorneys like Nissenbaum $700 an hour and up in order to jockey for position in front of an almighty judge.

As Nissenbaum explains, the importance of establishing the narrative first is extraordinarily important, whether it be a cheating husband or a greedy wife or simply a helpless housewife. That's because, as Hitner found out, once an alimony award was ordered, whatever it happened to be, modifying it would be next to impossible. Not only do judges like to maintain the status quo, but, in Massachusetts, they felt their hands were tied by the "lifestyle to which they have become accustomed" standard. David Hoffman, the Harvard lecturer whose law office is only a few minutes' drive from the statehouse, sums up the legal inertia that takes over in family court: "Lawyers have a saying," he says. "That there is nothing so permanent as a temporary order." With so many cases to churn, and so little time to consider the evidence, many judges will argue that they simply don't have time to modify existing orders, or even to rethink whatever precedent was set, however specious or misguided.

Things would get both better and worse for Hitner. As he did his research on other states, he realized that there was significant variation in how alimony is treated. Some states, like Massachusetts, require that alimony be paid for life with little flexibility for changes in the payer's income or health status. Other states require a second spouse to contribute to the alimony payments going to the first spouse. If the payer's income has dropped, causing the payer to not have enough income to make the full alimony payments, the courts will require a second spouse to make up the shortfall.

Like the former NFLer Bob Simms experienced in Connecticut, Hitner's judge refused to consider the negative trend in his income tax returns and business records, but the judge did consider something else: the income of Hintner's second wife, Jeannie, who is not much younger than Hitner and also approaching retirement. That the judge would ignore the fact of Hitner's greatly reduced income but invade his second wife's income for funds in order to pay Hitner's first wife her unchanged alimony award was not something that had occurred to him. As Hitner's own financial situation became even more desperate, the judge warned Jeannie that she might need to take on a second job in order to keep him out of jail. All to ensure that the first wife in Florida received her $45,000 per year.

Jeannie Hitner sits at a round Formica table in the customer room of her husband's printing shop. The shop, like the small town where they live, is quiet and feels a little abandoned. The town has somehow missed out on both the real-estate boom in Boston and Cambridge and the technology boom along Route 128. Wrapped in a wool sweater, her wavy hair pulled back with a barrette, she listens to her husband deliver a familiar diatribe about how ludicrous the system has become and how it runs afoul of traditional values like self-sufficiency and common sense. During a lull in her husband's speech, Jeannie is asked if, knowing what she now knows about family court, she would still have married Hintner.

"No," she says softly, "I would not have married him. I mean, I love him; but if I had known what we would go through, no."

This last lesson, which Hitner was soon to learn from personal experience, has given impetus to the formation of "Second Wives Clubs" in many states. And this latitude on the part of a judge to make the current wife help pay an ex-wife would become a critical component of gaining support from women's rights groups, which have typically demanded that alimony laws be more, not less, generous.

HEADS THEY WIN, TAILS YOU LOSE

Gale Candaras continued to push her bill forward over the summer of 2011, traditionally a dead time for legislation, a season when legislators are more focused on vacation plans than lawmaking. But she had gathered the support of a broad spectrum of constituents by then, mainly thanks to hearings in which dozens of financially ruined, stressed-out, and sometimes broken men and women had paraded to the microphone to tell their horror story. On Monday, September 26, 2011 at 4 p.m., Senator Candaras walked down the hall to the Governor's office and stood by him as he signed alimony reform into law. A press conference was held in the ornate rotunda, with both Steve and Jeannie Hitner in the audience. Soon after they returned to their printing office, which is decorated with dozens of his friends' cut-off neckties, Hitner changed the headline of his website to "We Did It!"

Over the next several months, there would be more reason to celebrate as Second Wives' Clubs formed around the country and alimony reform efforts got underway in many states. The Florida Legislature passed an alimony reform bill and sent it to Florida's governor for signature, and there is growing discussion in other states, including New Jersey and Ohio, to do the same. But a second look at the Massachusetts law inspires caution. Despite the elimination of mandatory lifetime alimony in Massachusetts, the new law still offers no equation for computing a standard amount of alimony or hard and fast rules regarding how long the commitment will last. An ex-spouse must now reopen the divorce case and argue all of the parameters that impact the alimony award once again, requiring more long waits in the parade of broken dreams and more rounds of expensive legal fees. At his last hearing on his ex-wife's lawsuit for half of his printing business, Hitner could not even afford an expert to value it. In the short term, at least, alimony reform will surely generate more, not less, business for family law attorneys—including, of course, Gerald Nissenbaum at $700 per hour. Perhaps that is why it passed in the Massachusetts legislature.

One of the major areas of argument going forward will be how to "impute" the income of the earner spouse. Courts will still be free to raid the earnings of a second wife (or second husband) in order to pay the first and to send the earner spouse to jail if he or she fails to keep paying.

For her part, Gale Candaras has moved on. A glance at her official website reveals nothing about this legislative victory. Curiously, her official bio announces that she once worked for Goldman Sachs and that she has sponsored both a drunk driving bill and an anti-drag racing bill, but it makes no mention of her pivotal role in reforming alimony in Massachusetts. It's hard to imagine a Democrat from one of the country's most liberal states being more proud of working for the world's most reviled Wall Street bank or consider illegal drag racing a bigger issue than one that affects 50% of married Americans. Then again, since the 1970s, family law has become a kind of legislative third rail. Just as divorce pits parent against parent, reforming the system can pit legislators, many of them lawyers themselves, against their fellow lawyers.

THROUGH THE LOOKING GLASS

"That would be ridiculous!" says Sorrell Trope, the nonagenarian dean of celebrity divorce, when asked about the prospects of alimony reform in the country's most populous state. According to Trope, fixed alimony payments or the elimination of alimony post-divorce would result in helpless wives being flung to the street by indifferent—and not a little spiteful—husbands. The idea is similarly a non-starter at the mid-Wilshire high-risc offices of feminist legal eagle Gloria Allred, whose substantial accomplishments include allowing women into the Friar's Club but who has lately started representing a parade of other women who have been involved in affairs with married men, including the alleged mistresses of Tiger Woods and Arnold Schwarzenegger. Allred and her clients clearly believe that women should be compensated millions of dollars for what is euphemistically referred to as a loss of reputation, remarkably blindly disregarding the fact that these women publicized the affairs themselves. In any event, it is interesting that Ms. Allred should now find common ideological ground in representing ex-spouses who demand payment for having been married as well as ex-mistresses who demand payment for providing certain unspecified contributions, always hidden deep within the subtext, to a relationship without the legal sanction of marriage. Are these lawsuits not an affront to the original spirit of feminism and a hindrance to true equality?

On one of the first episodes of his short-lived talk show, the journalist Anderson Cooper hosted a bevy of successful young women, all of whom were being sued by their ex-husbands and boyfriends for alimony. Why? Because the law entitles them to live in the lifestyle enabled by their ex-wives or girlfriends. The women in the audience seemed disturbed that men would claim equal rights under laws that were enacted to protect women. Obviously, in the United States, when it comes to the topic of divorce and gender equity, the laws, the culture, and the judges are disjointed and contradictions abound. Divorce Corp. takes full advantage.

Marilyn York, a pretty and bombastic divorce attorney in Reno, Nevada—once known as the capital of divorce—has started a unique practice on the principle that alimony is sexist and that the courts do not treat men and women equally, as the law requires them to do. York and her coterie of female attorneys only represent men. To win alimony for these male clients is a daily battle. "I will say to the judge, 'Your Honor, you know that, if my client was a woman, you would have given her alimony.'" But there is something in the old ways of our culture, the laws be damned, that prohibits judges from being gender neutral. Many still see alimony as a female entitlement.

The explanation for this sad uncoupling, between the laws that the judges are sworn to follow and the actual behavior of judges in the courtroom, might be as simple as the journalist Peter Jamison's wry summation: "Family court is American jurisprudence through the looking glass." In short, it just makes no sense. It simply does not add up except for the professionals who benefit from its inconsistencies and abuses.

But there are bigger issues in need of reform than alimony. At $9 billion per year transferred from earner spouses to supported spouses, alimony is small potatoes compared to the real money, which, as every good divorce lawyer knows, is child support. The kids, or as Gerald Nissenbaum calls them, the "little bags of money."

4 | Children

Is there any psychological evidence to suggest that a child going from one standard of living to another standard of living is harmed? What? No! So if the kid goes and visits his grandmother for the summer and she has a small place in the countryside, that's going to somehow psychologically damage the child? Of course not! It doesn't make any sense.
—Margaret Hagen, psychologist

Should the child be punished just because the mother happens to make less money than the father? No. That's not the way it should work and that's not the way it works. Children are entitled to the lifestyle of the non-custodial parent. If the child support payment happens to benefit the mother, then so be it.
—Gloria Allred, attorney

THE CUSTODIAL PARENT

The Bible tells the story of two mothers who lived in the same house with their infants of about the same age. One night one of the infants died of suffocation. Upon finding a dead child in her crib the next morning, that mother claimed the child was not hers and accused the other woman of switching the infants in the middle of the night. The other woman denied any such thing. The matter was brought to King Solomon. After hearing the women's stories, the King asked for his sword and said that he would solve the dispute by cutting the child down the middle, at which point the woman with the living child screamed, "Please don't kill my child, your Majesty. I love him very much, but give him to her. Just don't kill him." The woman with the dead child replied, "Go ahead, cut him in half; then neither of us will have a child." And thus Solomon determined who should have the child.

But determining the fate of children upon divorce, for most of recorded history, required no such drama. Women and children were the property of the man, and thus the children went with the father, no questions asked. But an extraordinary individual, Caroline Sheridan, who was born to an aristocratic English family in 1808 and blossomed into a beautiful young lady (Caroline was so beautiful that the novelist Mary Shelley wrote, "Had I been a man, I should certainly have fallen in love with her"), would change that. The fate of George Norton, a well-connected Tory with a seat in the English House of Commons, was sealed when he first set eyes on her. He proposed marriage when Caroline reached age 16. Although she never loved Norton, her mother pressured her into marrying him to shore up the family's finances, which had begun to crumble after Caroline's father died years earlier.

The loveless marriage was rocky. Norton was abusive and beat her mercilessly at times. Three years into the marriage, Norton lost his seat in Parliament. Caroline, meanwhile, had become a successful writer and had established many literary and political contacts, including Lord Melbourne, a widower and known womanizer 30 years her senior. As the friendship between Caroline and Melbourne strengthened, Melbourne arranged for Norton to be appointed magistrate in the Police Courts at a generous salary. Three children were born to Caroline, but a scandal broke when George Norton accused Melbourne, who had subsequently become the Prime Minister of England, of having an affair with his wife. In 1836, George Norton sued Prime Minister Melbourne for alienation of his wife's affections and "criminal conversation." Charles Dickens covered the trial as a reporter. Although Norton lost the case due to a lack of hard evidence, Melbourne tendered his resignation; but King William IV refused to let Melbourne go.

All of this drama eventually led to a Norton breakup, but women did not have the right to initiate a divorce in those days, irrespective of the behavior of the man; and since adultery had not been proven during the Melbourne trial, Norton had no legal grounds for a divorce either.

Under English law, the three young children were the "property" of George Norton. Licking his wounds after the trial, he prohibited Caroline from seeing them. Caroline, who was now an influential writer with "friends" in high places, began to circulate pamphlets arguing that a mother had a natural claim to her children that overrode the common law rights of the father. Her arguments were based on the concept that children of a "tender" age needed to be with their mother: ". . . that while the child is of such tender years that the custody of the father must, from the nature of circumstance, be purely nominal . . . during that period of its life which God and nature point out as only fit for female care and tenderness . . ."[8] This became known as the "Tender Years Doctrine." No studies had been done and thus there was no science behind the overarching claim. In fact, there was nothing to support the assertion of the importance of the mother to a child of tender years except persuasive arguments made by an exceptionally close "friend" of the Prime Minister of England.

Opponents to Caroline Norton's Tender Years Doctrine cited a number of reasons to grant sole custody to just one parent—the man— including that:

- The prospect of the wife losing her children would decrease the likelihood of her seeking a separation from her husband.
- The courts would find it impossible to decipher domestic quarrels and to choose a custodial parent.
- The mother, if given access to the children, would probably, if not certainly, abduct the children.
- A dispute over custody would afford a temptation to perjury.
- Reconciliations would be less probable.
- The education of children under the father's exclusive care (and financial support) would be disturbed.

---

8 "A Plain Letter To The Lord Chancellor On The Infant Custody Bill," communicated under the pseudonym "Pearce Stevenson, Esquire" and sent to all of the members of Parliament in 1839.

During a period of debate in Parliament, stories surfaced that Caroline also had affairs with the Duke of Devonshire and with an extreme radical Member of House of Parliament. Against what might have been impossible odds for any other person, Caroline eventually persuaded both houses of Parliament to change the law in 1839. The Custody of Children Act granted sole custody and control of children under the age of seven to the mother, and it secured the right of visitation for the mother until the child reached the age of 16.

What began with an aristocratic mother marrying off her beautiful daughter, in order to maintain financial stability and social status, exploded into a bitter martial dispute and political scandal the proportions of which would make Bill Clinton's televised impeachment hearings appear respectable. The situation ended with legislation that flipped child custody laws upside down, the effects felt for 150 years hence, and not only in England but in most English-speaking countries, including the United States. The tender years doctrine has dominated U.S. family law for decades, causing family courts to grant custody predominantly to women.

There are many instances when single parenthood is unavoidable, of course. One parent might abandon the family, become ill, or die. The role of a single parent can be grueling, with responsibility for supporting and rearing the children placed on a single individual. But statistics consistently show that children who have two parents in their lives fare better, on average, than children raised by a single parent. Two-thirds of all suicides are by individuals who have come from a single-parent family.[9] Three-fourths of children/adolescents in chemical dependency hospitals are from single-parent families. Why societies of past centuries did not recognize this and instead opted to give sole custody to one parent, even when two fit parents were available, can only be understood from the perspective that women and children were considered property.

That joint or shared custody arrangements were unthinkable less than 200 years ago might dumbfound a modern progressive-American,

---

9 http://www.photius.com/feminocracy/facts_on_fatherless_kids.html
   http://www.telegraph.co.uk/news/uknews/1419897/Suicide-risk-higher-in-one-parent-children.html
   http://www.news-leader.com/article/20121125/NEWS01/311250054/single-parents-Ozarks-poverty

but the idea of sharing the children was not considered an option until very recently. In the 1970s, higher courts in the U.S. found the Tender Years Doctrine to violate the equal protections clause of the Fourteenth Amendment of the U.S. Constitution because it discriminated based on gender. The Fourteenth Amendment states that no class of citizens can be treated unequally under the law. The Tender Years Doctrine has since been replaced, at least at the level of lip service, by the "Best Interests of the Child" standard (more on that later). But in spite of the decisions of the higher courts and the data on chemical dependency and suicide, the concept that custody of a child must be assigned to a primary parent, and not shared equally, has remained the unwritten law in the U.S. family court system to this day. U.S. family court judges will go to great lengths, causing great anxiety for the children and great expense for the parents, to examine and evaluate families in order to choose one parent over the other.

CHILDREN FOR MONEY

For Deb Singer, a single mother in Southern California, the head-scratching began well before the evaluation itself. Singer had by her own admission married the wrong man. She realized her mistake after her daughter was on the way and filed for divorce. That's when things started to get very, very bad. According to Singer, her husband was found guilty of domestic violence and raiding her trust fund. Even so, he claimed no assets or income in his preliminary financial statement. After a single 15-minute hearing that resulted in a judge's decision that ordered Singer to pay him child support, and that produced a custody schedule that made it impossible for her to work, Singer's first bill from her attorney, "Disso-Queen" Laura Wasser, totaled more than $100,000.

She found a private investigator to disprove her husband's financial statement and a new attorney who managed to reverse parts of the order. But there was one thing the new attorney could absolutely not convince the court to reconsider: the court's desire to have Singer and her husband evaluated as parents. There were several obvious reasons to object to a custody evaluation. For one, Singer had been the child's primary caregiver from birth. She had cared for her daughter for all of her life. And no one, not even her estranged husband, was arguing that she was an unfit parent. But there was an even more obvious reason to forego the evaluation. By the time the order requiring a custody evaluation was issued, Singer's ex-husband was in jail.

Singer's attorney persuaded her to agree to an evaluation anyway, if only to placate the court, and assured her that a judge had never sent a young child to live with her father in prison. Singer relented with one caveat: she asked the court to limit the cost of the evaluation to no more than $7,500. "By then," she says, "I knew that, if I didn't do that, I'd get a bill for $50,000 tomorrow." The judge accepted the limit and Singer was to be given a "list" of evaluators to choose from. But when the "list" arrived, it contained only two names. Based on previous experience, her lawyer advised her against the first name. The second was a prominent court psychiatrist, Dr. Joseph Kenan, M.D. Kenan's CV was impressive. He was the chief forensic psychiatrist at Cedars-Sinai and president of both the American Society for Adolescent Psychiatry and the California Society for Adolescent Psychiatry. The judge made it known that Dr. Kenan had the court's absolute faith and trust.

Driving to Dr. Kenan's office in Beverly Hills a few days later, Singer recalls feeling a sense of hope that, despite the expense and the absurdity of it all, the custody evaluation would establish that she was a fit parent and would put an end to any uncertainty over seeing her daughter. But her hopes began to evaporate when she pulled into his lot and parked next to a quarter-million dollar Aston Martin. When she entered his office, she discovered an expensively-dressed young man who had no idea who she was. Her lawyer had prepared a binder on the case that sat, unread, next to a pair of $5,000 Hermes computer bags. "He didn't even know my name," Singer remembers. "I was shocked."

According to Singer, Dr. Kenan shoved a microphone in her face and instructed her to talk about her own childhood while he opened his mail. Pretty soon she was as distracted as he was because of his unusual behavior. "There was sweat running down his face," she says. "He was agitated. When we took a break, I called my lawyer and said, 'I'm being interviewed by a drug addict!'"

Her lawyer tried to talk her down. Maybe, he suggested, this was an elaborate psychological trick and her response to his odd behavior was part of the evaluation. Court psychologists are fond of using inkblot tests, so this was not as much of a stretch as one might assume. Singer's lawyer instructed her to go back and finish as calmly as she could. Her daughter's life was now in the hands of Dr. Kenan, whoever and whatever he was. And even with her ex-husband in jail, her lawyer warned, she could not afford a bad evaluation. Theoretically, the court could suggest a third option, like foster care, or force her to only see her child in the presence of a court-approved supervisor. Or the court could order her to attend parenting or anger-management classes. In the name of the best interest of her child, in fact, the court could order just about anything, no matter the time or cost involved or the rational basis for the order. And it wasn't like the judge had given them a long list. Dr. Kenan might as well have been handpicked.

Singer finished up the interview as instructed, gave Dr. Kenan a check for the agreed-upon sum of $7,500, and left. Not long after, she received a call from the manager of her bank. According to Singer, the manager wanted to let her know that there was a Joe Kenan in the lobby. He was trying to cash a check on her account for $7,500. It seemed suspicious to the bank manager. Singer confirmed she'd written the check, but now she was even more convinced that something was awry. Why wouldn't a doctor, she thought, just deposit the check into his account?

A few days later, Singer's attorney received a call from Dr. Kenan himself. The evaluator immediately made it known that he was unhappy with the court order. Surely her attorney realized that $7,500 was too hard a bargain, Kenan reportedly said. According to Singer's lawyer, he demanded another 25. Singer's lawyer asked nervously, "Twenty-five?"

"Yeah," he says that Kenan responded, "25,000."

The lawyer took a deep breath. He knew that he couldn't say no to the man who held the fate of his client's child in the balance. So he punted, reminding the evaluator that any increase in his fee would have to be approved by the court and that he would see what he could do. He promised to call the judge and schedule another hearing, which seemed to placate Dr. Kenan. Then Singer's attorney hung up the phone and started typing a brief.

It is not unexpected that in any field or profession there might be some less-than-qualified individuals; but what was striking in this case, and what is striking in many other cases involving professionals who work closely with family court judges, is the lack of oversight, review, or certification of the professionals' competence, fairness, or behavior. As Singer's attorney would later observe, "Evaluators do not have to be competent or knowledgeable to be hired by the courts—they just need to get in good with the judges."

CHILD SUPPORT

"I'm just the numbers guy," Art Grater snaps when pressed for an opinion. Grater, a middle-aged software engineer from Wisconsin, is not here to opine on the morality of the family code. He is here, courtesy of his client, to show off a piece of technology—software that he and a divorce attorney developed in the mid-1980s known as the Disso Master. The program, which was sold to one of the world's largest information companies several years ago, was necessitated by the voluminous family code sections related to child support payments. Other than the federal tax code, the laws with respect to children and child support have no rival in terms of complexity, and this complexity can produce some head-scratching results. Grater claims that computing a single child support payment requires more than 10,000 separate calculations. "There's no way that I or anyone else could do that on their own," he says.

DissoMaster is one of those terms that means nothing outside of family court (like the "Disso-Queen," the prefix is a nod to the fact that in many states divorce is legally known as dissolution), but within family court, DissoMaster assumes a significance of nearly biblical proportions. Judges refer to it constantly, sending nervous litigants down the hall to have it recalculated whenever a new order is entered. *Pro pers* line up like hopeful game show contestants at the clerk's desk or, if the court has one, the legal services office to crunch the numbers themselves. Lawyers hold conferences perched around iPads and laptops running the software, hoping that the results will provide some leverage, or maybe a tax benefit. At least with DissoMaster, cooperation is sometimes rewarded. Although the DissoMaster software is based on formulas in the family code that judges can look up themselves, or even override or modify if they identify special circumstances, whatever the DissoMaster crunches out is almost always the "gospel" in family court. The formulas are just too complex for the average judge to decode.

Like alimony, child support represents a stream of monthly payments that the non-custodial parent (payer) must pay to the custodial parent (recipient). The presumption is that the custodial parent will bear extra expenses in raising the children and so the non-custodial parent must pay money to the custodial parent to contribute toward those expenses. How much will those extra expenses be? One might assume that there would be some uniform amount per month, enough to take care of the basic necessities of raising a child, and that this amount would be the same for every child within each state (or perhaps for every U.S. child). Otherwise the government would be aiding some children more than other children, and favoring certain children over others would violate the equal protections clause of the Fourteenth Amendment to the Constitution. Correct? And any monies transferred from the payer parent to the recipient parent would need to be spent on the children. Correct? Auditable and accounted for. Correct?

Wrong. Child support can be spent on anything the custodial parent wishes to spend it on without limitation, even legal fees to sue for more child support. And child support awards are based not on the needs of the child, but like alimony, on the income of the payer parent.

Although a very controversial subject, proponents of pegging child support to percentage of income argue that the payments are intended to equalize the standards of living between the payer parent and the recipient parent, and that this is good for the children. When asked if he knows of any proof that it is good for the children, however, retired Hon. Judge Robert Schnider says, "I'm not aware of any. But it just makes sense." Professionals who have looked at the question scientifically, like Dr. Margaret Hagan, Professor at Boston University, say there is no proof whatsoever. When given a hypothetical example of a non-custodial parent who had voluntarily lived at a lower standard of living than his or her wealth would allow, in order to *not* spoil the kids, Sorrell Trope, the nonagenarian attorney, says that the political message behind the law was to balance the lifestyles, but the law goes much further than that. "It's not really the lifestyle that the parents are accustomed to," he says. "It's the lifestyle that's possible given the earner spouse's income."

Although the higher courts have proscribed the Tender Years Doctrine for more than 40 years, the 2010 U.S. census reports that more than 90% of child support is paid by men to women.[10] While there is no legal justification for this, it is no coincidence that women file more than 75% of all divorce actions, and thus bring more than 75% of the business to the family courts and associated professionals. As private detective John Nazarian says, "This is a business. This is not social services." So, as with any other marketplace in which a given demographic provides the lion's share of the business, that demographic will be treated with greater deference.

In the 39 states that have adopted the "Income Shares" model into their guidelines for computing child support, there is a term known as the "K factor." This is the algebraic term that computes, in dollars and cents, what it means to have been granted a certain percentage of time with your own children. One legal website recently tried to explain the K factor in a single paragraph:

> The K factor is defined in subsection (b)(3) of section 4055 as being a function of the amount of time the high earner spends with the child(ren) multiplied by a statutorily determined fraction. If the high earner spends 50 percent or less time with the children, then the multiplier is calculated one way, and if the amount of time is greater than 50 percent, then the multiplier is calculated another way. If the percentage of time is 50 or less, the multiplier is equal to one plus that percentage. For example, if the amount of time is equal to 20 percent, then the multiplier is equal to 20 percent plus 1, or .20 + 1 = 1.20. If the amount of time is equal to 85 percent, then the multiplier is equal to 85 percent subtracted from 2, or 2 - .85 = 1.15.

The K factor may be impossible for non-mathematicians to wrap their heads around, but the bottom line is that the guideline child

---

10 In 2009, 6.2 million child support recipient parents were women and 0.7 million (700,000) were men. For every one man that is granted primary custody of his children, 9 women are granted primary custody.

support computation weighs each parent's assigned time with the children. Not the actual time that they spend with the children but the amount of time that the judge has granted to each parent.

Grater, the DissoMaster programmer, demonstrates this twist on one of the laptops he's brought along to an interview. With a few clicks on the mouse pad, he conjures up a nifty 3-D graph that shows how the K factor swirls around the universe of possible entries and affects how much money the non-custodial parent must pay to the custodial parent. The child is therefore transformed into a kind of money mule over which to fight. The more time the court allows the custodial parent to have the child, the more money the custodial parent receives. The more time the court allows the non-custodial parent to "visit" with the child, the less money the non-custodial parent has to pay. Child support can amount to half or more of the non-custodial parent's take-home pay. So the K-factor motivates parents to play tug-of-war with the children and argue over who can be a better (or worse) parent in front of the judge (and all too often in front of the children). The establishment of the K-factor in "guideline child support probably quadrupled the amount of contested custody cases," Sorrell Trope observes.

What Trope does not mention is an additional incentive to fight written into the family code. By making child support tax-free while other forms of support, such as alimony, are not, the stakes of fighting over custody even further have been raised substantially. "All else being equal," Grater says matter-of-factly, "you'd prefer to get child support rather than alimony." The numbers just come out better for the recipient that way. For a moment, it's easy to forget that the child support number is supposed to represent what it costs to raise a child.

And the DissoMaster does not stop with the K factor. It digs deeper, attempting to determine not just the parents' actual income but what a judge wants the income of a non-custodial parent to be (imputed income) based on nebulous circumstances that the lawyers can fight over, at hundreds of dollars per hour, and that the judge can manipulate. DissoMaster can be used to adjust the numbers for perceived hardships, perceived windfalls, and above all, relative tax rates. How a parent making a gift to, say, the Salvation Army, changes the amount of money their child needs from them is one of those pesky questions that the numbers guy, Grater, prefers not to delve into.

Although the fact that a computer, and not a human being, is producing the numbers may give them the appearance of accuracy and objectivity, DissoMaster is subject to the same principle as any other computer program: garbage in equals garbage out. If one parent chooses to lie about their income, charitable giving, hardships, etc., then Disso-Master will produce a skewed result. Alternatively, if a judge or opposing party wants DissoMaster to produce a certain result, it is remarkably easy to change the assumptions.

Sorrell Trope says that it is not uncommon for parents to agree to 50/50 custody for purposes of the DissoMaster computer program in order to minimize what the earning spouse has to pay while secretly agreeing to a less equitable custody schedule. That parents feel forced to go through this exercise, as collusive as the olden days in which husband and wife staged an affair together, demonstrates the twin shortcomings of the DissoMaster and the family code.

In Andrew Karres' case, this motivated his ex to hire experts who simply made up (or in legal jargon, "imputed") his income. In general, imputed income is determined the same way that a realtor decides on a price for a home, by assembling "comparables." If one auto broker earns $150,000 annually, so then, goes the theory, another auto broker should as well. The problem, of course, is that not everyone has the same level of experience, the same client base, or the same talent. Nor does the imputed income standard take into account whether or not a job is available in the first place. It simply assumes that it is.

Back in the 1950s and 1960s, when the economy was relatively stable and career tracks were secure, it might have been safe to assume that such jobs were there for the taking. But, as we all know, over the past 30 years the economy has been anything but stable and the job market even less so. According to the Bureau of Labor Statistics, the average American worker will only stay with their current company for about four years. Between the ages of 18 and 42, that worker will hold an average of 11 jobs. Whether this is due to the increased occurrence of economic boom/bust cycles over the past several decades, a decrease in company loyalty, or simply the increased velocity at which lives change these days, family courts once again pretend as though nothing has changed.

The consequences for the earner spouse can be severe. *Bloomberg News*, for example, recently ran a widely-read article on a 41-year-old former portfolio manager who is routinely sent to jail because he has been unable to find a job since the financial crisis of 2008 but his divorce judge continues to impute his income at its pre-crisis high. For others, the jail may be more metaphorical but no less punishing. Rather than take a job at a smaller firm with lower pay but greater opportunity, or start a business, or go back to school for a degree that would enable a higher standard of living a few years down the road, the earner spouse is forced to remain in whatever job allows them to keep making the payments—even if pursuing another career had been the intention during the marriage. Ironically, the supported spouse has the freedom to do all of these things but not the incentive since earning more money would reduce his or her support payments! For both parties, the right to life, liberty, and the pursuit of happiness gives way to a catch-22 of the court's making.

And who ultimately decides who the "earner" and the "supported" spouse should be in the first place? The court does, of course, and not necessarily according to the wishes of the parties or even the tradition of the marriage. The judge, for example, might decide that one parent should work full-time while the other parent is only obligated to have a part-time job or maybe no job at all because they would like to spend more time with the kids. In other words, the judge can apply his or her social or religious or gender biases to the situation and create an earner/ dependent model out of thin air, choosing who will be the earner and who will be the dependent.

It is not only the custodial parent who benefits by rigging the child support formula. Child support payments, being unrestricted, unauditable cash in the hands of a client, means that attorneys have a spigot to tap. Because custody time and child support calculations can be re-litigated at any time based on a "change of circumstances" such as a change in salary or expenses, allegations of incompetence or unavailability, remarriage, or a host of other life changes, attorneys can encourage their clients to seek frequent increases (for the custodial parent) or decreases (for the non-custodial parent) in the child support payments. And they can extract their legal fees from either the increased payment stream or from the savings due to a reduction in payment size.

In 2009, the total amount of child support awarded was $35 billion, a 47% increase since 1993 (a 14% increase after considering inflation). Yet the average worker's salary over the same time period, adjusted for inflation, did not increase at all. The conclusion: judges and lawyers are squeezing an ever-bigger piece out of the average worker's paycheck. Yet over the same time period there were fewer children subject to a written child support order; and the income gap between the sexes decreased dramatically. Both of these factors should have caused the aggregate amount of child support awarded to have decreased, not in-crease. But then, Divorce Corp is a self-perpetuating, self-serving, beast that has no master.

Part II

Follow The Money

I always tell my grandkids: If you want to know who gets helped and who gets hurt, follow the money.

—Gloria Allred

5 | Checks Without Balances

Divorce used to cost $1,500; an appeal was $2,500. These days, somebody sneezes and it's $2,500.
— *Thomas Zampino, presiding family court judge, retired*

We have the best system for divorce in the world.
— *Dennis Wasser, attorney to Steven Spielberg, Tom Cruise, and Kirk Kerkorian*

DIVORCE ATTORNEYS AND JUDGES ARE USUALLY QUICK TO WARN muckraking journalists and court observers that the divorces that end up on television or bandied about the water cooler are the exceptions and not the rule. The vast majority of marriage dissolutions, they point out, are handled efficiently—if not affordably. There is no way to measure the accuracy of such a claim, however. No one keeps track of contentious versus non-contentious hearings, nor is it clear, when parents appear for a modification down the road, whether they have come in harmony or one has been dragged kicking and screaming. But the huge difference in child support ordered and collected (only about 60% of awarded child support is actually paid) suggests that litigants often are not able or willing to comply with the orders issued by the family courts and/or that the family codes are not operating as effectively as the court's officers suggest.

If a payer faces a decline in income, they may be forced to go back to the court and petition for a reduction in a child support or alimony award. If a recipient parent is not receiving the full amount of child support or alimony, they may go back to the court and petition for enforcement. Either way, Divorce Corp. gets more business. While the courts keep no data on litigants who return to the courts—indeed, some family courts do not even log litigants' complaints—there is plenty of anecdotal evidence of what some court observers have come to call a "revolving door of services."

GUARDIAN BAGMEN

Defenders of the system could hardly find a better example of an amicable initial divorce than that of Wendy Archer, a pretty middle-aged mother of two who lives in a modest home outside of Dallas decorated with the artwork of her daughter, a talented young artist. Archer describes her divorce as being straightforward. She and her ex-husband, a successful businessman, reached a settlement on their own and the court approved it. The expense was minimal, and for a while their 50/50 shared-custody arrangement seemed to work well for themselves and their children. Then, some time after her husband remarried, he stopped adhering to the custody schedule. After repeated requests over a nine-month period for him to do so, Archer hired an attorney, who advised her to seek full custody of the children. This wasn't something she wanted, but the attorney advised her that to do so was standard practice in custody disputes. Archer didn't press for an explanation. She assumed that filing for full custody was either like sending a warning shot to her husband—that he could lose custody if he continued not to abide by the agreement—or it could be used as leverage to force him to adhere to their 50/50 schedule. She let her attorney file the motion. She expected a brief negotiation that would produce a new, shared custody agreement or at least a court order for her ex-husband to comply with the existing arrangement.

Instead, war broke out. According to Archer, her ex-husband hired a prominent Dallas divorce attorney, a man who had appeared in *Vanity Fair* and ran the largest divorce practice in the state, which according to Wendy's research, just happened to have contributed to her judge's re-election campaign. The first hearing was a disaster. Her ex filed a counter motion for full custody and the judge immediately appointed an attorney for the children, ostensibly because the parents now could not agree on a visitation schedule.

An attorney appointed by a family court judge in order to "assist the court" to protect the best interests of the child is known as an *amicus* attorney. In contrast, an attorney appointed by a family court to "represent the child" legally may be called minors' counsel or guardian *ad litem*, depending on the state in which the case takes place. Other states use a the term guardian *ad litem* more generally to describe an individual who may or may not be an attorney but who represents the child's best interests and, along with the judge, helps make parenting decisions. If the guardian *ad litem* is also an attorney, then they may serve dual roles—one representing the child's legal interests and the second helping the judge to make parenting decisions. For this reason, they are considered "friends" of the court. However, no matter in which capacity such individuals serve, the parents generally must pay their fees.

According to Wendy, her children's *amicus* attorney happened to literally be a friend of the court in that she was a close friend and perhaps a business partner of the judge. She had also done business for Wendy's ex-husband's law firm. "It felt like a setup," Archer says now, an observation that is hard to argue against in light of subsequent events. First, the *amicus* attorney showed up at Archer's house talking about how amazing her ex-husband's new family was, down to their pet cat. Then she informed Archer that she, and not the judge, would be making custody decisions. And then there were the bills, which Archer was not allowed to contest because technically Archer was not the client. Since the *amicus* attorney was working on behalf of the court, only the court could review her fees.

"It's a huge problem," says Richard Warshak, the Dallas-based psychologist who often works with Archer's ex-husband's firm but who would eventually become supportive of Wendy's struggle to hang on to a relationship with her two children. "The courts don't enforce the custody schedule and there's nothing parents can do to force the other parent to adhere to the schedule."

But that is not exactly true. What the court did in Archer's case was fan the flames of the conflict by not reverting to the original agreement but by bringing in another party, a party with layers of conflicts of interest, to poke around in the family's interrelationships and, of course, submit bills. Archer made under $30,000 a year, which she said amounted to less than one-tenth of her husband's income. There was no conceivable way that she could go toe-to-toe with her husband, but she tried because her children were hanging in the balance. The judge, who received periodic financial statements from both parents, watched Archer's bank balance shrink to zero and did nothing to intervene. There was no debate as to whether bankrupting their mother was in the children's best interest—quite the opposite. When, late in the case, the *amicus* attorney submitted a bill for $11,000, she attached a motion for contempt—a threat that if Archer didn't pay she would be sent to jail. "They knew I couldn't pay it," Archer says. She ended up asking her mother for money, and indeed, ultimately spent most of her mother's retirement account, which, just like her own bank account, now stands at roughly zero.

Archer's nightmare darkened when she began to look at records from the Texas Elections Commission, which revealed her ex-husband's law firm's contributions to her judge. It was in those records that she also learned that her ex-husband's law firm had represented the *amicus* attorney in a prior court case. According to Archer, the *amicus* attorney at one point asked the judge to ban Archer from accessing public records in the court's own records department, presumably because of her success in digging up so many conflicts of interest.

"When you look at the records," Wendy says, "you find that the law firms that give the most money to the judges win most of the time." A 2006 study of the Ohio courts by the *New York Times* found that contributors won their cases about 70% of the time, with one judge deciding in his contributors' favor in more than 90% of cases. Perhaps more disturbing, the *Times* also found that judges almost never recused themselves. In the 12 years in which the study was conducted, judges recused themselves just 9 times in the 215 cases with the most blatant potential for conflicts of interest.

A study of the Massachusetts family courts, conducted by Terrence Brennan of ACFC, showed that of 1,236 cases of potential misconduct by guardians *ad litem* involved in divorce actions since 1999, not a single guardian *ad litem* was ever removed or disciplined.[11] Mr. Brennan's study compared this to actions taken by the Board of Registration in

---

11 http://www.acfc.org/e-newsletter-archive/31313listserve/

Medicine during a similar time period. Of 312 cases of alleged wrongdoing by medical doctors, the Board of Registration of Medicine issued 59 Voluntary Agreements not to practice, 23 Resignations, 48 Suspensions, 43 Probations, 18 Revocations, 52 Reprimands, 26 Fines, 12 Practice Restrictions, 3 Admonitions, and 1 Censure. The disparity between the lack of disciplinary actions taken by the judicial system against guardians *ad litem* versus the diligent efforts taken by the Board of Registration of Medicine are striking, and reveal a complete lack of true oversight within the court system. Moreover, contributions by guardians *ad litem* to judicial election campaigns reflect an unhealthy level of collusion between insiders.

After two years of expensive litigation, Wendy had completely exhausted all of her available funds, gone into debt, and was forced to give up—which in her estimation amounted to more than a complete loss. But there was a silver lining: Her daughter had grown two years older and two years more mature and began to ask to see her mother again. Wendy and her ex-husband then reached at a new custody schedule, privately, one driven by the revised wishes of their daughter. So even though Divorce Corp. had failed to provide any help to the parties, cost both parents exorbitant sums, destroying one parent's finances utterly, the passage of time eventually opened a window of hope for some normality. Indeed, said hope was in spite of the arm of Divorce Corp. called family court.

The same year that Archer settled with her ex-husband, a Texas family judge by the name of Suzanne Wooten was found guilty of six counts of bribery as well as money laundering, record tampering, and engaging in organized criminal activity. Unlike Archer, Wooten received a full jury trial. And even though she was found guilty, Wooten's judge merely sentenced her to community service and a $10,000 fine and allowed her to keep her law license until the judicial conduct board finally suspended it some time later.

FRIENDS OF THE COURT

In addition to campaign contributors and guardians *ad litem*, family courts have attracted enough friends to make Facebook blush, and they all have one thing in common: money. There are visitation supervisors, custody evaluators, court reporters, anger management counselors, parenting counselors, judges *pro tem* (temporary judges), rent-a-judges, appraisers, income consultants (for computing what a parent "should" be making) and above all, psychologists.

When Debra Singer spotted the Aston Martin at the office of her custody evaluator, Doctor Joseph Kenan, she was simply discovering something that court insiders and observers have known for years: there is big money in court psychology, sometimes more money than in the law itself. That's not to say that all officers of the court think this is a positive thing. Margaret Hagen, the Boston University professor, was so disturbed by the quasi-science being performed by custody evaluators that she wrote an entire book about this phenomenon titled *Whores of the Court*. Gloria Allred, for her part, has called out guardians *ad litem* for being more worried about repeat business from the judge than the kids. "Not a positive system," she says. And Singer's attorney, Dennis Braun, is horrified by the way that family courts have become closed-loop collection agencies for their "besties"—mainly psychologists and attorneys. "The court will produce the customer for them," he says, "then order you to pay them upon threat of being jailed, and sometimes even collect the money for them! The best part of it is, all they have to do is get in good with the judge."

Even Dr. Kenan, the Los Angeles family court's favored child psychiatrist, is a critic. All it took him to become a custody evaluator, he says, was a course "I could have slept through" and a minimum number of hours doing evaluations. "I know for a fact," he says, "that certain law firms have certain evaluators in their back pocket. And I can assure you," he says with a creepy smile, "that's true."

In Deb Singer's case, the opposite was true, but her story still illustrates the odd loyalty dynamics of family court. When Braun, Singer's lawyer, requested a hearing before a new judge who had taken over Singer's case to determine whether or not Kenan should be allowed to increase his fee from $7,500 to $32,500—in order to determine whether or not Singer should retain custody of her own child while her ex-husband was in jail on a domestic violence charge—the new judge bluntly told Kenan that, if he was not prepared to complete such a simple evaluation report for the agreed-upon fee, she would find someone else. Braun let go a sigh of relief that the judge had told Kenan off and not forced him to do so. He imagined that his client was safe from another attempt at what Braun considered black-and-white extortion. But when he returned to his office that afternoon, Braun had received an e-mail from Dr. Kenan asking if he could send someone over with the check for $20,000. Now Braun was really stumped. At least, he thought, he had the e-mail to prove Kenan's refusal to abide by the judge's order. But what if Singer refused to pay or brought the psychiatrist's behavior to the judge's attention and the court decided to abide by Kenan's evaluation anyway? After all, Kenan was the Los Angeles court's go-to guy.

Luckily for Braun, he received the e-mail on a Friday. He had all weekend to prepare a brief that would attempt to negotiate a very delicate situation. He would not communicate his client's suspicion that Kenan was a drug addict—a suspicion that seemed to be bolstered by recent events—but he would lay out the case of alleged extortion, at least in so many words. But the following afternoon, while walking the neighborhood with a friend, Braun received an unexpected gift. Walking across the sidewalk was Dr. Kenan dressed in casual clothes. When Braun pulled his friend aside in order not to be recognized, explaining that the guy was his client's custody evaluator, his friend shrugged him off. "Dr. Kenan?" he said. "You mean, *Joe*?"

A few moments later, Braun's friend was scrolling Dr. Kenan's secret Facebook page, where he went by "Kegan" rather than "Kenan." According to Braun, Kenan, high on meth, had invited the friend back to Kenan's apartment one day and tried to have sex with him without protection. The friend left. Now Braun was scrolling down unlocked photos on Kenan's Facebook page that suggested drug use and unprotected anal sex with young men. There was even a photo of a poster that had apparently been posted in local bars showing Kenan kneeling naked except for a leather collar. Above him were two young friends throwing money. The title of the event was "West Hollywood's Most Dysfunctional Family." Not only was the poster advertising a reckless lifestyle, Braun thought to himself, but Dr. Kenan was openly mocking the families he was supposed to be helping in family court.

Braun called his client, who began copying the photos to her computer. "There were hundreds," Singer recalls. That Monday morning, Braun requested an emergency hearing and presented a thick binder to the judge, who immediately called the parties into her chamber. Dr. Kenan was taken off the case immediately and Singer's money was ordered repaid. However, Kenan did not lose his privileges in family court, and in fact, he received nothing but support from the court. One commissioner criticized Braun for bringing the photos to the court's attention, telling the local news that Kenan's personal life didn't have anything to do with his job (evaluating families for good parenting skills, and evaluating children for emotional problems). When Singer sent a letter to the presiding judge in Los Angeles, the judge sent back a terse letter telling her that the court would not address the matter. Once again, the litigants were to blame for causing trouble and the judges maintained their relationship with a longtime friend of the court.

Singer eventually went to the *L.A. Times*, which ran an article, and a local television station broadcast a story as well. Braun's telephone was flooded with calls from parents around the country who had dealt with nightmare custody evaluators. Braun says he has learned of horrific decisions made by Kenan; but despite the obvious evidence that he was, at best, guilty of serious misjudgment that might get a fast-food employee fired, and at worst, a hardcore drug, porn, and sex addict encouraging unsafe sex, the court refused to reconsider any of his hundreds of custody evaluations and recommendations. Singer remains outraged. "This is the guy who's going to tell *me* whether I'm a good mother?" she asks no one in particular. Apparently, for the Los Angeles Family Court, the answer remains a yes. As for the presiding judge, she has gone back to a lucrative legal career in the private sector.

Danielle Malmquist, the ex-wife of the FedEx pilot, has been through three psychological exams with three separate psychologists, all requested by her ex-husband and ordered by the judge. The first two described Malmquist, a UC-Berkeley graduate who holds bachelors and masters degrees, as fine. The third, however, for which $15,000 was billed to each Malmquist and her ex-husband, designated Malmquist a low-functioning individual. The third evaluation was used to deny her custody of her two sons by a judge who had been receiving campaign contributions from the ex-husband's lawyer. The experience left her believing that the court had allowed her husband to pay for the result that he wanted, a suspicion echoed by many litigants who remain anonymous for fear of retaliation.

But Malmquist's experience with "friends of the court" did not end there. When she filed her appeal, she was surprised to learn that she could not obtain a transcript of her trial without negotiating with the transcriber who, in the state of Tennessee, was free to charge whatever he wanted. His first quote was $12,000. When Malmquist sent him a certified check in that amount, however, he raised the price to $30,000—all for a record that in any other type of case would have been available for a nominal fee and for which the transcriber had already been paid a generous hourly rate. According to Malmquist, when she asserted what she believed to be her right to the transcripts as they were necessary to file the appeal, the transcriber mocked her in e-mails, writing that she had no "fucking right" to them. As in Deb Singer's case, the judge did nothing to correct the disturbing behavior of the transcriber, a person who happens to be regularly employed by the court.

The use of friends of the court has increased along with the amount of money flowing through family courts while court budgets have remained flat or decreased. Outsourcing justice, at the litigants' expense, has become a favored way to save on costs while rewarding those with whom the court will do business in the future. In California, after the cost of a case management program commissioned by the Administrative Office of the Court ballooned from $80 million to more than $2 billion, the court's knee-jerk solution was to hand the project over to a for-profit corporation, effectively privatizing all court records. If the plan proceeds, public records will effectively no longer be public. Litigants will have no rights to the transcripts of their own trials and any litigant who wishes to file an appeal will be at the mercy of a "friend of the court" whom the court has made very powerful and probably very wealthy.

Before going any further down this golden rabbit hole, however, it might be helpful to visit another part of the world where divorce and money rarely appear in the same sentence.

6 | Utopia

The kids will be just fine, because the family will rally round them and, likely as not, the parents will continue to have a civilized relationship, based on the usually automatic understanding that custody for the children will be shared.

— Oddny Sturludottir

When I decided to get divorced, I consulted my minister and a psychiatrist. Not once did I ever think I needed a lawyer.

— Eva Marie Jonsdottir

In 2008, the journalist John Carlin traveled to Reykjavik, the capital of Iceland, a Scandinavian nation of just 300,000. The country is known to Americans as the land settled by the Vikings and, more recently, the idyllic backdrop of the peace summit between Ronald Reagan and Mikhail Gorbachev—a summit that produced the first major thaw in the Cold War. Carlin, a cerebral and jolly cultural observer whose biography of Nelson Mandela is the basis of the critically-acclaimed film *Invictus*, had been sent by the British newspaper *The Guardian* to investigate a study showing that Icelanders were the happiest people on earth. Carlin was skeptical of studies in general—he wryly observed that the only reason to consider this particular one legitimate at all was its ranking of Russians as the least happy—and cynical about Icelanders in general. As the first two sentences of the article would point out: "Highest birth rate in Europe + highest divorce rate + highest percentage of women working outside the home = the best country in the world in which to live. There has to be something wrong with this equation."

Iceland's mix of "loads of kids, broken homes and absent mothers" sounded, he wrote, more like "a recipe for misery and social chaos." And, in most of the Western world, it would be, wouldn't it? Certainly in the United States, where this laundry list of social ills might be a rallying cry for a conservative politician running for high office or an evangelist lamenting the decline of family values and traditional morality. So how to explain the fact that Icelanders were not only the happiest people on earth, at least according to the study, but some of the most productive—their per-capita GDP was then ranked sixth in the world—and among the smartest, their children outperforming Americans in standardized math and science tests?

Perhaps *how* their families dealt with conflict was more important than the presence of conflict itself. Perhaps if you ditched the paternalistic mindset and considered men and women truly equal, they would make better mothers and fathers. Perhaps, if you did not link money to children (or, more specifically, child "custody") you would not fester lengthy and punishing legal battles. Perhaps this would leave more money for things like education and living expenses so parents would not have to fight over what was left.

Carlin talked to dozens of Icelanders, from the president to a doctor-filmmaker to a local soap opera heartthrob named Baltasar Kormakur. The result is an often incredulous look at a people who have decided that there is no such thing as an "earner spouse" and a "dependent spouse," that freedom means being able to move on with one's life as a self-supporting individual, and that "the best interest of the child" is served by resolving the divorce quickly and out of court with the child maintaining a relationship of equal weight with both mother and father.

A DIFFERENT KIND OF WOMAN

The centerpiece of Carllin's article would turn out to be a 31-year-old city councilor named Oddny Sturludottir.[12] Like many of her generation, Sturludottir is the mother of a so-called patchwork family

---

12 In Iceland, the suffix to the last name identifies gender, i.e. "dottir" for daughter and "sson" for son.

consisting of two children by different fathers. The father of the younger child is her husband. The father of the eldest is a German who visits for weeks at a time, crashing at their apartment as a member of an extended family might. Five years after the article, Sturludottir is still young and beautiful in a natural way. She strides into a hip bar on the roof of an apartment building in Reykjavik around 10:00 p.m. and orders a beer. Out on the deck, young British and American tourists are staring sky-ward, awestruck at the Northern Lights putting on their ethereal show above the atmosphere.

Sturludottir is no longer a politician. She now writes books and translates the works of others into Icelandic. Like her fellow coun-trymen and women, she is a survivor of the financial meltdown that occurred the same year as Carlin's article, a meltdown that exposed Iceland's banking system as largely a house of cards but Iceland's people to be as sturdy as their Viking ancestors. The bankers who defrauded regulators have been sent to prison, unlike the bankers and regulators who defrauded the American people in our banking crisis; and the in-vestors lured by unrealistic returns have eaten their losses because the taxpayers rejected their prime minister's attempt to make them bail out the banks, as happened in Europe and the U.S. The currency has sur-vived. Sturludottir notes that Iceland's voters have always challenged the status quo and their politicians have become a reflection of themselves. They passed the first equal rights legislation for men and women in the 1920s, and in 1980 they elected the world's first female president, who also happened to be a single mother.

In America, a mother, particularly one with two children by two fathers, would presumably have heard of plenty of legal divorce battles. She might very well have had a story of her own. In contrast, Stur-ludottir cannot think of a single friend or acquaintance who has even gone to court for a family matter. The thought of doing so is foreign. "Can't two adults figure these things out by themselves?" she asks. When pressed that a housewife, for example, might be scared to make it on her own, she bristles. "Why would a woman want to depend on an ex-husband? An Icelandic woman would lose her self-respect if she took money from an ex-husband." Fighting over support payments, Sturludottir concludes, seems like it would be horrible for the kids, not only the effects of enduring the fighting but teaching them the wrong lessons about conflict and self-sufficiency. When asked why there are no divorce lawyers listed in the phone book, she can't imagine why any would be needed in Iceland. In fact, there are no family courts or family judges either. "Why would there be?" she asks with a shrug. It seems very confusing.

Stefan Olafsson, a professor at nearby Reykjavik University and Iceland's most famous sociologist, offers an explanation the following morning in his spare office. Icelandic women, he says, grew accustomed to their fishermen-husbands going off for months at a time. They learned to become independent, and their husbands learned that they liked it that way. So Icelandic women, like most Scandinavian women, learned to support themselves. If a marriage did not work out, both parties went their separate ways. That is why there is no alimony after marriage in modern-day Scandinavia. Marriages are generally equal partnerships with equal responsibility. If a Scandinavian couple wishes to live under an earner/dependent family model, they can sign a private agreement that provides for a certain period of alimony should the marriage end. But, unlike in the United States, alimony is not written into the law.

But what about jealousy and anger in Scandinavia, retribution and the human instinct to battle over stuff? Olafsson shrugs his shoulders. "Of course the ending of a relationship can be difficult at first," he says, "and there are bad feelings. But over time the rifts heal, and everyone shows up to the kids' birthday parties and just get along." Why is it so much easier to "just get along"? Perhaps the absence of a court battle in which your government encourages you to criticize your spouse has something to do with it.

Like Sturludottir, Olafsson cannot relate a single divorce horror story. Nor can he explain how it is that, given a similar divorce rate, the outcome in the United States and Iceland could be nearly opposite. One could argue that Iceland is small and homogenous and therefore less conflictual, but all family courts in the United States are essentially mini-fiefdoms and many operate in demographically homogenous places. One could also argue that Americans are simply more litigious people, but everyone, even Icelanders, must file for divorce; it's what happens *after* the filing that matters. And one could say that

Scandinavians are just not that wealthy or sophisticated, but the Scandinavian economies, including Iceland, are all highly advanced and boast some of the highest per-capita GDPs in the world. Scandinavian companies are leaders in shipping, manufacturing, biotech, telecom, oil, technology, entertainment . . . You name it. To say that Scandinavians must be genetically averse to conflict would be just as inaccurate. The Vikings were among the most aggressive settlers and violent warriors in history. So what is so different about the way they divorce?

A POSTAGE STAMP

Alexandra Borg sits on the couch of her cousin's home outside of Malmo, a medium-sized industrial city in southern Sweden less than an hour's drive from Copenhagen. In her mid-20s, Borg seems much younger. Her frizzy hair and loose clothes recall the 1980s, and when she talks, she giggles a lot. At the moment, she is waiting for a callback from *Swedish Idol*, a spin-off of the hugely popular television talent contests *British Idol* and *American Idol*.

When asked how much her recent divorce cost, Borg doesn't seem to understand the question. "Not a single krone!" she finally says before correcting herself: "I spent five krone on the stamp for the envelope!" She giggles. There was no finding a divorce lawyer. There was no retainer. There were no fees for psychological evaluations or mediators. Instead, Borg went on the Internet, found the court website, and downloaded a simple form. She filled it out, put it in an envelope, affixed the stamp, and dropped it in a mailbox. Six months later, she says, she and her husband were legally divorced.

So what about dividing the assets? Borg shrugs her shoulders again as though she doesn't understand. "What's his was his and mine was mine." Another pause. "We did argue about a couch that we both liked," she suddenly remembers, "but that has been settled." Bad feelings? "Of course I would never say that he's an asshole or something," Borg says. Pause number three. "I mean," she adds, "not in front of the children. Probably to my friends." She laughs again. Like Sturludottir, Borg finds the notion that her husband would support her after the divorce patently offensive. "I wouldn't be able to respect myself if I thought I needed some man to support me," she says. When a job took her several hours away from where they lived, she left her son with her ex so he would not have to change schools, but no court intervened and no judge made a decision. Nor did her ex sue her for support. Had he done so, the most he would have received was roughly $150 a month, which is what the government figures it takes to pay for a young child's food and clothing. So why bother? "The thing about it here is," Borg says. "You don't get rich taking care of your own child."

LITTLE BAGS OF LOVE

After a week of talking to residents of Scandinavia, only two people with personal knowledge of custody battles emerged. The first is a member of Parliament and longtime judge, Sigríður Ingvarsdóttir, who estimates that in her last two decades or so on the bench she has adjudicated maybe two custody cases a year. But even these are not custody cases in the sense of the term known to Americans. The way that Ingvarsdóttir describes them, such cases are more about parenting than about money. How does the judge handle them? Well, she says, speaking in the calm, deliberate, and compassionate tone that one would expect—or at least *hope*—of a judge, "I come down from the bench, take off the black robe, and sit down with them. I make it very clear that I am not acting as a judge but as a mediator to see if we can come to an agreement." How much time does that take, she is asked, more than 15 minutes or so (what Emily Gallup was allowed in the "emergency room model" preferred by Nevada County)? "Oh yes," the judge replies. "I usually take two or three days." In the unlikely event that the mediation doesn't work, Ingvarsdóttir returns to the bench and comes to a decision. By then, of course, there is no question that both parties have had their say. And there is another difference. Rather than return to the bench alone and order up an expensive psychological evaluation, the judge invites two others, including a psychologist, to serve with her on the bench. This eliminates the chance that any one person's bias will determine what happens to a family.

The other Scandinavian familiar with custody cases is the former soap opera heartthrob interviewed by John Carlin for his article in *The*

Guardian, a still smoldering man named Baltasar Kormakur. Kormakur is now a hugely successful Hollywood producer and director. His latest film, a thriller starring Denzel Washington and Mark Wahlberg, reached number one at the North American box office. Like many Scandinavians, he is part of a patchwork family; Kormakur lives with his wife, their children, and a son from a previous relationship. But unlike most, he is very familiar with a custody battle. He describes a case involving hugely expensive attorneys, sensational allegations, and prolonged arguments over things like whether or not the children were entitled to fly in private jets versus first class on commercial airliners. But this was not his custody case, or in fact, not the custody case of anyone in Iceland. Kormakur's familiarity with a custody battle is entirely a result of working in the United States, and the case involved two American friends fighting over custody of their American child. The idea of parents fighting each other, even over alimony and child support payments, seems to bewilder Kormakur. He says that his American friends spend much time and money trying to convince a family court that certain material things are "in the best interest of the child," but he believes they make no difference at all to the children. He wonders what kind of person would use their child to extract money for themselves and asks why any legal system would even make that possible. In Scandinavia, he explains, child support is always a modest fixed amount. Parents are free to voluntarily pay more if they like, and of course either parent is free to spend as much money on their child as they wish. But that is their decision, not the court's. When child support is paid, he adds, the check is sent from a government agency and then the amount is collected from the payer parent. The result is that the parents are no longer directly connected monetarily. No one needs to drop off a check, and no one needs to wait or beg for one.

Divorce is not a business in Scandinavia because there is no money in it. Neither is being a divorcee who "married well" or getting pregnant with some highly-paid athlete's child just to collect child support. There is no alimony at the end of the marriage and child support amounts to about $150 to $200 per month regardless of how much either parent makes. It is perhaps no wonder that much of the adversarial behavior that is commonplace and viewed as normal in the United States is absent in Scandinavia.

Is there a downside to a system with no family court and no divorce lawyers? If the impact to a country's gross domestic product of eliminating a $50 billion per year transfer payment from the general public to a cadre of family law professionals is viewed as a downside, perhaps; but the Scandinavians seem to be happier, live longer, have lower unemployment, and score better on standardized tests than Americans. Of course, cultural differences must be taken into account, but overall the lack of a financial incentive to fight in court seems to benefit everyone, and most of all, the children.

And there is the great irony of the two systems. As Kormakur explains, the Scandinavian system, while not shoveling money back and forth in order to equalize lifestyles, is very much designed in the best interests of the child. "Since the government sends the check," he explains, "the child never knows whether the money has gone unpaid or is sent late." In other words, parents have no incentive to disparage a child's mother or father and the kids are not subjected to the indignity of watching their parents waiting for a check to arrive so they can eat or have clothes or go to the movies. "Is that not how it works in America?" he asks, scratching his graying beard.

7 | The Best Interests of the Child

In 1979, less than one year out of Harvard Law School, the future constitutional scholar Erwin Chemerinsky submitted his first article for publication in a national law journal during a stint at the Justice Department. He'd settled on a topic that not only raised the kinds of abstract and serious constitutional questions favored by academic publications but one that affected millions of families every year: the "best interest of the child" standard then used by nearly every family court in the country.

Just as the established paternalistic mindset enabled family courts and legislatures to establish guidelines for alimony and legal fees, the "best interest of the child" standard gave courts the ultimate authority over the lives of children whose parents happened to be going through a divorce. And like the delineation of an "earner spouse" and a "dependent" spouse" that justified alimony and legal fee awards, the "best interest of the child" standard rested on an antiquated premise: that families in which the parents were divorcing or already divorced, so-called "broken homes," were automatically troubled and therefore fundamentally less healthy than other families. This distinction, which once allowed judges to force dysfunctional families to stay together, now gave the court the moral authority to ignore the presumption expressed in certain landmark Supreme Court decisions[13] that both parents had an equal right to see and to support their children. In its place was a web of guidelines, expert opinions, and ultimately, judicial discretion.

Prior to 1979, the year Chemerinsky's article appeared in the *Journal of Family Law*, "in the best interest of the child" tended to be interpreted narrowly. Most judges preferred to leave the parenting to the parents unless they had been proven unfit—a term that implied either neglect or abuse. As Chemerinsky noted in his article, however, by the late 1970s judges were beginning to take a much more active role. This, he said, raised serious constitutional issues, since what was in the best interests of a child was obviously a vague and highly subjective standard. While the assumptions contained in the so-called Tender Years Doctrine that were transplanted to the U.S, and ultimately deemed unconstitutional, the assumptions underlying the best-interests-of-the-child standard created a more nuanced issue: the standard essentially said that decisions regarding children are not the purview of their mother *or* their father but a state-run court.

Egging on this power grab by the state was a chorus of child psychologists led by the sixth and youngest offspring of Sigmund Freud. Beginning six years before the time of Chemerinsky's article, Anna Freud published no less than four books on the subject: *The Best Interest of the Child*, 1973; *Beyond the Best Interests of the Child*, 1980; *Before the Best Interests of the Child*, 1984; and, finally, *In the Best Interests of the Child*, 1986. Freud's premise was that the very term "parent" is simply a legal invention. In her opinion (and it should be noted, in direct opposition to what the U.S. Supreme Court has stated in multiple opinions) parents do not necessarily act in their child's best interest. Children, Freud claims, are simply "assigned at birth to their biological parents or, where this relationship either does not develop or fails to function, assigned by later court proceedings to parent substitutes. This intimate group of adults and their children constitutes the central core of a family." Rather than acknowledge biological parents as profoundly interested in the well-being of their own—blood being thicker than water, after

---

13 Troxel v. Granville (99-138) 530 U.S. 57 (2000). Also, for an excellent review of the related cases see "Not In the Child's Best Interest", Ron. B. Palmer and Sherry L. Palmer, 2013 available through www.FixFamilyCourts.com

all—Freud tosses both mothers and fathers aside as though they are mere accidents of biology and wholly interchangeable with another "intimate group," say, a group or institution or household chosen by a family court. For married parents, or even single parents, who are never subjected to the "best interests" standard, Freud's perspective was an irrelevant curiosity, the platitudes of an intellectual who never had children of her own. But for the millions of parents who entered family court in the 1980s, 90s, and beyond, the stakes were much higher and the influence of this "expert-by-heritage" has had a profound effect. Freud's ideas would mean that, as soon as they filed for divorce, their status within their own family was immediately and irrevocably subordinate to a stranger in a black robe.

In fact, a family court judge can act in the role of surrogate parent. Thomas Zampino, the retired presiding judge in New Jersey, speaks proudly of the many children whose lives he has managed as though they were his own—deciding where they went to school, where they vacationed, even what clothes they wore. "Their parents were perfectly lovely people," he explains. "They just couldn't get along!" Zampino chortles.

Ask any family court judge why they would make highly invasive decisions on behalf of parents and they will likely say the same thing: *The parents made me do it!* What the judges fail to acknowledge, though, is that the K-factor of the child support formula often encourages at least one of the parents to disagree on decisions involving their children. If the parents agree, they have no basis for going to court to ask for more custody time. But if they disagree and bring the matter to a family court, they can petition to be the primary custodial parent; and if they win that battle, they might be granted more than 50% custody time and therefore be awarded more money. The system rewards people who resist compromise, who refuse to get along.

To make matters worse, rather than be satisfied with breaking deadlocks in situations where the parents cannot agree, judges have, over the past few decades, become remarkably proactive about asserting their power to determine which parent will have greater influence over the fate of the children even when the parents get along reasonably well. Some argue that the court must select a custodial parent so that decisions can be made efficiently. What if, for example, a child would be happy to either join the school soccer team or join the marching band but one parent wants the child to join the soccer team and the other parent wants the child to be in the marching band? By granting one parent the final word, there are no deadlocks. Decisions get made.

But which parent should be given the last word? Which parent should be awarded legal custody? Who is more likely to act in the best interest of their child—the mother or the father? Answering these questions typically means evaluating both parents, a process that can be extremely expensive, comprehensive evaluations sometimes running $35,000 to $100,000 and including multiple tests (like IQ tests and Rorschach "inkblot" tests) that require additional evaluation by additional experts. All of this can be extraordinarily jarring for the children, who are often interviewed along with friends and relatives. And it is more than jarring for their parents, who have suddenly been thrust into a position of being judged without any information as to how or why this is all necessary.

There is an alternative. When siblings argue over who gets to sit in the front seat versus the back seat of the car or who has to take out the garbage, good parents find solutions that are fair. For example, one sibling might get the front seat on Saturdays while the other sibling might get the front seat on Sundays. Johnny might have to take out the garbage on Tuesdays and Lauren might have to take it out on Fridays. There is no reason the courts cannot find similar solutions for giving parents the final word. Perhaps one parent makes final decisions from August through July in odd numbered years (e.g., August 2015 to July 2016) and the other parent makes them in even numbered years (e.g., August 2016 to July 2017). Or the parents could simply flip a coin each time a deadlock is reached. These simple schemes would avoid the time, enormous expense, and psychological trauma of detailed custody evaluations used to determine which parent is "better." In short, there are simple ways to assign responsibility and authority without choosing one parent over the other, and yet family courts fail to even consider these less traumatic, less expensive alternatives.

One simply needs to compare the U.S. Postal Service to Federal Express or the U.S. public education system to private schools to see the fallacy that is the assertion that a public institution should be in charge of parenting on any level. Yet it is surprising, and indeed a reminder of the entrenched power of Divorce Corp, that there has been no effective challenge to Freud's ideas about placing the government in charge of parenting more than 50% of U.S. children.

THE GADFLY

There is little disagreement that fighting over who is a better parent, with the accompanying accusations, true or false, of parental incompetence, abuse, or neglect, is not good for the children. The family courts naively warn the parents that "nothing is to be discussed with the children," but in reality, negatively manipulating the children's views of the other parent can improve one's chances of gaining more custody time because custody evaluations routinely involve interviews with the children. Young children are gullible. They will parrot certain phrases they hear from their parents. And a manipulative parent can use this to their financial advantage, unfortunately at the grave detriment to their children's future social skills, family values, relationships, and happiness.

There are no statistics kept on how many evaluations have been done since the adoption of the "best interest of the child" standard or what those evaluations have cost litigants. It is safe to assume, however, that Erwin Chemerinsky's 1979 law review article was prescient. As predicted, the vague standard has made judicial discretion so expansive as to make parental rights meaningless. Ask family judges what the standard means and you will get as many answers as there are judges. Retired Los Angeles family court judge Robert Schnider sums it up well: "It means," he says with a grin, "pretty much whatever we decide that it means."

In 2011, nearly four decades after the publication of Anna Freud's first book, a Northern California medical doctor named Michael Newdow filed a taxpayer lawsuit alleging many of the same points in Chemerinsky's article and claiming that the standard had not only resulted in the pain and suffering of untold parents (in his pleading, Newdow calls the "best interests of the child" standard an "inane, vague and gross misnomer" and suggests renaming it the "arbitrary, unwarranted government infliction of life-shattering abuse standard") but that courts had wasted hundreds of millions of dollars in taxpayer funds fomenting child custody battles. Newdow is well known in legal circles. After being ordered to pay $320,000 to his ex-wife's divorce lawyer years before, the result of a custody battle that ended in him receiving only 30% of his daughter's time, Newdow acquired a law degree. He gained national celebrity when, in 2008, he invoked the wrath of religious conservatives by suing his local school district in order that his daughter not be compelled to say the words "under God" when reciting the pledge of allegiance before class. That lawsuit went all the way up to the Supreme Court where Newdow argued on behalf of himself. Although most observers had expected him to fall apart before the nine justices and his opponent, the Solicitor General, Newdow presented a cogent, confident argument. Ultimately, however, the Supreme Court refused to rule on the case it had handpicked among thousands. In an about-face, the justices side-stepped the main issue and wrote that, because a family court had only awarded Newdow 30% custody of his daughter, he did not have the authority to advocate on her behalf.

Sitting in the backyard of his modest home in a suburb of Sacramento, Newdow enumerates his arguments in a rapid-fire and slightly bewildered tone while he gesticulates with thin, muscular arms. The same Supreme Court, he notes, that said he was not allowed to act on behalf of his daughter has ruled time and again that parenting is one of the most fundamental constitutional rights in existence. Most recently, Justice Anthony Kennedy went a step further, stating in a published opinion that family court judges must assume that parents will act in the best interests of their child—even if the court believes otherwise. That, of course, contradicts the assertion of family court judges that they, and not the parents, are the automatic arbiters of the child's best interests. When asked to square the two, Schnider, the retired judge, offers a hedge. He agrees that there is a presumption that parents act in their child's best interests. "Unless," he says, "we find that the parents actions are detrimental." Who decides what is "detrimental"? The family court judge, of course!

It's this sort of overreaching that gets Newdow particularly exercised. Courts, he says, are not supposed to get involved in parenting children unless there is proven neglect or abuse. For a judge to unilaterally decide that the way a child is being parented is "detrimental" unleashes a flurry of unanswerable questions. "Which is better?" he asks rhetorically. "A big house or an apartment? Tennis or swimming? Studying or playing with friends? The old movies or the new movies?" And on and on. "It's just so insane!" he concludes. Not only does the "best interests of the child" standard constitute a violation of due process in that divorced parents are assumed to be unfit and must, through evaluations, prove otherwise, but Newdow believes it a very serious violation of the equal protection clause in the Fourteenth Amendment to Constitution, which states: "[no] state shall make or enforce any law which shall . . . deny to any person within its jurisdiction the equal protection of the laws." If a judge can mess with a divorced family but not a family where the parents are still married, then we are not giving divorced parents and their children the same protections under the Constitution that we are giving married families. We might be tempted, he points out, to assume that parents who have kept the marriage together are automatically better parents, but that is clearly not always the case. And what about single parents? Is it fair to assume, for example, that a teenager who got pregnant by a man who has long since disappeared, a girl who had a baby out of wedlock, is a better mother than a woman who waited until marriage to have her child but whose husband divorced her after 10 or 20 years? Or, as in Deb Singer's case, a mother who made a questionable choice of husband but has always loved and provided for her daughter?

Defenders of the system will claim that family courts can and do interfere with the parenting choices of married persons when those choices are contrary to the best interests of the child, such as in cases where parents want to deny conventional medical treatment to their children, perhaps due to religious or counter-cultural beliefs. But the counter argument is that such denial of medical treatment can be viewed as neglect or abuse, and therefore should fall within the jurisdiction of the courts. Simply filing a petition for divorce is not evidence of abuse or neglect, and although the petition technically gives the family court jurisdiction over the dissolution of the marriage, why should it also give the court jurisdiction over a parenting, absent evidence of abuse or neglect?

The irony, as Newdow sees it, is that the "best interest of the child" has mainly served up an issue over which both sides can endlessly argue. Moreover, judges can use the standard to justify just about anything. From hugely expensive psychological evaluations performed by their close associates, to micromanagement of children's lives, to anger management classes taught by friends of the court, to arbitrary awards of custody time, all of which ultimately add up to litigants spending much—if not all—of their time and savings while Divorce Corp. banks enormous profits. Deb Singer's legal bills, for example, are now approaching the million-dollar mark, and her divorce has thus far lasted twice as long as her marriage.

Erwin Chemerinsky, the constitutional scholar, believes that the "best interests of the child" standard has survived for a simple reason. Legislatures and courts don't know how to replace it. Ergo a catch-22: While it's clearly not in the best interests of the child to provoke hugely acrimonious and expensive battles over their best interests, how does the government protect the children without giving the courts the authority to do so? Newdow has suggested changing the standard itself. Perhaps the family courts should only have jurisdiction over custody if criminal abuse is first proven in criminal court, for example.

But "best interests of the child" reaches past the children in that the standard has proved a remarkably useful tool for silencing criticism of the court itself, particularly questions about the behavior of judges and friends of the court like Deb Singer's custody evaluator, Dr. Joseph Kenan.

HE (OR SHE) WHO CASTS THE FIRST ACCUSATION WINS

Custody battles are like typical lawsuits in reverse. Rather than file a claim, enter mediation, or go to trial where evidence is considered by a jury and then decided, resulting in an order from a judge, in family court the judge makes up a custody order before any of the evidence is established and then, only months and sometimes years later, hears the case. This has a few important implications that litigants usually fail to appreciate. For example, a "temporary" order is temporary in name only. The initial hearing may be short, but since family court judges can handle dockets of more than a thousand cases each, the judges tend to do little more than revert to their original decisions in subsequent hearings. In Deb Singer's case, for example, her first 15-minute hearing resulted in being ordered to pay her ex-husband $3,000 per month in support as well as abide by a visitation schedule that forced her to stop working. Singer recalls her attorney glibly telling her on the way out of the courtroom, "It was a good day!" This was true in one respect: the judge's terrible, and legally incorrect, order would allow Singer's attorney to bill thousands more in order to get his order fixed, a process that Singer's new attorney likens to turning around the Titanic.

The stickiness of "temporary orders" makes the court's first impression of the litigant extraordinarily important. And because the custody case effectively moves backwards, if there are any allegations (e.g., postpartum depression, drug use, alcoholism, and so on), temporary custody can be influenced by these mere allegations because, in family court, the accused parent is guilty until proven innocent. The chances that litigants will be allowed to submit real evidence at the first hearing to rebut such charges are remote, to say the least. In the family courts in many states, litigants do not even have the right, as they do in criminal and other civil courts, to cross-examine a witness who makes an allegation against them or to present evidence in open court. The judge simply decides who they believe is more credible based on the direct testimony. And this testimony is often delivered via written "declarations."

Under the adversarial system of law, if one party makes an allegation in a declaration and the other party does not respond, or does respond but with a weak argument, the judge can accept the allegation into evidence and then make a ruling based solely upon the written allegation and the written rebuttal (or lack thereof). In family court, serious allegations can go unchallenged for months and even years. The journalist and family court observer Peter Jamison describes the process thus: "It's not so much whether you did it or not but whether or not the judge thinks that you're the *type* of person who might have done it."

The end result is that, for the parent/litigant who presumably has no pre-existing relationship with the court, what really matters is choosing a lawyer who does. Litigants, like Ulf Carlsson's wife, who choose an attorney with a friendship or special relationship with the judge, are at a huge advantage over those who, like Carlsson, do not. The reasons for this may be entirely innocent, albeit no less wrong, since judges are more likely to trust those with whom they have a history, as will be discussed shortly. But regardless, those who are faced with an unfair "temporary" order will be forced to spend a lot of money on attorneys' time fighting for modifications. The thousands spent on the preliminary hearing can quickly become tens of thousands on the modifications, which becomes hundreds of thousands as the case is bounced back and forth, like an endless game of pong but with two glaring exceptions: unlike pong, there is no time limit and there is no end to the game. Whenever one player doesn't like the score, they can simply start it over—unless they insult or otherwise anger the judge.

Mike Newdow, the emergency room doctor turned constitutional lawyer, racked up a bill in the low six-figures fighting for equal custody of his daughter years ago. He offers a simple solution that adheres to the precedents set by the United States Supreme Court. Unless there is proven abuse or neglect, temporary custody orders should always be for equal time with mother and father and for joint legal custody, meaning that parents have an equal say in major decisions affecting their kids. If the parties want to reach another agreement, Newdow says, that's fine with him. But if the family courts were instructed to adhere to the Supreme Court's precedents in favor of gender neutrality and the right of any parent to raise their children as they see fit, they would have to assume that spending equal time with the parents is automatically to the child's benefit.

Newdow is well aware that attorneys and judges will dismiss this thinking as simplistic, and for years he has searched in vain for the science upon which child support is based. He has found none. Even prominent academics like Margaret Hagen at Boston University and Richard Warshak, a Dallas-based child psychologist who has testified in hundreds of trials and written several books on the harm that custody battles can do to children, have criticized the use of inkblot tests and misuse of the lifestyle-equalization standard as misguided. Newdow, who has developed an attorneys' proficiency in logic and argument, has also tried to rationalize the tying of child support dollars to the time each parent gets with the child. So far he has concluded that the intended benefit is superseded by the destructive effect of fighting that results when parents realize that their financial situation can be improved if they can convince the court that seeing both parents equally is not in the child's best interest, a fight that many judges are all too willing to enable. Newdow's conclusion is that the entire child custody and support apparatus is an arbitrary system that leads to the under-funding of children of poor non-custodial parents and the over-funding of the children of wealthy non-custodial parents. This argument formed a major part of the lawsuit that he submitted to replace the "best interests of the child" standard with a presumption that "fit" parents automatically share custody of their children 50/50.

Newdow's lawsuit pertaining to the "best interests of the child" was officially pronounced dead on November 20, 2012, when a state court of appeals in Sacramento affirmed a lower court's decision dismissing his case. While the appeals court stated that Newdow had chosen the wrong branch of government for redress, it nonetheless shed some light on the court's way of thinking. "To the extent plaintiffs' claim in this regard rests on the premise that every fit parent has a constitutional right to 50 percent custody when the parents cannot agree between themselves on how to divide the custody of their child," the opinion stated, "the law does not support this premise." The court declined to elaborate, perhaps because it is impossible to prove a negative—or perhaps because the assertion is absurd on its face. If the Supreme Court has ruled that there may be no gender bias in assigning custody rights to parents and that those parents must be presumed to act in the best interest of their children, then what argument is there to presume that the parents should have anything other than equal parenting time?

As for Newdow's assertion that the "best interests of the child" standard is vague, the court did not disagree. It did, however, assert that laws could only be found *unconstitutionally* vague if the law involves a certain type of constitutionally protected "conduct." For example, if a law allows restaurants to deny service to patrons who perform religious rituals prior to eating, the law might be struck down because the term "perform religious rituals" is vague and such rituals would be considered "conduct." However, according to the California appellate court deciding Newdow's case, a law that gives a judge the right to choose one parent over the other involves judicial discretion, which is not a type of constitutionally protected conduct. So the law cannot be struck down due to vagueness, even if it is in fact vague. If the appellate court's rationale itself sounds vague unto confusing, unfortunately the court has no obligation to explain itself clearly.

So the standard, and the wars between parents, will presumably continue. Newdow's lawsuit received virtually no coverage in the press and disappeared into what amounts to a pauper's grave. The first page of the appellate court's decision is even stamped with the command "NOT TO BE PUBLISHED." But stroll through any family court in the country and phrases from Newdow's complaint come to mind, none so much as the courts' manufacturing of what he termed "severe and prolonged conflict that results in little but increased inter-parental animus, increased parental distress, wasted parental time, wasted familial financial resources, and the shattering of a parent's life (as he or she is marginalized in the ability to love and nurture his or her children)." The appeals court dismissed Newdow's language as "hyperbolic," but anyone who has stepped inside of a family court knows exactly what Newdow was talking about.

WINNERS & LOSERS

Not that a trip downtown is necessary to understand what Newdow is talking about. Trolling the news websites on the Internet or watching television provides daily examples of custody battles gone awry. There is, for example, the bizarre case of basketball star Steve Nash. When the 39-year-old point guard was traded from the Phoenix Suns to the L.A. Lakers, it seemed like a dream come true for both Lakers fans and for Nash. His ex-wife and mother of their two children soon announced her intention to bring the children to California, where they could attend better schools and continue to see their father on a regular basis. But that would mean exposing Nash to child support payments of more than $1 million per year. His ex-wife had received a $5 million divorce settlement but had not been awarded child support in Arizona. Nash opposed the move. He said that he would be able to spend as much time with his children in Arizona whether he played for the Suns or the Lakers, and that a move could be disruptive for his children. The parents went back to court for an order on whether or not Nash's ex-wife would be allowed to move the children out of Arizona. Nash's lawyers presented an e-mail that purported to show the ex-wife scheming to

wait six months and then run to a California family court and secure
her $1 million-plus annual windfall. She countered that her wealthy ex-
husband was thinking of himself rather than his kids. Reading accounts
of the public court hearings, one could imagine Newdow tearing his
hair out at the insanity of it all—a parent with $5 million fighting over
more money at the expense of their children being thrust into an unnecessary battle. That the system was responsible for the conflict by
providing a giant financial disincentive for a father to work closer to his
children and a huge financial incentive for a mother to want to uproot
the children and move them to a new school, a new house, and a new
set of friends was self-evident.

But that is how the modern child support system works. Certainly,
there are winners, like the model-turned-reality-star Kimora Lee Simmons, whose child support payments of roughly $600,000 per year
help finance the over-the-top lifestyle familiar to viewers of her show,
The Fabulous Life of Kimora Lee. But there are losers, too, like the actor
Jon Cryer, who was ordered to continue paying a huge amount of
child support every month to his ex-wife. She had lost custody of
their son because of an injury sustained to the boy on her watch, but
the judge decided that the amount being paid in child support would
allow the ex-wife to maintain her standard of living, which, theoretically, might benefit the child someday if she regained partial custody
of the child.

To Simmons and Cryer's former wife's advantage, the court has no
interest in auditing the payments to make certain that "child support"
actually goes to supporting the child, which would be impossible anyway considering that the amount is not calculated based on the child's
needs in the first place. Interestingly, if an adult cashed an elderly parent's
social security check and spent it on themselves, they would probably
go to jail for fraud. Yet "supported" parents routinely spend their children's "support" money on themselves and the court not only turns a
blind eye but rewards them when they come back to fight for more.

DEADBEAT MOMS & ATHLETES

In 2011, a rare event propelled child support into the news: the twin
lockouts of NFL players and NBA athletes by the owners of their teams.

The average NFL player then made close to $2 million a year (before taxes and agency commissions) while the average NBA player made about three times that. But, as the head of a NFL players association estimated, roughly four out of five players were paying child support. So the media was treated to the specter of hundreds of millionaires lining up in family court to have their child support payments modified, at least until they started getting paid again.

Of course, many of the players' ex-wives lined up too. After all, a lowly athlete grossing one million a year could be expected to pay nearly $150,000 in annual support, an amount to which the ex-wives claimed they had become entitled. "It takes money to raise a child!" one of them protested to a journalist who asked if she could empathize with her ex. So here was a bizarre situation: fathers who had temporarily lost their jobs paying attorneys thousands of dollars to beg judges to lower what they paid their wives to raise their children, while the wives argued—often successfully—that the husbands should be forced to sell their homes, cars, and even their championship rings first. The NBA players union issued a 65-page booklet on how to cut expenses, but the players would have to abide by what the judge decided anyway. In an intact family, a father's job loss would have triggered sacrifices all around. This practice of making the non-custodial parent pay no matter his or her circumstances has created a kind of reverse double-standard: children of intact families are expected to sacrifice when times are tough while children from divorced homes are protected from circumstances by the expectation that they should enjoy the "intact" lifestyle until they graduate high school (and even long after in some states).

Of course, most of those lining up in the "parade of broken dreams" are not professional athletes making seven-figure incomes. They are fathers and mothers whose incomes, according to the statistics, have not kept up with the expense of feeding, housing, and educating their children while the amount of debt they have been forced to take on has skyrocketed. That family court judges treat these folks as though they were immune to economic hardship shows up in a sobering statistic that stayed relatively consistent when the economy was good. Of the hundreds of billions of dollars in child support that courts awarded from

1999 to 2009, only about 60% was actually received. And over the past four years, as unemployment has remained stubbornly high, the amount received has dropped 12%, suggesting that the ability to pay—and not attitude—is the primary driver of payment.

The reaction of legislatures has generally been to toughen child support collection laws, denying drivers licenses to men who are behind on support, for example, or publishing their names in the newspaper, even sending them to prison.[14] At present, approximately 50,000 fathers who are behind on child support are languishing in jail, where they obviously have little to no chance of earning the money needed to get them out.[15] That's because the conventional family court wisdom has been that fathers choose not to pay child support out of spite. The presumption is that a judge—or DissoMaster—would not force a father to pay an amount that he could not afford.

Katherine Porter, a professor of bankruptcy law at the University of California, Irvine, disagrees. In 2006, Porter was part of the Consumer Bankruptcy Project, a landmark study to determine why people go bankrupt. Since then, she has become a bankruptcy project fellow at Harvard and studied the topic for the World Bank. She was recently appointed by the California Attorney General to oversee a $21 billion mortgage relief fund, the purpose of which is to keep debt-ridden families in their homes.

Porter's research has yielded two revelations: divorce is one of the top three causes of personal bankruptcy, and the vast majority of people fail to pay an obligation like child support because they don't have the money—not because they don't want to or because they chose to spend the money on something frivolous. "You have families who are barely keeping their heads above water already," Porter explains, "and then the divorce court comes in and says that, after the families split, they should both maintain the pre-divorce lifestyle. That's mathematically impossible." While the court insists that the provider parent

---

14 http://www.acfc.org/e-newsletter-archive/31313listserve/

15 http://www.bergendispatch.com/articles/30734235/New-Jersey-Supreme-Court-Orders-Empty-the-Cells-At-The-Bergen-County-Work-Release-.aspx

achieve the impossible, they must bend to reality. Consequently, what often happens is that that parent starts using credit cards and other loans to make the child support (or alimony) payment in order to stay out of jail, digging a deeper hole.

In most cases, an individual—or a family—who ended up unable to make their obligations would share the pain and ultimately avail themselves of their constitutionally guaranteed bankruptcy rights. A judge or bankruptcy trustee would modify their support payments to a manageable level and they would have a chance at a fresh start. But here again, family court orders trump the Constitution. In fact, in this case family court orders trump a right, bankruptcy, that predates the Bill of Rights! Only the family court judge can modify support payments, which it turns out, they almost never do. While an intact family is thus able to move on with their lives, divorced parents often remain mired in an impossible situation.

As soon as the NBA and NFL lockouts ended, the child support modification story disappeared from the news cycle, replaced by the familiar story of deadbeat dads like Dallas Cowboys wide receiver Terrell Owens and Baltimore Ravens cornerback Chris McAllister, both of whom had been cut from their teams and then pleaded their inability to keep up with oversized child support awards. There is traditionally little to no sympathy for men, particularly strong, successful men, who fall on hard times and can't make child support payments—even if those payments are in the hundreds of thousands of dollars a year. Maybe it is hard to feel sympathy for anyone of such means, even if that means was fleeting, but professional athletes are far from the only ones penalized by the family court's intractability. In many states, such as Texas, the non-custodial spouse is required to pay child support, even if their ex-husband or ex-wife happens to be wealthy while they themselves are barely—or not quite—making it. For these litigants, the term "child support" is especially quixotic and the suffering particularly brutal.

8 | Courts of Equity

. . . judges . . . are liable to be tempted by bribery; that they are misled by favor, by relationship . . . and that the opinion of twelve honest jurymen gives still a better hope of right . . .
— *Thomas Jefferson, 1789*

In my world, there are no juries. I'm more comfortable with that.
— *Hon. Thomas Zampino, presiding family court judge, retired*

ULF CARLSSON, THE SACRAMENTO MAN WHOSE WIFE'S ATTORNEY HAD A close relationship with the judge, was lucky in one respect: his attorney had convinced him to pay a court reporter to transcribe the entire proceeding. The cost for three days was roughly $2,000, but Carlsson considers it money very well spent. Unlike Danielle Malmquist, owning a copy of the transcript allowed him to immediately file an appeal.

In family court, however, the "right" to file an appeal means little more than the "right" to spend $40,000 more on legal fees in order to go back to square one. As Mike Newdow points out, family court judges are effectively protected by the vagueness of the "best interest of the child" standard. Appeals courts cannot reverse a judge's assessment of character or weighing of the evidence unless it would be inconceivable that any judge in the state would make such a ruling. They can only reverse legal errors, and so, if a family court judge decides that it's better for a child to be with one parent rather than another, which, in effect, allows the judge to game the child support calculation, the parent losing custody has no recourse. No appellate court will second-guess such a determination. "What is there to appeal?" Newdow asks rhetorically. If the family court judge evaluated the parents first-hand in the courtroom and decided that one parent was more "fit" than the other, what can an appellate court say? Appellate court judges do not meet the parents; they merely read legal briefs and search for legal errors. They cannot claim that they can make a better assessment of character by reading a document. As a result, in California, where both Newdow and Carlsson were divorced, only a small fraction of family court cases are overturned on appeal.

THE DO-OVER

Carlsson was unique in the sense that his judge had not only ruled inequitably on every issue —he lost custody of his daughter, was forced to pay his ex-wife's attorneys, and was ordered to sell his house rather than be allowed to pay his ex-wife for her half of the equity—but that the judge had committed a blatant procedural error. He had left the courtroom while his attorney was in mid-sentence (Carlsson's ex-wife's attorney had finished her case a day earlier). In other words, the judge had not followed the rules, which is very much something that can be appealed. The only problem was that Carlsson had gone broke paying the attorneys and his ex-wife. So he did what Andrew Karres and Wendy Archer and a lot of other litigants do. He went to his elderly parents and asked them for a loan. It was humiliating for a middle-aged man, especially one who had left Sweden in pursuit of happiness and wealth in America. On May 8, 2008, two years, two months, and a day after the conclusion of Carlsson's divorce trial, the appellate court ruled in Carlsson's favor and ordered a new trial with a different judge (citing a Greek proverb in the decision: Only judge when you have heard all). But the appellate court did not reach any decisions with respect to Carlsson's underlying divorce case. In other words, even if appellate courts overturn a ruling, they rarely substitute their own ruling on the underlying matter; they merely send the case back to the original court for a do-over.

At this point, Carlsson had another problem. The appeal had caused his parents to reach the limits of their savings and max out their home equity, so neither Carlsson nor his parents could afford a new trial.

Nor would the government pay for a new trial, even though a government employee, the judge, had committed what could be equated to malpractice by walking out of the courtroom mid-trial. Ulf was left in the unfortunate situation of having to pay two attorneys (his and his wife's) for two trials in order to get a single fair one. Adding insult to injury, even though the appellate court had vacated (thrown out) the judge's original order, Carlsson's ex-wife's attorney refused to give back the $40,000 that the vacated order had required Carlsson to pay her. And he had no chance of forcing her to give the money back unless he could afford to go back to court in hopes that another judge would order her to do so. It was the classic case of winning the battle but losing the war.

CHALLENGING BIAS

Carlsson possessed two remaining options. He could file a complaint against the judge, whose behavior the appellate court had excoriated in its reversal, and he could sue the judge for denying his right to due process. He decided to do both, thinking that he had nothing else to lose. He could not have been more wrong.

Of course, if most Americans can no longer afford a divorce attorney, the number who can afford to file an appeal is almost negligible anyway. For the masses, then, there is effectively one recourse: to prove that the judge is biased or possesses a conflict of interest and have them removed from the case (recusal).

Wendy Archer, the Dallas mother who filed an enforcement motion only to lose custody of her two children and all of her money, felt confident that she had built a compelling case for recusal of her judge. After all, her ex-husband's law firm was one of the judge's top campaign donors, the firm had had a prior business relationship with the judge, and the *amicus* attorney also had an existing relationship with the judge. It made perfect sense that a judge would favor a campaign donor over a non-donor and that an *amicus* attorney would help her friend and benefactor, the judge, arrive at the judge's desired result. Archer's motion for recusal, filed atop a stack of documents from the Texas Election Commission, was transferred to a judge a few doors down, where it sat for weeks while Archer—and her children—waited and worried.

It is difficult, maybe impossible, for those who have not gone to family court to understand the particular dread that this kind of waiting inspires. Elena Haskins, a litigant from Nevada County, California, describes constantly wondering if she would get "the good judge or the bad judge" before a given hearing. And by that she meant which personality her judge would display. Emily Gallup confirms that Haskins' judge was known to have a far more professional demeanor before lunch but became irascible after her hour break, leaving everyone to conjecture what, exactly, she had consumed. Gerald Nissenbaum, the Boston attorney fond of bow ties and suspenders, says that family law judges are often unfamiliar with the law itself and naturally insecure. As they approach retirement, Nissenbaum says, they tend to get "burned out" and impatient—hardly good qualities for someone who will decide what happens to a family. Joe Kenan, the psychiatrist, says that he's observed a lot of anti-social behavior on the bench and that some people become family court judges "in order to hurt people." During his appeal, Ulf Carlsson learned that his judge had been convicted of wrongdoing twice before. In the last instance, he had illegally cut down trees on public property to enhance his view of the American River, and then he lied about it when he was caught. The episode earned the judge, Peter McBrien, the nickname "Chainsaw McBrien" but did not get him removed from the bench.

The decision on the recusal of Archer's judge—by a judge in the same courthouse—is a stunning document. In refusing to assign a different, less conflicted judge to Archer's case, the neighbor judge excoriates not only Archer but all litigants for not donating money to the re-election campaigns of judges! The resulting shortfall, writes the judge, leaves only the attorneys to donate money to these campaigns. Not to worry, however, he concludes, because attorneys only donate money to "good judges." That this begs the question of what constitutes a "good judge" seems obvious, but litigants like Archer assume the term refers to judges who rule in that attorney's favor.

One of the most bizarre recusal cases occurred in the case of Malmquist versus Malmquist, the Memphis divorce between the FedEx pilot and his ex-wife, Danielle. While preparing her appeal, Danielle Malmquist discovered—by accident—a police report that had been filed against her by her own judge. Apparently, the accusation stemmed from a run-in that Malmquist had with a private investigator hired by her husband, an unlicensed investigator who had used her own husband, a police officer, to illegally run checks on the targets of her investigations, including Malmquist. The private investigator had secretly made sinister allegations about Danielle Malmquist to the judge in clear violation of Malmquist's due process rights, assumedly in order to further bias the judge in favor of Malmquist's husband. When Malmquist brought it to the court's attention that she knew about the police investigation that the judge had initiated and kept secret, both the private investigator and her police officer husband were reprimanded, though not seriously.

Malmquist then filed a motion for the judge to recuse himself. Shockingly, he refused, stating that he bore no ill will to the woman he had earlier suspected of being a threat to his life. The judge did, however, order her to take down her blog through which she gave her account of these convoluted events. He also sent her to jail a couple of times on contempt charges, the result of her wanting to see her sons. His rationale: Malmquist's writing about her case was not in the best interest of her children, who were not yet old enough to read or access the Internet. Malmquist did manage to get a couple of local television stations to cover the story, but while such stories seem to shock the general public, nothing changed for Malmquist or her sons. The judge remains in complete control of the case, lawyers continue to make money off of it, and Malmquist has not seen her children in over four years.

THE PALACE OF PERJURY

Bonnie Russell, a Southern California journalist who publishes familylawcourts.com, laughs. "He who lies first lies best," she says. Privately, judges and attorneys bemoan the pervasive courtroom culture of lying while doing almost nothing to stop it. As predicted in Caroline Norton's 1839 letter to the Chancellor of the House of Lords, lying has become so common that Steven Kolodny, a Los Angeles-based attorney who teaches family law and has represented the billionaire Kirk Kerkorian's ex-wife and movie star Mel Gibson, among others, calls the downtown Los Angeles courthouse the Palace of Perjury. But Kolodny is one of the few family court professionals who get worked up about it. He would prefer to cross-examine every witness under oath, as is common practice in criminal and civil courts, but the family courts claim that there is no time. Instead, the litigants typically remain at a table with their lawyers, raise their right hand, and take a truncated oath before engaging in brief exchanges with the judge. "So many times," a now-retired New Orleans judge named Sol Gothard says, "Litigants swear to tell the truth, the whole truth, and nothing but the truth. And then they proceed to lie like hell!" Gothard claims that if he had enforced the rule against perjury in his courtroom, everyone would have gone to jail.

Thomas Zampino, the New Jersey presiding judge, is more optimistic. "There was a study," he says, "that the best people at determining whether someone was lying were FBI agents and family court judges." Schnider, the retired L.A. judge who now rents out his services for $500 an hour, thinks he's pretty good at discerning the truth but admits that, while he was on the bench, he "must have been fooled by some pretty good liars." In his more than half-century in family court, Sorrell Trope cannot recall a single instance of perjury being punished.

Malmquist never had a chance to disprove the investigator's lie because she was not even aware of it. At least, in her case, the police conducted an investigation and concluded that there had never been any merit in the investigator's allegations. But of the millions of lies told in family court, most go unchallenged and many, as we'll see, have consequences more dire than prison. Most troubling, perhaps, is how the non-enforcement of the oath litigants take to tell the truth has eliminated one more check to keep the scales of justice in balance.

JURIES AND OTHER SAFEGUARDS

For centuries, civilized courtrooms have separated the role of the decision maker (jury) from the role of the referee (judge). Thus, civil and criminal courts in the United States operate with both a jury and a judge so that no one person, as the saying goes, can be "judge, jury, and executioner."

But in family court, a judge does act as judge, jury, and "executioner." And, as mentioned earlier, the appellate courts are essentially powerless to overturn a family court judge's decision. As illustrated in Shakespeare's *Macbeth* and later paraphrased by Lord Acton: "Power tends to corrupt, and absolute power corrupts absolutely." Family courts suffer terribly from this human failing, and yet our judicial branch of government justifies the lack of checks and balances by claiming that the family courts are not "courts of law" but, rather, "courts of equity."

The sixth amendment of the U.S. Constitution states, "In all criminal prosecutions, the accused shall enjoy the right to a speedy and public trial, by an impartial jury . . . to be confronted with the witnesses against him; to have compulsory process for obtaining witnesses in his favor, and to have the Assistance of Counsel for his defense." But the judicial branch of government has sidestepped all of these protections by arguing that family court cases are not criminal prosecutions and therefore the court need not be speedy or public, need not provide a jury, need not allow the litigants to confront the witnesses who testify against them, and need not allow the litigants to call witnesses in their favor. And, as mentioned earlier, there is no right to counsel paid for by the state. Even though a family court judge can send a litigant to jail, the judicial branch of government argues that traditional constitutional protections do not apply in family court because the name plate that covers the front entrance to the family courthouse does not say Criminal Court.

Citizens might hope, then, that the seventh amendment to the U.S. Constitution would protect them: "In suits at common law, where the value in controversy shall exceed twenty dollars, the right of trial by jury shall be preserved . . ." Family courts should at least provide juries, correct? Wrong, according to the judicial branch of our government, which has determined that family courts are not courts of common law but of equity. Remarkably, it is not stated anywhere in the U.S. Constitution that there are any such things as courts of equity, nor does it state that courts of equity would be exempt from providing the protections of the sixth or seventh amendments. In fact the U.S. constitution only mentions "equity" once, in Section 2 of Article 3: "The judicial Power shall extend to all Cases, in Law and Equity arising under this Constitution . . ."

Courts of equity originated in England around the time of Henry VIII. They were essentially courts of appeal, where citizens could appeal to the king in the event that the law may have produced an unfair result based on the particular circumstances, such as fraud or deceit, or where a fair result could not be quantified with money. Henry, being too busy putting his wives to death at the time, delegated these appeals to his Chancellor, who also was too busy to be bothered with boring matters such as justice. And so the Chancellor set up the Courts of Chancery, as written about by Charles Dickens, and delegated these matters mostly to clerics of the Church of England.

Prior to the American Revolution, some of the early U.S. colonies also established courts of equity, but the federal government freed itself from many old English traditions, particularly ones that had demonstrated abuses against individual freedoms. The Constitution thus set up the Supreme Court and gave Congress the power to create "inferior courts." In short, congress never created courts of equity. Instead, the Constitution granted the judiciary the power to make decisions "in equity" and "in law" both within the same courtrooms. In other words, the judiciary has the power to deviate from or add to written law in situations where fairness would be better served.

In general, suits brought in equity today are over non-monetary disputes, the idea being that monetary relief would be inadequate or the damages unquantifiable. An example would be blocking a developer from building on land protected by an open-space easement. The original intent of the open-space easement was to protect the natural beauty of the land in perpetuity, and thus arises an important question: How does one quantify in dollars the harm inflicted by altering that natural beauty? Reasonable people might come up with very different numbers, and so a court of equity is granted the power to devise other remedies such as ordering the developer to tear down the offending structures and pay for the restoration of the land. The English kings of yesteryear believed that a judge, not a jury, could best craft such one-off solutions. Thus the lack of a jury is purely historical in nature, not Constitutionally mandated, although beloved by the judiciary who do not have to deal with the extra work of a jury trial.

Suits based in law, on the other hand, are usually quantifiable. And according to the U.S. Constitution, when that quantity is more than $20, the parties are entitled to a jury trial.[16] Civil suits that involve both issues of equity and issues quantified with money are heard by a judge for the equity part and a jury for the monetary part. A judge does not decide the monetary issues without a jury in civil court.

However, divorces and other family matters have been deemed "equitable" matters, again primarily for historical reasons. Until the 1900s, women were not allowed to file suits against their husbands because women were the property of their husbands and had no independent protection under the law. Therefore, the only possible recourse for a woman, if she lived in a U.S. colony that still operated a court of equity, was to have the matter filed there. If she did not live such a colony, then her only option was to find an agent to take the matter up as an issue "in equity." Another historical reason for treating divorce as an equitable matter is that marriage was considered a lifetime contract of a personal nature for which there could be no monetary relief. You could not take an amount of money and go out and buy a new husband (at least not legally). If a woman lived in an age when non-virgins were viewed as unsuitable for marriage, what law could quantify monetary damages that were appropriate to compensate a woman for her husband breaking a marriage contract?

But society has changed and so has the law. Women now have an equal right to work and to earn a living. With the advent of no-fault divorce, marriage is no longer looked upon as a lifetime contract requiring so-called equitable remedies if broken. In fact, modern-day marriage, as seen through the lens of the law, is more like a business partnership than anything else. And the dissolution of a business partnership typically proceeds according to the law, not the vague notions of equity. Divorce court today is about dividing the joint assets, not about who was at fault (or at least it is not supposed to be about who was at fault). So why doesn't a jury decide these cases?

---

16 The founding fathers never anticipated that Franklin Roosevelt would alter the price of gold or that Richard Nixon would take the United States off the gold standard, respectively giving birth and vigor to modern day inflation.

One could argue that the fate of children is not a monetary issue, but as we've seen, in most states *the custody of the children is directly related to the amount of child support to be paid each month*. If two parties each claimed that they owned a plot of land and one party started to build on the land, the other party could bring a suit in equity to ask a judge to halt the construction until a determination is made regarding true ownership. That would not demand a jury, but deciding who actually owns the land and how much that owner had been damaged requires a jury. How then, by analogy, do family courts justify not only deciding who in effect takes possession of the children but, in the absence of a jury, how much cash must be paid every month by the other parent? And although some states compute such amounts based on computer-automated statutes, the family court judge has the discretion to override the computer's results and change the amount based on circumstances—and without a jury.

All of this raises a simple question: Why is it that a single person has the power to dissolve or not dissolve a marriage, to divide the assets, assign custody of the children to one parent or the other, and to set or vary the amount of support payments one spouse must pay to the other, all without a jury? And how is it that a single judge has the power to send the parties to jail, again without a jury? Because that's what the king of England once did? Are we that illogical and bound by tradition? You might argue that we still measure in pounds, ounces, feet, yards, miles, acres, and other ill-conceived and cumbersome standards because the cost of conversion to a better system is too great and so why not keep this one for like reasons? But what if the cost were minimal? Or what if conversion could save us $50 billion per year?

A MODEST PRESCRIPTION

Occasionally when a patient is nearing death in a hospital, the doctors, out of complete desperation, stop all medications. And sometimes the patient "miraculously" improves. Through this exercise, the doctors might learn that the patient was not dying because of a failure to respond to the medications, but because the mixture of medications being administered was toxic. The Scandinavian countries have demonstrated that, when it comes to the dissolution of a marriage, the medicine prescribed in the U.S. is worse than the cure and that divorce and custody can be resolved not only without juries and lawyers and custody evaluators and thousands of pages of family codes, but also without judges and family courts.

Tear down the family courts? Not necessary. Leave the buildings as they are. Just convert them to day care centers with a fraction of the $50 billion per year savings.

9 | Who Me? Biased?

*I was given an award by the Defense Bar. That trip was
to Spain, all expenses paid. And we had two other judges
along . . . and there was no conflict whatsoever . . .*
—*Hon. Sol Gothard, retired judge*
New Orleans, LA

I<small>T MUST HAVE BEEN A COOL AFTERNOON IN LATE</small> M<small>AY WHEN</small> U.S.
Supreme Court Chief Justice John Roberts penned the dissenting
opinion in the case of Caperton v. Massey Coal Company[17] because the
issue at stake, campaign contributions to judges, fuels a fever in the
mind of just about any judge. Five of the other justices had ruled
that judges must recuse themselves when a "substantial campaign
contributor" is a party in a case. It was the first time in history that the
U.S. Supreme Court acknowledged that a "probability of a conflict
of interest" was a concern. Justices Scalia, Thomas, and Alito joined
Roberts in the dissent.

The case involved a campaign contribution of $3 million made,
both directly and indirectly, to a candidate for a West Virginia State Supreme Court seat. The candidate won the election and subsequently
ruled, on appeal, in favor of the donor of the $3 million. The question
before the U.S. Supreme Court was whether the West Virginia justice
should have recused himself from hearing the case.

---

17 Caperton et al. v. A.T. Massey Coal Co., Inc., et al. 556 U.S. No. 08-22,
June 8, 2009.

THE BRAIN VAULT

In Justice Roberts' dissenting opinion, he lamented that raising the specter of judicial bias might erode the public's perception that judges are honest, wise, and fair individuals: "There is a 'presumption of honesty and integrity in those serving as adjudicators.' All judges take an oath to uphold the Constitution and apply the law impartially, and we trust that they will live up to this promise." And citing another opinion, "We should not, even by inadvertence, 'impute to judges a lack of firmness, wisdom, or honor.'"

The dissenting justices focused on a potential gray zone between *de minimis* campaign contributions and contributions warranting a self-recusal. Where does a judge draw the line, they argued: $100, $1,000, $10,000?

The judicial branch of government operates on the assumption that judges can cordon off the portion of their brain where they store prejudicial information and ignore it. Bias in their decisions is presumably eliminated by teaching the judges to consider only information stored in the "evidence" part of their brain when formulating a decision. The judicial branch does not believe that the general public has the ability to ignore prejudicial information, however, and so juries are protected from hearing information that might engender bias. Since family courts have eliminated the safeguard of a jury, in their role as substitute jury, judges are exposed to all types of prejudicial facts.

Although the judicial branch believes that family court judges are capable of being unbiased in their decisions, one would be hard-pressed to find a neuroscientist who would offer a plausible neurological model to support such a controllable split-brain model. To the contrary, Nobel prizes have been granted to behavioral scientists who have demonstrated that cognitive bias is both powerful and difficult to detect. The very fact that the judiciary believes that judges are capable of suppressing bias in and of itself exemplifies "belief bias," "self-serving bias," and "confidence bias." Given this culture of denial within the court, however, it's not that hard to understand how four of nine Supreme Court justices would think that a judge could completely ignore a $3 million campaign contribution.

When there is a vacancy in the U.S. Supreme Court, the President nominates a candidate for the open position and then Congress essentially interrogates the nominee, looking for inherent prejudices. Why does Congress go to such extremes? Because people outside of the judiciary know that human beings are subconsciously influenced by our biases and prejudices. We safeguard the Supreme Court by requiring nine justices to sit on the bench. Our founding fathers knew that human beings, no matter how well-meaning, see things differently and that nobody is capable of providing impartial justice in all situations. A panel of nine individuals is likely to have a spectrum of biases and prejudices that hopefully negate each other. Shine red light, green light, and blue light at the same spot, and you create white light. The individual light frequencies, in aggregate, produce a different, more neutral result than any of the light frequencies alone. Yet in family court, you either get the red judge, the green judge, or the blue judge; and each of them thinks that any bias they may bear can be cordoned off into a hypothetical sector of their brain that science has yet to discover. The victims interviewed in conjunction with this book leave little doubt that our judicial establishment is either grossly naïve when it comes to human psychology or callously negligent when it comes to providing impartial justice in family court.

While the 2009 Supreme Court case was about campaign contributions, Justice Roberts went on to explain that campaign contributions are not the only factor that can give rise to a probability or appearance of bias. He wrote:

> In any given case, there are a number of factors that could give rise to a "probability" or "appearance" of bias: friendship with a party or lawyer, prior employment experience, membership in clubs or associations, prior speeches and writings, religious affiliation, and countless other considerations. We have never held that the Due Process Clause requires recusal for any of these reasons, even though they could be viewed as presenting a "probability of bias."

Precisely! Although the dissenting justices argued that a $3 million campaign contribution was only one among many reasons why a judge might be biased, they seemed to have missed the larger point. All of these factors are apt to create bias! Precisely the reason no single human being should be judge, jury, and executioner.

RELATIONSHIPS WITH LAWYERS

Take, for example, "friendship with a party or lawyer." Who among the entire human race can completely disregard a friendship when trying to act impartially? Or take "prior employment experience." In Danielle Malmquist's case, her judge once worked at the same law firm as her ex-husband's attorney. Did it influence how the judge saw the case, treated the ex-husband's lawyer, or treated Danielle?

"They have a family law section of the Los Angeles County Bar," says retired judge Robert Schnider as he sits in his bright yellow living room, "that's very active, that puts on programs. Some judges will sit on that executive committee from time to time. Judges will be in all of the programs that they present. You work together with them on panels, on presentations. So there's a lot of contact and communication, and you see these same lawyers all the time." In other words, a group of lawyers called a "Bar Association" has organized committees, panels, programs, and presentations to mingle lawyers and judges together in what the four dissenting Supreme Court justices identified as "membership in clubs and associations." In fact, bar associations create all-expenses-paid junkets for judges so that they may socialize with well-connected lawyers in pleasant surroundings.[18] Judge Sol Gothard described a trip to Spain organized by and paid for by the Louisiana Association of Defense Counsel (LACD). A brochure for this sponsored event offers a description of the lodgings in the Palace Hotel that states ". . . cocktails will launch the program," and then goes on to tout "excursions" and "beaches, bars, shops, restaurants, and vineyards." When asked how he felt about this, Judge Gothard said, "It was no conflict whatsoever . . . I love my lawyers."

In March 2014 the LACD will organize a ski trip to Beaver Creek, Colorado. Should judges and lawyers be free to have fun? Of course.

---

18 http://ladc.org/associations/12861/files/2011-09-12%20LADC%20
   Costa%20Rica%20Annual%20Meeting%202012.pdf

Should they do it together? Probably not, especially when a judge who has enjoyed the hospitality of such lawyers later finds him or herself trying to decide on the fate of a family, one of whose members is represented by such a lawyer, and the other is there alone without representation.

Pasadena family law attorney and "Super Lawyer" Mark Baer's bio on the *Huffington Post* website, a favorite forum for divorce attorneys seeking publicity, reveals that he is "recognized as a 'thought leader' in many areas of Family Law for his provocative and forward-thinking ideas on improving the way in which Family Law is handled." A popular post on his personal website concerns the potential for judicial bias and what his firm does about it:

> EVERY judicial officer has their own personal biases in the family law court. We therefore try to determine whether the judge assigned to a particular case is biased for or against our client. We select custody evaluators that are hopefully biased in favor of our particular client. The same exact case would have incredibly different results from one court to the next. The bias impacts the judge's factual findings, the great discretion they are given and how they opt to apply the law. This bias exists in no other area of law to this degree. No amount of bias elimination training can educate a judge to forget about their life experiences, assumptions, personal beliefs/views and biases. This issue alone makes family law litigation very unfair and inequitable.

Baer's frank admission of judicial bias might seem provocative to those unfamiliar with the workings of the family court, but he actually understates the problem while not fully assigning blame for its cause. Judicial bias is not only an inevitable fact of life, as his article suggests, but is it not necessarily passive, the natural result of, say, religious convictions or a particular upbringing. Much, if not most, of the time bias is manufactured by the very law firms and bar associations that support judges. In Baer's court in Southern California, for example, the family law bar throws an annual awards ceremony for their "Family Judge of the Year" in an elegant ballroom overlooking the San Gabriel

Mountains. Although the price of such an event, including crystal chandeliers, a cocktail hour, and "old Hollywood glamour" ambience, begins around $10,000. The meal alone costs a minimum of $70 per plate, but the judge pays nothing. The bar even produces a glossy video of the tribute for free.

Savvy lawyers who understand the importance of getting in good with the judge can lavish attention—and money—on the men and women who hear their cases in a host of other ways. There are committee appointments for judges, and even the spouses of judges, that can pay in the range of five and six figures for very little work and no responsibility. There are gatherings held by the Inns of the Courts— exclusive social clubs that bring together attorneys, judges, and law school professors for closed-door sessions—their dual purposes advertised as discussing matters of law and "breaking bread." This despite federal and state canons that bar judges from social and professional relationships that might prejudice their judgments or give the appearance of favoring one litigant over another.

EXTRACURRICULAR ACTIVITIES

While family court judges in most states are forbidden by law from accepting direct gifts in excess of several hundred dollars, they remain free to moonlight for and schmooze with the law firms whose cases they hear, just as long as they claim that they won't be biased by the money or the perks—a loophole that even the judges themselves seem to find laughable. As retired Los Angeles family court judge (and current private judge) Robert Schnider admits, "We aren't much different from any other segment of society in terms of money calling the shots."

What did the four dissenting Supreme Court justices mean when they wrote "and countless other considerations" that could create a probability of bias? There is a little known jackpot at the end of the rainbow for some judges who play their cards right. In many states, a judge need serve only 10 years before retiring, and that retirement often comes with a near-full-salary pension for the rest of their life. So what does a judge do at age 50 after 10 years of "serving the public"? Play golf every day? After 10 years of listening to people complaining and whining and lying, who can blame the ones who choose to do so? But more ambitious judges have found ways to double or triple their retirement income.

Some jurisdictions are short of judges and need to fill public courtrooms with judges "pro tem" (temporary judges). Like substitute teachers, these judges come in for a day, a week, a month or more to fill spots left vacant by judges who have left for political office or because of age-related issues or for health reasons. Pro tem judges can even be used to fill their old courtroom now vacant because of their retirement. So a judge can retire one day with a $150,000 (or more) per year pension and come back the next day to do the same job for yet more money. Or a retired judge can come back the next day as a lawyer to the same courtroom that they presided over for 10 years and appear before judges who were peers, and perhaps friends, the day before.

But the fastest-growing source of judicial bias—and the biggest monetary prize by far—is private judging. While public courts pay judges $50 to $125 per hour for their work, private law firms can arrange for the judges to earn $500 or more per hour participating in a process called "alternative dispute resolution," ADR for short. And how does a retired judge entice a law firm to hire them for a $500 per hour assignment? According to a prominent national association of family law experts, by getting in good with these firms while they are still seated on the bench.

THE SECOND SYSTEM

Across a wide promenade on the west side of Los Angeles, above the glittering Century City Mall, sits a massive new glass office building, the middle cut out to give the effect of an arch. The building is known in entertainment circles as The Death Star. It houses Hollywood's premier talent agency, Creative Artists Agency, which manages the careers of such celebrities as Steven Spielberg, Tom Cruise, and Alec Baldwin. Rising far above this building are a pair of massive white triangles known as Century Park East and West. The buildings are surrounded by manicured gardens and parking is valet-only. The address is so exclusive that the Bank of America on the ground floor doubles as an art museum.

It is here, in expansive offices on the 12th floor, that Dennis Wasser, an elegantly thin man in his 60s who favors tailored suits and expensive ties, and his daughter, Laura, decked out in gold jewelry and fitted designer dresses, ply their trade as celebrity divorce attorneys. When asked what justifies their hourly rates, reportedly more than $1,000 per hour for him and nearly that for her, Wasser smiles and ticks off a number of items, most of which don't have to do with the law at all but with accounting and asset valuation.

"No-fault made divorce into a business-type trial," Wasser says by way of establishing the terms of the debate. He means that his clients need someone to hire the experts and to manage what amounts to a merger in reverse that, for the Wassers' clients, can routinely reach into the hundreds of millions, if not the billions, of dollars. But apart from the amount of money at stake, it turns out that the family code has remarkably little in common with the laws governing commerce—or anything else for that matter. There is no other body of law that automatically assumes that one side is entitled to receive and the other to pay. Nor under any other legal code does the outcome rely on individuals who are not, in any meaningful way, a party to the dispute: the children. And the temptation to manipulate and even corrupt what would amount to innocent bystanders in any other court, while always present, becomes exponentially greater when more money is at stake. This is something that the Wassers know all too well.

In 2002, Dennis Wasser was hired to represent Kirk Kerkorian, a very private man who, at the time, just happened to be the billionaire owner of MGM. Kerkorian had been led to believe that he had fathered a baby girl with a much younger woman, a tennis pro by the name of Lisa Bonder. He believed this because, as it turns out, Bonder had convinced Kerkorian's real daughter to give her a buccal swab.[19] The older woman claimed it was necessary for a school project. She then presented the swab as if it was her baby's and the results came back that Kerkorian was the father of the younger child. He then briefly married Bonder so that the child would not be illegitimate. Not surprisingly, the marriage quickly fell apart and he filed for divorce. Bonder then

---

19 A cotton swab taken from inside of the real daughter's cheek

demanded $320,000 a month in child support, including $70,000 for her infant's birthday party at the Beverly Hills Hotel. She claimed that amount was necessary for the child to be raised in what her lawyer called "the lifestyle consistent with the daughter of Kirk Kerkorian"— even though she knew that her daughter was not his and even though common sense would suggest that an infant did not require $4 million a year to live on.

Convinced that Bonder was lying, Wasser did something straight out of the pre-no-fault playbook. He hired a Hollywood PI named Anthony Pellicano, a shadowy figure fond of explosives, dead fish, and wiretaps. Pellicano bugged Bonder's phone and listened in on her conversations for weeks, gathering evidence of her legal strategy as well as tidbits that could be leaked out now and then to intimidate her. As it turned out, however, the FBI was listening in on Pellicano, who is now serving hard time in a federal penitentiary for illegal wiretapping, among other crimes.

In the end, Kerkorian discovered that the true father of his "daughter" was a wealthy film producer (his lawyers' attempts to involve the real father in his daughter's life proved fruitless, probably because of the threat that the child support battle would then be thrust into his lap), but the billionaire agreed to continue making payments of more than $50,000 a month in child support—the settlement reached with his ex-wife and approved by the family court. Wasser was named a "person of interest" in the FBI investigation of Pellicano, though he was never charged with any crime, but the episode was a major embarrassment for both Wasser and Kerkorian. It was for Bonder as well, who tried to justify her child support claim in a disastrous interview with Katie Couric and was universally labeled a fortune hunter by the media. What was not reported in the media was the role of the family code in encouraging the fraud and the reaction to it, which have left Bonder's young daughter with nearly a million dollars a year in disposable income but without a father. Her only role model is a mother who used trickery and deceit to manipulate laws that equate "the best interests" of her daughter with cash.

Sitting in a leather chair in the sleek conference room of his office, Wasser seems above the dirty war in which he played a central role and disconnected from the straight line that connects the family code to such tactics. "We have the best system for divorce in the world," he says in a measured, earnest baritone—utterly cognizant of the rarefied atmosphere in which he and his daughter operate. "But don't take our clients as examples of the status quo," he warns. These are people, after all, who live in homes worth well into eight figures and travel the world in private jets that cost more to operate in a year than most families will earn in a lifetime. Access to the best—attorneys like Wasser and private investigators and forensic accountants—is just one more perk of being ultra-wealthy. What may be more surprising is that they now have access to something far more valuable: fast and discreet justice.

Apart from the huge numbers, it turns out that the Kerkorian divorce was not so extraordinary in two major respects: it spawned a battle royal in the name of the best interests of a child and was played out in full view of the public. As Wasser points out, the State of California considers all family court documents public unless the litigants are able to seal them, a lengthy and expensive process that the courts are reluctant to entertain. He has found the solution to this last issue in a burgeoning spin-off of the family court business: alternative dispute resolution. ADR allows attorneys to hire a private judge quickly and to conduct mediation and even a divorce trial in the confines of a private office.

Hiring retired judges to mediate disputes is nothing new. The world's largest alternative dispute resolution company, JAMS, was founded in 1979. Whether using rent-a-judges to dissolve marriages is a good idea, or even ethical, however, is a matter of opinion. Wasser is a fan—in no small part because it dovetails with his notion of divorce as business litigation. His concerns are more abstract. "It creates two systems," he says. "One for the rich and one for the poor."

Sorrell Trope's well-honed legal instincts sense an older problem rearing its head: judicial bias. He suggests that the rent-a-judges might favor those represented by law firms who bring them the most business. Trope prefers to go to court. But as it turns out, the mere existence of private judges has engendered a troubling conflict of interest, whether one uses them or not.

In Wasser and Trope's state, one of the oldest and largest associations of family law specialists, known as ACFLS, the Association of

Certified Family Law Specialists, has documented a disturbing trend. Non-family law judges, according to one of its recent reports, are requesting family law assignments on the eve of their retirement. Those judges may not know much about family law, but they do know that, even with the weakest of credentials in family court, they can snag hugely lucrative cases as a rent-a-judge upon their retirement. That, according to the ACFLS report, creates a biased courtroom. In the words of the report:

> Some judicial officers make transparent efforts to develop relationships with those of us who have clients who can afford private judges. More importantly, the availability of family law judges for hire compromises the appearance of judicial independence and increases the disparity between the quality of and access to justice available to the wealthy and that enjoyed by most people.

One prominent law firm boasts in advertisements and on their Internet site that their team of more than 600 lawyers nationwide wins their cases over 85% of the time! How do they accomplish this? Are all 600 lawyers in the firm mind-readers, capable of selecting only clients who are destined to win their cases? Does the firm turn away wealthy clients who are unlikely to win? Nothing like this is mentioned on the firm's web site. The real answer is obvious.

Not everyone who decides to rent-a-judge is rich and not everyone who waits in Bob Simms' parade of broken dreams is poor. For those with the ability to choose, meaning those who not only can afford to shell out the additional fees for the private judge but who can convince their spouse to do the same, choosing between a courthouse and a private office is placing a bet on where justice is most likely to happen. A public court, where the officers have all sworn to uphold the Constitution and who work beneath majestic seals and beside oversized flags, would be the obvious choice for a fair, if not expeditious, resolution of disagreements in an unbiased system. But it turns out that this assumption is false because the general public does not know who has raised money for whom, who is friends with whom, who used to work side-by-side with whom, who is in the same club or association or church or synagogue or serves on the same committees as whom, who has been invited on which junket and by whom, and who is a few months from retirement and is jockeying for plum assignments at $500 per hour or for an "Of Counsel" corner office at a big law firm in a high-rise across the street.

As Bonnie Russell, the journalist and publisher of the family court watchdog website www.familylawcourts.com, observes, "Most people hire an attorney and assume that person will be their advocate. But that's only partially true because the relationships between the attorneys and the court existed before they arrived and will remain long after they leave. The attorney/client relationship is temporary. A the end of the day, the litigants are basically grist for the mill."

IMMUNITY FOR JUDGES

Linda Sparkman was 15 years old when her mother brought her to the DeKalb Memorial Hospital in DeKalb County, Indiana. Linda had been told that she was to have her appendix removed. Instead her fallopian tubes were cut and tied. The doctor sterilized her. Although this might seem like the buildup to a medical malpractice case, here the courtroom proceedings took place before the surgical procedure.

Linda's mother had not been happy with her daughter's behavior. Linda had been seeing "young men" against her mother's wishes, and she had stayed out with them overnight on several occasions. Linda's mother consulted with a lawyer who filed a petition with the DeKalb Circuit Court to have Linda sterilized. Even though Linda attended public school and was promoted each year with her class, the petition claimed that Linda was "somewhat retarded."

Judge Harold D. Stump did not demand a hearing on the matter. Nor did Judge Stump appoint a guardian *ad litem* to look out for Linda's best interests. Linda was not examined or questioned by the court. She did not appear in court, nor was she told about the petition. She was just taken to the hospital.

About two years later, Linda married, and when she was unable to become pregnant, she and her husband investigated. They learned that Linda had been sterilized. They filed a federal lawsuit pursuant to

42 U.S.C. Section 1983 against Linda's mother, the mother's attorney, Circuit Judge Stump, and the doctors who performed the sterilization. Because federal law 42 U.S.C. Section 1983 pertains only to the actions of a state or someone employed by a state, the federal court dismissed the suit regarding all individuals other than Judge Stump, a state employee. But the court found that Judge Stump was immune from the suit because he was acting in his capacity as a judge, and judges have absolutely immunity from lawsuits.

Linda and her husband appealed, and the Federal Court of Appeals reversed the lower court's decision regarding Judge Stump, finding that he had not acted "within his jurisdiction" when issuing the order to have Linda sterilized. They found that sterilization of a minor at the request of a parent is not part of a judge's normal duties and, therefore, not within his jurisdiction. Judge Stump then appealed to the United States Supreme Court, which heard the case.

In what is now the leading Supreme Court decision regarding judicial immunity, the Court found that Judge Stump was in fact immune from being sued based on its interpretation of Indiana statutes giving judges broad general jurisdiction.[20] The Supreme Court recognized that Judge Stump had made several procedural errors and that there was no specific Indiana law granting a judge the authority to approve a parent's request to have their minor child sterilized; yet it held that: "A judge will not be deprived of immunity because the action he took was in error, was done maliciously, or was in excess of his authority, but, rather, he will be subject to liability only when he acted in the 'clear absence of all jurisdiction.'"

A family court judge cannot pull out a gun and shoot someone in the courtroom. That would not be within their "jurisdiction," but they can jail someone, take away their children, force them to pay an unobtainable amount of money to their ex-spouse, or force the sale of their home to pay an *amicus* attorney or a custody evaluator that they, the judge, chose in the first place and with whom they might have a relationship. All of these acts would be within their jurisdiction, and our

---

20 Stump v. Sparkman, 435 U.S. 349 (1978)

government grants them absolute immunity from a lawsuit in response to such egregious acts.

It's no wonder then that family court judges can become tyrants. They act alone. While they are instructed to consider only the "evidence" in a case, they are the sole arbiters of what is and is not evidence. They have broad powers to punish people, and citizens have no direct recourse for an action a judge "took in error, was done maliciously, or was done in excess of authority."

So, with no juries to look out for the interests of the general public, little effective power of appeal, almost no right to demand a recusal, and no right to sue a judge for blatant bias, cruelty, or malpractice, what recourse does a citizen have? Most states have judicial "oversight" committees that review complaints from the general public, but as Ulf Carlsson found out when he complained about the actions of Judge McBrien, these committees are made up of judges and lawyers and rarely take effective action against a wayward judge. How ironic that a committee created to police judicial incompetence and bias might serve as another venue for lawyers to become cozy with judges?

Unfortunately, the press finds little interest in publishing stories about malicious or incompetent judges. So this has left victims with one last resource—the Internet. If they only knew . . .

10 | Enemies of the State

Sometimes there were people in my court who I just did not like.
—Lynn Toler, Presiding Judge of Divorce Court

When the people fear the government, there is tyranny.
When the government fears the people, there is liberty.
—Barnhill-Tichenor debate on Socialism, 1914

ULF CARLSSON WILL NEVER KNOW WHY THE JUDGE HE AND OTHERS call Chainsaw McBrien took such a strong dislike to him. Maybe it wasn't personal. Maybe the relationship between McBrien and Carlsson's wife's attorney, who just happened to serve as a temporary judge in the same courthouse, was too close, as the first few divorce attorneys Carlsson interviewed had suggested. Was it possible that McBrien, presumably of Irish descent, didn't like Scandinavians? Maybe the judge had something against mild-mannered civil servants with an interest in ancient African masks. Or maybe, after years on the bench, he had just become ornery, as Gerald Nissenbaum observed that family court judges do, and the diminutive Carlsson was an easy target for his rage. Maybe the reason for his dislike does not matter because, the bottom line is the U.S. family law system allowed Judge McBrien to be as arbitrary, nasty, abusive, biased, and vindictive as Judge McBrien chose to be.

Carlsson, sitting on the back patio of his modest home in a leafy suburb of Sacramento, sips coffee from a steaming mug. He is dressed in a pressed pale-blue oxford and blue jeans. His narrow shoulders are tight. His expression conveys controlled disgust and a little resignation. He is describing the final humiliation, the last and fatal blow to his life in

America, delivered personally by the Chainsaw. Carlsson had worked almost 20 years for the State of California, rising up the ranks in the planning office where he had an exemplary work record and was looking
forward to a generous pension. But one afternoon during the nightmare,
a superior called him into his office and told him to pack up his personal
things and leave within an hour. "There was no explanation." Carlsson
sighs. "After nearly 20 years, it was just basically 'you're fired.'"

A SLAP ON THE (JUDGE'S) WRIST

Only later, when the judicial oversight commission released its findings publicly in response to a complaint filed by Carlsson, did he learn
what had really happened in his divorce. After Carlsson filed his appeal,
Judge McBrien called the general counsel of the planning commission,
a personal friend, and said something that led to Carlsson's firing. Much
like the judge who had filed a police report against Danielle Malmquist
without her knowledge, McBrien had gone behind his own litigant's
back and maligned Carlsson outside of the courtroom, and yet he did not
recuse himself afterwards. In Carlsson's case, however, the damage was
far worse and far more calculated. McBrien's unofficial actions meant
that Carlsson not only lost his job and his pension but, in the process,
the funds needed to continue to fight McBrien publicly after the appeal.

Carlsson's voice quivers as he wraps up his story. He says that fighting the family court is like fighting the mob. The oversight panel called
McBrien out for his misdeeds and, considering the judge's checkered
past, wrote that his behavior would probably continue. But, Carlsson says,
it allowed him to not only remain a judge but to remain on the bench
of the family court. That was the final insult. Carlsson lost everything,
including his daughter, and the judge received a light slap on the wrist.

Like most litigants, Carlsson did not know that the oversight committees rarely discipline judges in a meaningful way. In the same year
that he filed his complaint, for example, there were more than 1,000
similar complaints filed by California litigants; none of the judges in
those cases were fired or removed from the bench. The committees
will sometimes write a private letter to the judge in question, apprising
them of the committee's findings. Occasionally, if they want to send
the judge a warning about some particularly abusive and potentially

politically unpopular behavior, they will release the letter to the public. But they rarely fire a judge. In the year that Carlsson's complaint was reviewed, the judicial ethic board did, however, raise the limit on gifts that judges could receive.

Carlsson has done everything he could possibly do, filed every grievance that the system allows. He has even made a YouTube video to oppose McBrien's reelection and attended weekly protests in front of the Sacramento Family Court, but it has been a losing battle. As he sat on the patio of his house, movers were arriving to pick up the furniture, and the keys would soon be turned over to someone else. Carlsson was on his way back to Sweden where, in his mid-50s and broke, he would move in with his elderly parents and try to begin a new life.

Carlsson belongs to a loose confederation of family court litigants around the country who have been singled out and punished for what they consider standing up for their constitutional rights in a system that is based upon the sovereignty of a single individual: the judge. Sometimes they meet in person, at protests, or in groups like Emily Gallup's Nevada County Reformers; but mostly they just hear about one another in the press or on websites like www.familylawcourts.com or, more and more, on blogs. The ability of litigants to publish first-hand accounts of their experience in family court has provided an outlet for frustrated parents and a target for judges. What is most interesting about many of these blogs is that they are not, as one might expect, he said/she said accounts of nasty divorces but categorical attacks on the family court system itself. Though their audiences are small—often limited to a circle of sympathetic friends and relatives—their perceived threat to the system is anything but. Few of these websites have been as cheeky, comprehensive, and feared as the one started by a 31-year-old Indiana father of two named Dan Brewington: www.dansadventuresinfamilycourt.com.

FREEDOM OF SPEECH

Describing Brewington is next to impossible because he has been locked away for more than two years, the last six months in a medium security prison outside of Indianapolis known as the Farm. Visitors are not allowed, nor are cameras. Brewington, once an overweight but jovial young man with a receding hairline, has reportedly shed more than

100 pounds from two hunger strikes and now sports a beard. According to e-mails that his mother, Sue, receives and sometimes posts to his website, Brewington's fellow inmates are mostly drug dealers and rapists, though there are a few killers who cannot imagine why he is living among them. But like these men, Brewington too is dressed in a blue jumpsuit and known by a ten-digit number. Brewington is not sure why his neighbors (many of whom appeared on a reality show approved by the Indiana Department of Corrections called *Inmates Got Talent!*) have been interviewed extensively on television while the system considers Brewington so dangerous that a documentary crew was recently turned away and a visit with a journalist was denied both by the warden and by then-Governor Mitch Daniels.

The crimes that landed Brewington in prison for the next five years[21] were intimidation of a family court judge, that judge's wife, as well as a psychologist, though an interview with the district attorney who prosecuted the case, Aaron Negangard, yields another answer. "Brewington," says the prosecutor, "just didn't know how to play ball." He had become a vexatious litigant, an irritant and potential threat.

Dan's adventures began several years ago when his wife filed for divorce. They had, according to his mother, never been a particularly good fit. Both had mild psychological issues—his wife suffered from depression and Dan from attention deficit disorder (ADHD). But after having two daughters, Dan at least proved that he was a loving father, more maternal, says his silver-haired retired fifth-grade teacher of a mother, than his wife. He took the girls camping, set up a trampoline at the family farm, taught them about the stars, and played Disney princesses with them. He also taught them how to use the computer and built them a tree house. Nearly all of these actions would later be framed in a negative context during Brewington's divorce.

What is clear is that Brewington did not want to divorce his wife and, perhaps because of that, he turned out to be a terrible client of

---

21 On September 5, 2013, Brewington was released from prison after serving only 2½ years, including credit for time spent awaiting trial and good behavior. The release came in the few months leading up to the publication of this book and documentary film of the same name.

two law firms before being forced to represent himself because of a lack of funds, a decision that did not sit well with his judge, a silver-haired outdoors enthusiast named James Humphrey. Brewington's first order of business was to get his custody evaluation report thrown out. The report, he claimed, was riddled with errors and irrelevant tidbits like the fact that there had been breadcrumbs on his kitchen counter during a visit by the custody evaluator. The evaluator had not interviewed his mother or brother but concluded that Brewington was a narcissist and that his personality was not appropriate for joint legal custody. The psychologist's recommendation—of joint physical custody but with legal custody assigned to his wife—stung. It would not allow Brewington to contact teachers and doctors and make decisions about his daughters' welfare. It would not even allow him to leave his girls with their grandmother. So Brewington did some digging. He found out that the psychologist had made some bizarre decisions in the past, including awarding custody to a known drug addict, and that he was not even licensed to practice in Indiana, where Brewington's divorce was being adjudicated. Brewington called and e-mailed the psychologist's office, demanding to see the case file upon which the report was made. The psychologist initially said yes, then claimed it could only be released to Brewington's attorney. Brewington said that he was his own attorney, that he was representing himself, like most people. The psychologist still refused.

Brewington motioned for the psychologist's report to be thrown out. The judge refused. The transcripts are painful to read—a self-represented father trying to assert his right to parenting to a family court judge who seems to consider him little more than an obnoxious pest who doesn't understand the rules. Thus swatted down, Brewington took to the Internet, registering the URL DansAdventuresInFamily Court.com as a way to document his experience with the custody evaluator. The website gained a handful of followers, mainly his relatives, and contained next to nothing about his children or his ex-wife. Brewington wanted the site to be about the court and not his family. Nor did he wish to disparage his wife or expose his daughters to any kind of negative feedback.

When Brewington's ex-wife found out about the website, her attorney filed a motion to have it shut down. Brewington's blog about his experiences with the custody evaluator, the attorney argued, was not in the best interest of his daughters. After considering her argument, Judge Humphrey refused to order the website shut down, but he also issued a veiled threat to Brewington in his opinion. Although he would not shut down the website—presumably based on First Amendment grounds—he warned Brewington that his continued blogging would be considered in the permanent custody order. In retrospect, that the judge would use Brewington's daughters as pawns in order to get him to stop writing about his custody evaluator was a chilling warning, but Brewington didn't get the message. He continued blogging to his tiny audience.

Two months later, after two years of co-parenting and a psychologist's report that recommended joint physical custody, Judge Humphrey made good on his threat. Brewington's right to see his daughters was terminated completely and indefinitely pending a raft of conditions, including undergoing additional psychological testing, which he could no longer afford, and taking down his blog.

Brewington was apoplectic. And because he had no longer afford an attorney, when he next confronted Judge Humphrey in court, there was no filter to hide his resentment and disdain for what the judge had done. The chemistry between the two men—one a loving father who had been diagnosed with ADHD and the other a judge who had just taken that father's young daughters away from him for no discernibly judicious reason—was toxic. And rather than calm the waters, both men would ratchet up the stakes. Humphrey by awarding a quarter of the Brewington's family farm, which was held in trust for Brewington's widowed mother, to Brewington's ex-wife; and Brewington by writing about the judge's decision on his website, in which he questioned whether the judge and the psychologist who he felt had conspired to take away his children from him (and conversely, taken away the girls' father from them) were guilty of child abuse. He then found the webpage for the court's Ethics & Professionalism Committee, posted a contact name and address on his website, and encouraged his handful of readers to write a letter protesting Humphrey's order. The name of the Ethics & Professionalism Committee member that Brewington posted was Heidi Humphrey, an airline gate attendant and housewife—and she was also the judge's spouse. She had been an adjunct member to the Ethics & Professionalism Committee, which is supposed to monitor the performance of the State's judges, but the mailing address was the Humphreys' home. Brewington would claim that he did not know if Heidi was the judge's wife or simply shared the same last name. He said that he was only concerned with the fact that she was a member of the Ethics & Professionalism Committee. The local district attorney would initially claim that Judge Humphrey's wife was not on the committee, then acknowledge that she was but that, despite the title, the committee was actually just a social thing and that Brewington should have known this.[22] Then the DA dragged Brewington, representing himself, before a Grand Jury and recommended charging him with a raft of crimes, including intimidation of a judge, a judge's wife, and the psychologist, a friend of the court. For good measure, the DA claimed that Brewington had also committed a crime when he told the psychologist he was an attorney in the hopes of getting his case file (a common misunderstanding among *pro pers*, who are, in every meaningful way, their own attorneys in the eyes of the court).

Brewington was charged and immediately thrown in jail. His bail was set at $600,000, an amount that Brewington could not possibly afford, especially given that Brewington's mother could no longer borrow against the land that Judge Humphrey had tied up with an ownership encumbrance. Though Brewington had never so much as attempted to contact anyone in a non-professional context and had no history of violence, the DA compared him to a cop killer. And the authorities in

---

22 Ironically, politicians like Negangard do seem much more likely to understand that oversight committees, such as the one Heidi Humphrey served on and the one that investigated Ulf Carlsson's judge, are more about attorneys, judges, and former politicians getting together to collect a paycheck than dispensing oversight. Appointments to these committees are often viewed as favors for friends or fellow politicians who voted the right way. In California, salaries on committees that meet a few times a year can run into the six figures. It is highly unlikely that an average citizen like Dan Brewington understood any of this, in large part because states tend to make finding information on how committee members spend their time and how much they are paid very difficult.

his county led Brewington's guards to believe that he was an especially dangerous inmate, an assertion that surprised them after they got to know him. Brewington is a mild-mannered, if somewhat scatterbrained individual. To Brewington and to his family, it felt like he was being set up, but there was nothing they could do. Brewington was broke, and the real property lien on the family farm prohibited the family from getting a loan that could potentially fund a defense. Brewington's criminal fate would be in the hands of a public defender chosen by the same court system that was trying to put Brewington behind bars for years.

In a cramped office across from a run-down strip mall on the outskirts of Cincinnati, Bob Kelly, a family friend and attorney, portrays what happened to Brewington as an example of small town justice—an incestuous system wherein the judge and his acquaintance, the district attorney, can intimidate litigants that they don't like. "What happened to Dan Brewington," Kelly, who is on the far side of middle age and resembles an older version of the television police captain Barney Miller, "is absolutely a violation of his First Amendment Rights." Kelly helped Brewington prepare some of his pleadings but is not licensed to practice in Indiana, which is across the river from Kelly's Cincinnati office. The intimidation and perjury charges, Kelly says, are disgraceful. He's never seen anything like it in his decades as a lawyer. "Even convicted criminals are allowed to see their kids," he says, shaking his head. What has happened to a father like Brewington is cruel, vindictive, and according to Kelly, unconstitutional.

CARROTS AND STICKS

But the court's treatment of Brewington is not as uncommon as one might assume. In family court, alternately using the threat of jail and the reward of time with one's children in order to get parents to behave in a desired manner is known as the "carrot and stick" approach. If a litigant plays by the rules, they receive a carrot. If not, they get the stick. The stick may initially be a small jail sentence for contempt, but if the parent fails to get the message, they often end up losing custody of their children—a penalty that activist Mike Newdow believes meets the Constitution's "cruel and unusual punishment" standard. Were these parents at risk of being imprisoned in criminal court, of course, they would have the right to an attorney and a trial by jury. In family court they can be sent to jail and lose their children without any representation.

Andrew Karres, the used car dealer who has befriended Ulf Carlsson, recalls being in court one day when Karres' ex-wife's attorney (who also happens to be Carlsson's ex-wife's attorney and a member of what he calls the "five karat" club, as in you can buy a five-karat diamond ring with the fees from a single divorce) actually suggested to the judge that he implement the carrot-and-stick approach after Karres refused to attend anger management classes taught by another divorce attorney. Karres' terse response: "My daughter is not a carrot or a stick." His comment was ignored by the judge, who later revoked his custody entirely.

The advent of Facebook and micro-blogging has led to an explosion in carrot-and-stick conflicts that involve a litigant's First Amendment rights. In the space of just a month in 2011, for example, a mother in Minnesota named Lea Banken was ordered to take down her private Facebook page by her judge and subsequently stripped of custody of her children when she refused. She then published a transcript of her next hearing, at which, to Banken's surprise, her judge admonished her that she had no constitutional right to parent her own children.

Then there was Mark Byron, a young photographer whose second wife had accused him of domestic violence. Byron shares custody of a nine-year-old son he had with his first wife without incident. His first wife has never made an accusation of neglect or abuse or incompetence as a father. Byron, sitting in his warehouse loft studio and wearing a sky-blue t-shirt sporting the phrase "Freespeech," describes how the Cincinnati police came to the Byron house on the evening that his second wife reported physical abuse. "Even though the domestic violence laws require the police to arrest someone," he says, "they saw no signs of even an argument, never mind any evidence of physical abuse, and so they chose to leave without an arrest." However, Byron's second wife, already twice divorced, followed the advice of the lawyer who had helped her secure custody of her children in a prior divorce and filed a restraining order in family court and also pressed criminal charges. Byron had never been guilty of more than a speeding violation, but he was detained and processed for domestic violence charges. As a result, the family court ordered him to leave the house and, except for two short visits per week under a supervised visitation arrangement, took away his right to see the infant son he had with his second wife. It took months for his domestic violence criminal trial to take place, during which time he says he had to explain to his nine-year-old son why the boy could not see his infant brother. Byron chokes up trying to describe his nine-year-old's bewilderment and sadness.

Byron was found not guilty at his criminal trial, and afterward he went to family court to ask the judge to allow him to see his younger son without supervised visitation. To Byron's complete shock and dismay, the family court judge again denied his request to see his younger son except under the supervised visitation schedule and only two times per week. As a result Byron missed the boy's first footsteps and his first birthday party.

Friends asked why he could not see his youngest son. After all, he had been exonerated of any charges of domestic violence in criminal court. Byron finally succumbed to the embarrassment and perceived injustice of the family court's ruling and, months later, posted a mini-rant on the private wall of his Facebook account. It read in part, that ". . . if you are an evil, vindictive woman who wants to ruin your husband's life and take your son's father away from him completely—all you need to do is say that you're scared of your husband or domestic partner . . ." When a friend slipped Byron's second wife the friend's Facebook password, she printed out the post and motioned for the court to order it taken down. The judge, in a very unusual move, drafted a groveling apology on Mark's behalf addressed to both Byron's very attractive second wife and to the family court itself. The judge ordered Byron to publish the apology on his Facebook account for 30 days or else go to jail for 60 days. After nearly three weeks of posting the apology, Byron took it down and went to the media. Forced to back down in the face of public outcry, a second judge nevertheless publicly excoriated the young father from the bench and then vacated the court's earlier ruling. From the perspective of the mob, the first judge's mistake may have been taking the child away too soon, leaving himself without the carrot and only the stick of a prison sentence.

Dan Brewington did not fare as well. On October 6, 2011 he was convicted on five of six counts, including intimidating the judge and the judge's wife. A few days later, he was allowed to beg for a lenient sentence. The psychologist and judge were also given time to publicly condemn his behavior, which they did, taking a few extra shots at his mother and his brother for supporting him. The criminal court judge sentenced Brewington to five years in a federal penitentiary, and he was soon shipped off to the Farm to spend years around violent criminals and lose all contact with his young daughters, save occasional letters that he can send his ex-wife in the hope that they are passed along. The irony is that Brewington's only hope for contact with his daughters now is the blog that caused him to lose custody in the first place and which he has never taken down. From a prison phone somewhere deep within the bowels of the Farm, Brewington offers his hope that, if his daughters know nothing else of their father, they will know that he fought like hell just to be their dad. And some day, when they are grown, he hopes they will know what Judge Humphrey, the psychologist, their mother, and the American justice system did to their father.

THE EAT THEIR OWN TOO

Michelle MacDonald is a bright-eyed family law attorney who practices in Minnesota, three states west of where Brewington is doing hard time. After 25 years of family law practice, MacDonald has seen it all, and she is appalled by the system. She believes that family courts actually harm children. She has grown used to seeing a 10-minute initial hearing involving flimsy evidence, or no evidence at all, result in "temporary" custody orders that end up lasting years, often demoting one parent to the role of visitor in their children's lives and sometimes eliminate both parents entirely. She has seen incompetent child protective service departments commit gross malpractice when placing foster children into abusive homes, and grown to believe that family courts and associated social service departments simply do not have the time, resources, or competence to serve the basic needs of children. Like Emily Gallup, the Sacramento mediator-turned-whistleblower, MacDonald is more qualified than the average person employed by the system in which she worked.

Also like Gallup, MacDonald was well-liked until she crossed an invisible line by challenging the system, in her case filing a federal lawsuit against a family court judge, David L. Knutson, a former state senator and the son of a former state senator.

MacDonald had a client who was the mother of five children. The mother had primary custody of the children and had been doing the lion's share of raising them in their middle-class neighborhood. The two older daughters claimed that they were afraid of their father and alleged that he warned that he would shoot the whole family someday. The father claimed that he threatened to kill himself, not the family, because the mother was alienating the children against him. Neither parent alleged that the other was physically abusive or incompetent, and yet, based on a theory of parental alienation, Judge Knutson ordered that the mother leave the family home immediately and not return and the children were taken away. The whereabouts of the children is not public information.

These situations are very difficult. Are the children truly at risk when they are with their father, or have they been brainwashed by their mother? Advocates make strong arguments on both sides. The case would be commonplace except for what happened next. Mac-Donald filed the federal lawsuit against Judge Knutson alleging that he violated the mother's constitutional rights by ordering her out of her own home and banning her from seeing her children in the absence of any clear physical abuse or neglect, claiming that she was being deprived of life, liberty, and happiness without due process of law. In addition, because the measure was enacted through a temporary restraining order, the mother had no right to appeal it. MacDonald claimed that the judge failed to make the order permanent so that it could not be appealed, again a violation of the mother's constitutional rights. According to MacDonald, state judges may be immune from prosecution under the laws of their state, but they are not immune from prosecution under federal law. MacDonald cites Federal Law 42 U.S.C. section 1983, which provides in part:

> Every person who . . . subjects, or causes to be subjected, any citizen of the United States . . . to the deprivation of any rights, privileges, or immunities secured by the Constitution and laws, shall be liable to the party injured in an action at law, suit in equity, or other proper proceeding for redress.

MacDonald alleges that Judge Knutson is in violation of this federal law because he deprived her client of her constitutional rights without sufficient evidence or sufficient due process. Although the U.S. Supreme Court ruled that Judge Harold Stump was within his jurisdiction and thus immune from being sued when he ordered the sterilization of Linda Sparkman, perhaps Judge Knutson had stepped outside his jurisdiction when he ordered MacDonald's client to abandon her home and children. Or perhaps Judge Knutson, by failing to convert his "temporary" custody order into a permanent custody order, had trampled on the mother's right to an appeal. However remote the chances of winning, the arguments were made in a civilized manner under the laws of our land.

When MacDonald next appeared in his courtroom with a motion for Judge Knutson to recuse himself, she was worried that the judge might reprimand her for filing the federal lawsuit or might try to game the courtroom procedures to trip her up on some technicality. There had been a prior dispute over the judge's calendar, which is posted in clear view in the courtroom, and so MacDonald used her smartphone to record a picture of the calendar before the judge entered the courtroom. She was also friendly with the bailiff, who offered to pose for a friendly photo prior to court being in session.

When Judge Knutson walked into the courtroom, MacDonald could sense that something was seriously wrong. According to MacDonald, he said little but glared at her. In so many words he asked her if she wished to postpone the recusal motion. She said no. He walked out of the courtroom.

At that point, according to MacDonald, three bailiffs approached. Two of them seized her and she was escorted from the courtroom and to a holding cell. She was stripped of her jewelry, phone, and eyeglasses and handcuffed to a wheelchair. She was grilled intensely. Her smartphone was searched without warrant. When she asked why she was being detained and interrogated, she was given no answer except a reference to a courtroom rule about taking photographs.

After a couple of hours she was wheeled back into Judge Knutson's courtroom still handcuffed to the wheelchair. Judge Knutson asked her if she wanted to continue the hearing. Shaken but undeterred, she said yes. As one might expect, her motion was unsuccessful. But the battle

was not over, at least not for Judge Knutson. MacDonald was not released. In fact, the handcuffs were not removed. Instead, she was wheeled
back to the detention area, placed in a cell overnight, and forced to sleep
on a bench with no mattress or pillow or blanket for the majority of the
night, neither under arrest for any crime nor held in contempt of court.
She was imprisoned with no explanation. She was not released until
5:00 p.m. the following day by another judge. She was not arraigned for
any crime, and no explanation was given for her imprisonment, humiliation, or intimidation.

With no juries to look out for the interests of litigants like Mac-
Donald's client (or even for fed-up lawyers like MacDonald), little
chance of appeal, almost no right to demand a recusal, and no right to
sue a judge for blatant bias, cruelty, or malpractice, what recourse does
a citizen have? Most states have judicial "oversight" committees that
review complaints from the general public. The First Amendment guarantees the right to petition the government for a redress of grievances,
but when the only ones to petition *to* are the perpetrators, that right
seems meaningless.

Which leaves the ordinary citizen with the media, if they are fortunate enough to attract their interest, and the Internet if they are not.
But both have ultimately provided little more than a temporary podium
from which to rail against their judges and their injustices in family
court. Whether you are a lowly citizen like Ulf Carlsson, Dan Brewington, Mark Byron, or Daniela Malmquist or a lawyer seeking justice for
his or her clients like Michelle MacDonald, the system will use anything
in its considerable power to silence you. With the court and its friends
above reproach or rebuke, parents and spouses are left with only one
person to blame: each other.

11 | Parental Disparagement

On the stand, I can make any father look like a piece of shit in two seconds because I know what they don't know: What's the name of your daughter's teacher? What's the doctor's name? Dads don't know these things. Are they good dads? Excellent! They can tell you all about their kids' homework and other super important things, but I can make them look like they don't care about their kids because that is not a man's strength.
　　　　　　　　　　—Marilyn York, family law attorney

MARILYN YORK, THE LITHE RENO DIVORCE ATTORNEY WHO PRIMARILY represents men, considers herself a spine-giver. Her profanity-laden pep talks are designed to get husbands, who she considers far too passive and gentle as a group, in the mood for battle. If they don't engage, York says, they'll lose the kids and the money. When asked what role acrimony has in a "no-fault" divorce state, York almost laughs off the question. It is no-fault in name only, she says. Litigants always slip in tidbits about the ex—alcohol use, drug use, dirty habits, and on and on. A recent national study of court records revealing that nearly 70% of divorce cases now involve Facebook seems to back her up. Disparaging the other parent has never been more important, and accumulating ammunition against them has never been easier.

York says that she draws the line at the kids. When litigants introduce their children to her—"this is the lady that's going to protect you from your bitch of a mother!"—she claims to recoil.

"If you bring your kids to my office," York says, "you better tell them that I'm a realtor."

But by her own admission, she practices a blood sport, and thinking that the kids don't know what's going on is wishful thinking. "Girls," she says, "want to know everything." This is not the era of Kramer vs. Kramer, when the loving father offers up his son to the prodigal mother in order to protect him from having to take the stand against one parent or the other. Either people have become more desperate, the system more cruel, or there is simply far more at stake. York recalls stepping out into the hallway during a lull in a hearing to find the opposing attorney coaching her client's young son with some colorful language. "Don't forget your dad's a piece of shit!" the attorney was telling him. York was furious. "Did you really just say that to my client's child?" she admonished. But she said nothing to the judge. She's seen worse. The implanting of false memories—"remember when your father touched you that time?"—is a known technique to corrupt children's memories. Bribes are also common. Depending on the age, kids love toys, nice clothes, cars, freedom, even alcohol and drugs. The goal is to win custody and, ultimately, either score (or avoid paying) a generous monthly child support check.

PARENTAL ALIENATION

While a spike in the number of divorces and resultant fee-gouging by attorneys were both anticipated in the lead-up to no-fault divorce, no one seems to have anticipated the danger of one parent turning the children against the other. The assumption was either that parents would never use their own progeny as weapons or that judges would not allow them to air the family's dirty laundry in court. Both assumptions turned out to be wrong. By the mid-1980s, it was commonplace in custody battles that the children had sided with one parent and against the other. Typically, the "alienated" parent was the non-custodial one, and typically this meant the father. More disturbing, there were often serious allegations made by the mother that were offered up to explain or justify the kids' behavior, and no one could be sure if they were true. Was the mother so self-absorbed and obsessed with boosting the size of her monthly child support check that she would risk the mental health of her own children by telling them lies about their father and then fabricating false allegations of abuse to support the lies? Or was Dad really a monster?

In 1985, a prominent child psychologist and frequent expert witness in custody cases named Richard Gardner gave the most severe cases of disparagement a name: Parental Alienation Syndrome, or PAS. Not since Anna Freud coined the phrase "in the best interest of the child" had the family court something so profitably vague to fight over. Gardner himself defined the syndrome as unique to custody battles and marked by eight symptoms: 1. A campaign of denigration; 2. Weak, absurd, or frivolous rationalizations for the deprecation; 3. Lack of ambivalence; 4. The "independent-thinker" phenomenon; 5. Reflexive support of the alienating parent in the parental conflict; 6. Absence of guilt over cruelty to and/or exploitation of the alienated parent; 7. The presence of borrowed scenarios; 8. Spread of the animosity to the friends and/or extended family of the alienated parent.

Over the next quarter-century, the prevalence of PAS and its symptoms would be debated endlessly and often heatedly. Many parents who had been alienated from their children during a divorce would latch on to PAS as a clinical explanation for what they were enduring. Others ridiculed it for its distinctly unscientific etiology. A nascent "father's rights" movement tended to embrace the idea of PAS as an explanation of how women had used allegations of molestation, domestic violence, and abandonment to turn their children against their fathers in order to gain custody, and therefore money, or perhaps simply retribution. Women's rights organizations scoffed at the implied misogyny of a "syndrome" perpetuated almost entirely by the female sex. When Gardner committed suicide in 2003, reportedly despondent over an incurable neurological disease that he had been diagnosed with, his critics pounced. Gardner, they said, was the classic case of the doctor being sicker than the patient. In 2009, a California Assemblyman even introduced a bill that would have made evidence of parental alienation inadmissible in family court. The bill was ultimately voted down, though only after its opponents asked father's rights advocates to back off, worried that the debate would degenerate into a battle of the sexes.

Despite the controversy over whether or not PAS should be recognized by the psychiatric (or legislative) community, the idea of parental alienation has lived on in books, articles, and most of all, in family court. In the Reno courthouse where Marilyn York practices, the willingness of one parent to share custody is now the top consideration for dividing custody time, the theory being that the parent least willing to "alienate" the other should be rewarded for their equanimity. In Emily Gallup's court in Nevada City, the same principle prevailed unto sex offenses and domestic violence being overlooked in the interest of no parent being "alienated" from their child. Gallup, of course, thought that was wrong and lost her job for speaking up. Bonnie Russell, the publisher of www.familylawcourts.com, is deeply suspicious of PAS, though for somewhat different reasons.

Russell, a vivacious two-time divorcee, lost contact with both her son and daughter in a custody dispute years ago when a judge determined that her allegations of child abuse against her ex-husband, an attorney, were not valid but instead constituted "parental alienation." She received the stick: total loss of custody. Russell is philosophical about it now, saying that she's happy that her adult children can at least move on with their lives without ambiguity. Her son is in school and her daughter is a congressional staffer in Washington, DC. What irks Russell is not the slapping of a catchphrase on a parent's motives but the fact that serious allegations like sexual abuse end up in family courts in the first place. On her website she has published a recent form made available by her local court. Seven boxes next to offenses ranging from sexual abuse to abduction are printed for litigants to check—allegations against their spouse. "What the hell is this doing in family court?" Russell asks rhetorically. These are serious allegations that should be adjudicated in criminal court with real evidence and a seated jury. That one can lose their children based on what side of a philosophical debate a judge falls is, she says, nuts.

On the other side of the PAS debate is Glenn Sacks, the former executive director of Fathers & Families, a father's rights organization. Sacks, a passionate conservative with a degree in Latin studies from UCLA, got involved in family court issues after hearing horror stories from litigants on his radio talk show. One involved a father who had flown from Los Angeles to Arizona in order to see his young girls.

It was the father's "weekend," Sacks recalls, and Dad had promised to meet them at their favorite restaurant for the exchange. But when he arrived, the girls were not there and his ex-wife would not answer her cell phone. The father called his lawyer in California, who told him that there was really nothing he could do about it. So he flew home. On his way back from the airport, his wife called with the girls on the line. She had made it seem to the girls that he had simply failed to show up to see them. "Where were you?" she asked. The girls had been waiting for him, she said, and he'd promised to be there. These are the kinds of games that people play, according to Sacks.

But there are more insidious ways to alienate a child from a parent. Sacks cites a common case known as the "move-away." The parent with custody will move to a less expensive city or state in order to make their support payments go further. If the earner spouse, however, wishes to follow the children, they must first go to the judge and seek a modification of the support award, since they probably would not be able to find a similar paying job in their children's new home. Considering that the children now need less money for housing and other staples and that the earning spouse wants to be close to his or her children, one might assume that the judge would oblige. But, Sacks says, the opposite is actually true. Judges often refuse to modify, and the earner spouse is stuck living in the higher cost city or state so they can maintain the higher level of support payments for children they can no longer see, at least with any regularity.

The "middle" of the PAS debate may be Wendy Archer, the Texas woman who didn't see her daughter for more than two years. She now speaks regularly on the topic of parental alienation, not as a syndrome but as a strategy that ex-spouses use to woo their children in an attempt to tilt the infamous K-factor of the child support calculation in their favor. Archer believes that her daughter was alienated from her through a series of gifts, such as a brand-new sports car, as well as a string of disparaging comments made by her ex-husband's new wife.

Legislators and judges seem split on parental alienation. Marilyn York, the fathers-only attorney in Reno, says that the Nevada Legislature made the non-disparagement of the other parent the number one consideration for granting custody time. Sol Gothard, a retired family court judge in New Orleans, says that he's "sure it happens" but dismisses it as a fact of life, the natural consequence of an adversarial and acrimonious system.

Even Sacks seems a little conflicted. The father's rights advocate is uncomfortable with calling parental alienation a "syndrome." Parents in intact marriages sometimes disparage one another, after all. In the midst of a heated divorce, well-meaning fathers and mothers will say the wrong thing in front of the kids from time to time. When they are fighting over limited resources and bound together by a monthly check, when their children become the multipliers of the amount they must give or receive each month, the resentment simmers and sometimes boils over.

But doesn't it "just make sense" that the turning of children against another parent seems evil, cruel, and maybe even psychopathic? "Doesn't putting one's financial status ahead of one's children's mental health and well-being seem like the definition of an unfit parent?" asks Baltasar Kormakur, the Icelandic film director. "You have to ask yourself: What kind of person would do that?"

Then again, Kormakur is from Scandinavia, where there is no financial incentive for such behavior to exist. Where he lives, parents create child-sharing arrangements themselves, and so they are natural arrangements that fit both the parent's work schedules and the children's needs. They focus on the well-being of their children first. In contrast, in the United States it appears that the financial incentives placed into the family codes by special interest groups at the latter half of the 20th century have significantly increased alienating behavior, and the adversarial nature of family court proceedings have kept it alive, if not actively encouraged it to increase.

THE REHABILITATIVE PSYCHOLOGIST

Dr. Richard Warshak may not have the name recognition of Anna Freud or Richard Gardner, but in family court circles, the Dallas psychologist looms large. A surprisingly gentle man who could be Kenny G's father, Warshak has written dozens of articles on parental alienation, even while the American Psychiatric Association repeatedly declines to include the syndrome in its bible, the *Diagnostic and Statistical Manual of Mental Disorders*, or *DSM*. Warshak himself questions whether or not it really qualifies as a syndrome. Maybe, he tells an interviewer in a gentle therapist's voice, it is best described as a tactic used to gain custody and thereby win more child support. Nevertheless, Warshak offers 19 products designed to combat Parental Alienation on his website, from a journal article titled "Parental Alienation Among College Students" ($5.75) to the Parental Alienation Deluxe Bundle, which features, among other things, his book, *Divorce Poison"* and a DVD, *Welcome Back, Pluto*—Pluto being the small planet that was recently kicked out of the planetary family by a panel of rocket scientists who considered it too small.

Like Forrest Mosten, the mediator, Warshak has built a children's playroom off of his modest office in North Dallas and decorated the walls with children's crayoned interpretations of parental alienation. The effect is at once comic and depressing, a reminder both of the human cost of custody battles and how commonplace they've become. Warshak has personally testified in dozens of custody cases, served as a consultant on child custody for the White House, and recently spoke at a parental alienation awareness rally in a neighboring suburb organized by Wendy Archer. He can personally attest to the damage done to children by custody battles, though good statistics are hard to come by. The numbers most often used are in regard to kids who have grown up in single-parent households. Since, in the vast majority of cases, the father is the one alienated, one can point to government studies on fatherless households (though these also include situations where the father simply left or might even be unaware that he has a child). The numbers are stark: children who grow up without their father present are twice as likely to drop out of school, five times as likely to be poor, far more likely to do drugs and alcohol, and as a result of the previous facts, more prone to become criminals. Warshak says that, after alienation, it can take years for children to reconnect with the alienated parent. Alienation, he says, can be as simple as one parent bad-mouthing the other continuously until the child absorbs their hatred.

What does *not* create a distance between children and their parents, according to Warshak, is the one thing that psychologists, legislators, and judges have insisted harms them so terribly: the disconnect in lifestyle, say, going from a father's mansion in an upscale suburb to a mother's apartment in a middle-class neighborhood, or vice-versa. "There's really no evidence of that at all," Warshak says, dismissing four decades of family court tradition. "In fact," he adds, "seeing a parent of lesser means might actually make the child more sympathetic to that parent."

That is the (sort of) good news. The bad news is that there is no cure for alienation once it happens. Warshak advises judges to assign more time between the child and the alienated parent as a means of bringing the two back together, though preventing the alienation in the first place is preferable. How to accomplish that? Assign equal time between the parents and limit the opportunities for conflict. Now in the latter years of his career, Warshak prefers to meet with both parties and work out a solution outside of litigation rather than work for one or the other parent. He has also begun to eschew most of the psychological tests, like the inkblots, for lack of evidence that they reveal much, if anything, about a person's parenting.

But in the event of serious alienation, Warshak offers a final product not listed on the website: a weeklong intensive de-alienation program. The cost is upwards of $20,000, and can in fact go much higher, he says, which means it is out of the reach of most families. Then he corrects himself with a soft smile. It's not really that expensive, he hedges, when you consider how much one-on-one time the child gets and, of course, when you realize what's at stake. As every divorce attorney knows, people rarely put a price ceiling on getting their children back.

Twenty miles northeast of Warshak's office, in the dining room of her modest home across from the strip mall shopping center, Wendy Archer displays a trove of paintings that her daughter has allowed her to reveal. The paintings were done spontaneously out of grief. The paintings are dark and oddly mature, and there is something Munchian about most of them—black holes and clouds and vortexes punctuated by childish cries for help: "I feel sad." Archer hints that her kids' alienation had something to do with her husband's second wife, though she claims not to resent either of them now. Nor does she blame the psychologists or the attorneys or even the *amicus* attorney who formed what she feels amounted to a racketeering ring or a mob. "If I could blame one person for what happened," Archer says, wiping a tear from her right eye, "I would say the judge. She could have stopped this at any time. She chose not to."

Part III

Unintended Consequences

*Family law litigants do not receive equal services or equal
dignity compared to other litigants.*
*—Report of the Association of Certified Family Law
Specialists, 2011*

12 | Domestic Violence

Battery? Sexual abuse? Kidnapping? What the hell is this doing in family court?
— *Bonnie Russell, activist*

How could they be married for 20 years–a great husband and wife to each other. Then they get divorced. Suddenly he's a pervert, a drug dealer. He's doing all these horrible things. She's an alcoholic, a drug dealer, and sleeping with everybody. Did this just happen in the last week or two? Mother Teresa does not marry Attila the Hun.
— *John Nazarian, private investigator*

BREAKING THE GLASS CEILING

From Jeannie Suk's official bio: "Born in Seoul, Korea, she immigrated with her family to the United States as a young child. Before college, she studied ballet at the School of American Ballet and piano at the Juilliard School. She earned her B.A. in literature from Yale University. She was awarded a Marshall Scholarship to study literature at Oxford University where she earned a D.Phil. in Modern Languages. Her doctoral dissertation, *Postcolonial Paradoxes in French Caribbean Writing*, was published by Oxford University Press in 2001. She attended law school at Harvard, where she studied as a Paul and Daisy Soros Fellow. As an editor of the *Harvard Law Review*, she was Chair of Articles, Book Reviews, and Commentaries. After graduating, she served first as a law clerk to Judge Harry Edwards on the U.S. Court of Appeals for the D.C. Circuit, and then to Justice David Souter on the United States Supreme Court. She also spent a brief time prosecuting as an Assistant District Attorney in the Manhattan District Attorney's Office. Four years after graduating from Harvard Law School, she was appointed to its faculty in 2006. Her book, *At Home in the Law: How the Domestic Violence Revolution is Transforming Privacy*, was awarded the Law and Society Association's Herbert Jacob Prize for the most outstanding law and society book published in 2009. Her writing has appeared in the *Yale Law Journal, Stanford Law Review, Columbia Law Review, Wall Street Journal, Slate,* and elsewhere . . . She has given congressional testimony on law and innovation in the fashion industry. She has been awarded a Guggenheim Fellowship, and has been a Senior Fellow of the Humanities Center at Harvard. Her numerous recent honors include recognition as a Top Woman of Law by *Massachusetts Lawyers Weekly* and the Trailblazer Award from the Korean American Lawyers' Association of Greater New York."

Suk is not only a tenured professor at Harvard Law School, but the first Asian-American woman who can claim that honor. One might assume, then, that this telegenic over-achiever would be celebrated by feminists for shattering another glass ceiling, but Suk's writings on family court have instead earned her some vicious nicknames. "I've been called Hitler," she says with a heavy shrug. Suk's explorations into a double-standard in the law, which has led to countless families being unwillingly "divorced" by the courts—a phenomenon she calls "de facto divorce"—are considered a betrayal to one of the tenets upon which both feminism and family law are built: that men are the earner-aggressors and women are the supported-victims.

Coincidentally, Suk's first glimpse into family law was watching the ER doctor-turned-constitutional-law-specialist Mike Newdow argue his first amendment case before the Supreme Court, the case in which he demanded that his daughter not be forced to say "under God" during the reciting of the pledge of allegiance at her school. She was then a clerk but remembers everyone being impressed with Newdow's eloquence and his passion for parental rights. Even those who disagreed with Newdow's religious views, and there are many, would have a hard time arguing that he was a passive or uninvolved father. Except for the court, which, after choosing the case for adjudication from among thousands of submissions, suddenly decided that he had no standing since a family court judge in California had only awarded him 30% custody.

There is no telling what impression Newdow's arguments or the Court's decision made on Suk. But a short time later, as an assistant district attorney in New York City, the issue of custody once again arose in an indirect, but powerful, way. Women—and a few men—were making allegations of domestic violence against their spouses. When the police showed up, the law required them to make an arrest, which was then referred to the prosecutor's office where a "no-drop" law required them to prosecute. The laws had been written in order to protect women from being intimidated into not seeking justice but had resulted in nearly anyone who wanted to smear a spouse for whatever reason to do so with the law automatically on their side. "The law defines domestic violence so broadly," she explains, "that almost any household could claim to experience it."

Suk witnessed one case in which a husband had thrown a basketball at his wife and missed. This was ruled to be domestic violence and he was arrested and ordered to stay away from his home. In another instance, neighbors had called because of what they considered overly loud arguing in the apartment next door. An arrest was made and the case was teed up to the judge, whether or not the police or the prosecutors felt that there was a case.

So now it was up to the family court judge to decide the outcome. (In larger courthouses, there is typically at least one courtroom devoted to domestic violence cases.) Rather than refer the case to a criminal court, the judge would often give the accused a choice: cop a guilty plea and get out of jail immediately, or sit in jail for weeks or months and hope that a public defender can get you in front of a jury. For wealthier litigants, the choice was obvious: make bail, hire an attorney, and beat the rap. After all, in many cases, the "accuser" refused to press charges. But for many, especially the poor and immigrants with little understanding of their rights, the choice was the lesser of two evils: cop the deal and get out of jail or wait around for a public defender and a trial,—and lose their jobs and their livelihood in the interim.

Suk noticed an even more stark bargain being made. Judges would typically require the accused to sign a "no-contact" order to get out of jail. This meant that the accused would be guilty of a felony if he or she so much as picked up the phone to call home—even if their spouse and/or their kids wanted them to. So the choice was actually between losing their livelihood or losing their family. That, Suk believed, was an obvious violation of due process. Courts were essentially forcing litigants to give up their constitutional rights—their right to a trial, to parenting, etc.—for no other conceivable purpose than expediency. And there was another angle that disturbed her. The government had a long tradition of recognizing the sanctity of the home, but now, as she saw it, the government was invading the home and making decisions for the family. The home was no longer an inviolable space, as it had been for decades, and there was no expectation of, or right to, privacy. Once someone called 911, a court could step in and force a family to break up.

Women's rights advocates tended to see this as the lesser of two historical evils. Over the past 100 years, after all, women had gone from being considered property (and as a result could be beaten and other-wise abused by their husbands without recourse) to being considered equals under the law. In the 1970s feminists launched ambitious initia-tives to combat domestic violence, and they had achieved some notable successes, such as halving the murder rate between "intimates" between 1976 and 1993. The explosion of domestic violence accusations, they claimed, was not fraud, but a function of the issue finally bursting out of the closet because women were less afraid to report abuse. And no one could really know how much abuse existed until the curtain was pulled back on the family home. Indeed, statistics suggested that many women—and men—failed to report domestic abuse, though this might have been less an issue of a fear of reprisal than a fear of losing privacy and harming their spouse, or a choice between enduring an imperfect situation and creating a calamity. By the 2000s, according to the Bureau of Justice Statistics, domestic violence awareness programs had pushed women to report abuse in more than half of instances versus a small minority of men doing the same.

Suk realizes that a serious question—whether women were over-reporting domestic violence or men were victims of a hopelessly vague legal standard—ultimately devolves into an unknowable he said/she said-type debate. But her research is less about the rates of domestic violence in general and more about how the allegations are handled in family court. And in this context, the statistics are stunning. While the

Bureau of Justice Statistics estimates the incidence of "non-fatal intimate partner victimization" among adults at a little more than three per 1,000 individuals, in 2003, the California Administrative Office of the Courts reported that, in 76% of its child custody disputes, at least one litigant claimed that inter-parental violence had occurred in the relationship. That dichotomy might be shocking to even the most committed anti-DV crusader. To put these numbers in perspective, the incidence rate of domestic violence skyrockets from 0.3% to 76% after Divorce Corp. dangled a financial incentive to make accusations.

TILTED SCALES

That the incidence of domestic violence allegations would be far more common in custody cases as in the general population is no surprise to family court professionals. Gerald Nissenbaum, the bow tie-wearing Boston divorce attorney, says that making an allegation of abuse is a common strategy. "Even if the charge is tossed out," he says, "you have a leg up on getting custody of the kids and maybe the house as well." The court will make the ruling first and look at evidence later, if at all. For those who cannot afford a well-connected attorney, claiming that the husband or wife has physically abused them or the kids is the easiest way to establish an advantage.

"I've counseled a lot of women, and a few men, on how to get the ex out of the house," brags John Nazarian, a flamboyant Los Angeles-based private investigator whose vanity plates read "SPYGAME." Nazarian, a burly ex-prison guard and police officer who now prowls the city in a fleet of six-figure luxury cars, remembers the days when he was the one making the arrests. He says that he became expert on who was telling the truth and who was telling stories. Ditto Lynn Toler, the TV judge, who recalls accusations flowing in during her eight years on the bench in Cleveland and becoming cynical. "It's too bad for the women who are being abused," she says. "Judges have become very skeptical when they hear claims of domestic violence in family court."

Perhaps none of this would matter if the case ended up in a jury trial wherein evidence is presented and an attorney is provided for the accused. Instead, domestic violence cases are sucked into family court, the case heard before an overloaded judge with no time for evidence. If the parties happen to be involved in a custody battle, the chance of a safe let alone just resolution seems even more remote.

DOUBLE STANDARD

"If you call the police in San Diego," Bonnie Russell, the activist behind www.familylawcourts.com, says, "The first thing that they now ask you is: 'Are you involved in a custody dispute?' And if you say yes, they tell you to take it to family court. Then they generally leave."

That family courts deal with domestic violence cases at all infuriates Russell, a feminist of such near-obsessive focus that some lawyers fear her taking an interest in their case. Actually, the mention of domestic violence at all grates on her. "There is no such thing as domestic violence," she claims. "There is only battery and rape and assault. These things belong in criminal court!" She is equally blunt regarding the consequences of what she considers de-criminalizing criminal behavior with acronyms like DV: "Family courts are getting women killed." Russell then launches into a description of violence that is the inverse of the one described by Jeannie Suk:

"Let's say a wife is abused," Russell says. This woman gets bounced to family court, where the judge decides whether he believes her or not. Maybe the judge thinks, as happened in one of Emily Gallup's cases, that the wife is histrionic, or that she is making up an allegation in order to win custody or stay in the house. In that case, the wife is actually far worse off than before. She has done what the law requires and reported abuse, but the judge has essentially told her to go away. Now the husband, rendered above suspicion by the court, is free to do virtually anything. He knows that the judge is in his corner, and the fact that the judge has ruled that he does not believe the woman sets its own kind of precedent. To later acknowledge that he was wrong, that the husband is really an abuser as the wife claimed, would be to admit to being a bad judge of character, which is pretty close to admitting to being a bad judge, period.

"Now," Russell says, "consider the other scenario." The judge believes the woman. She is not histrionic or scheming. Maybe she rolls up her sleeves and shows bruises, or maybe the judge just doesn't trust her ex-husband. One of two things happens: the judge orders a mediation in which the ex-wife is pressured to agree to a stipulation, a voluntary but legally binding agreement between the parties, stating that her ex-husband will keep his distance from her; or, as is more common, the judge will grant a restraining or no-contact order.

The trouble with stipulations, Russell points out, is that the police do not know what to do with them. They look like an agreement between two people but nothing else, and so the police won't enforce it. The problem with restraining orders, she says, is just as simple: "You can shoot through a piece of paper." Which, according to Russell, happens on a regular basis in her hometown of San Diego.

Two years ago, Russell decided to retire from being a full-time gadfly and offered up her services as a publicist to a GPS monitoring company. GPS bracelets and anklets have long been used in both civil and criminal court, where they are used as part of a sentence in order to keep track of serial DUI perpetrators and violent criminals out on bail, probation, or parole. Why not, thought Russell, order GPS monitoring rather than simply issuing a restraining order? That way, if an angry ex got too close, the other ex would receive a notification on their cellphone. The notification would give them time to get away while the police received a location to find the offender. She thought this pitch would be a slam dunk, but the family courts weren't interested. She did, however, find a state representative in Oklahoma willing to push GPS legislation in his state.

What Russell does not seem to appreciate is that attaching a monitoring device to someone who has not been convicted of a crime is a potential violation of the constitutional right against self-incrimination, never mind causing embarrassment and potential damage to reputation when one needs to explain to one's employer, or TSA agent, why one's ankle has been encased in a steel tracking device. Although Russell believes that the family courts are dysfunctional, and should be torn down, she shares their philosophy of guilty until proven innocent, especially if the accused is male, which tracks a common misconception about domestic violence – that it is predominantly perpetrated against women. Like much of our society, gender-based behavior is changing rapidly. According to the 2011 National Intimate Partner and Sexual

Violence Survey (NISVS), funded by the Centers for Disease Control and US Department of Justice, "an estimated 5,365,000 men and 4,741,000 women were victims of intimate partner physical violence".[23] This is a significant change from the 2001 National Violence Against Women Survey (NVAWS) in which an estimated 1.2 million women and 835,000 men were reported to be victims of intimate partner violence.[24] Critics might argue about differences in how these surveys were conducted and what they measured, but regardless of which survey is considered, the numbers make it clear that domestic violence is not strictly a one-sided problem, and the trend is moving in a direction counter to stereotypical views.

Entrenched, gender-biased positions are common amongst family law activist groups (both father's rights groups and feminist groups), almost as common as amongst family court judges. Although just about everyone admits that the family courts are broken, they fail to realize that positive legislative change will only come about if both sexes support the proposed reforms. While injustices and disparities have been perpetrated against both sexes in the past, the rules of the game are changing rapidly as our society transitions toward the Egalitarian norms demanded by our Constitution as interpreted by our Supreme Court. The time has come for the courts and the gender-polarized activists to reformulate their actions and positions according to gender-neutral concepts, and align themselves with modern America.

---

23 Hoff, Bert H., *US National Survey: more men than women victims of intimate partner violence.* Journal of Aggression, Conflict, and Peace Research. Vol. 4, No. 3, pp. 155 – 163, 2012.

Black, M.C., et. al., *The National Intimate Partner and Sexual Violence Survey (NISVS): 2010 Summary Report,* National Center for Injury Prevention and Control, Centers for Disease Control and Prevention, Atlanta, GA.

24 Tjaden, P.G. and Thoennes, N. (2000). *Full report of prevalence, incidence and consequences of violence against women: findings from the national violence against women survey,* Research Report November 2000 NCJ 183781, US Department of Justice, National Institute of Justice and Centers for Disease Control and Prevention, Washington, DC.

13 | Cracks in the Pillars

*Okay, so who is watching the court? I've come to the
unfortunate conclusion that no one is holding them
accountable for their actions.*
        —Emily Gallup, family court mediator

On Friday, October 12th, 2012, Emily Gallup, the former mediator,
strode up the steps of the federal courthouse in Sacramento to hear
the conclusion of her years-long battle to save her reputation and
reform the Nevada County Family Court. The weather was about
20 degrees cooler than normal but still pleasant, in the low-60s, and
she had eschewed her favored summer dresses for a more businesslike
dark skirt and blazer. Gallup was nervous but relieved all at once. She
had spent the past two years fighting the system at great stress to her
family's finances, her marriage, and her mental well-being. The past two
weeks had been a crescendo of that conflict, with the family court's
attorneys and CEO portraying her as a disgruntled former employee,
an unethical mediator, an immature human being, and even a thief. Her
legal bills had soared into the six figures and she required wine and pills
in order to sleep most nights. She was ready for her travails to be over,
but because she was still a very young woman and her entire future
hung in the balance, she could not afford to be ambivalent.

Gallup's attorney, Kathy Jones, a tiny but athletic woman her client nervously chided for wearing a mullet into the 21st century, held
her hand as they entered the courtroom. Unlike her client, Jones was
confident. She felt that Gallup had charmed the jury, and after all, Jones
had handily won the "binding" arbitration of Gallup's original work-
place discrimination complaint against the Nevada County Court.

This trial was the court's response to that stunning rebuke. But this time, better still, Jones had gotten to present her case to a jury rather than merely a retired attorney-turned-arbitrator who happened to be an older white guy.

Gallup was still focused on the negative, the risks. It still didn't make sense to her that the court could challenge the outcome of a "binding" arbitration with a trial. Most worrisome, the judge presiding over her jury had been picked by the Administrative Office of the Courts, the overseer of the courts she had initially called for help. After they'd passed the buck, she had lost faith that the AOC was interested in ensuring justice and had criticized them in interviews with the local paper as well as in meetings with the Reformers.

But when the judge announced that the jury had sided with her on all counts, awarding her more than $300,000 in damages, Gallup was momentarily stunned. Jones gave her a hug after the judge dropped the gavel and proclaimed the trial over. They had not just won but won big. The jury had been disgusted by what they'd seen of Nevada County's family court and decided to send a very strong signal.

Outside the courthouse, Gallup paused to give a brief interview to her friend Liz Keller, a reporter for the local newspaper, *The Union*. Keller was the same reporter who had earlier been kicked out of the courthouse by its testy CEO, Sean Metroka. Gallup was surprised to find herself so composed at such an emotional moment. "Those awful accusations have been exposed for what they were," she told Keller. "As hard as this has been, I'm not sorry for what I did. I'm glad I blew the whistle because people were being hurt . . . I think the court should be ashamed it treated employees the way it did, and that the employees have treated clients the way they did."

Keller later interviewed Metroka, who said he would respect the jury's decision but wasn't sure yet if the Nevada County court would appeal the trial. Despite the jury's clear message, he offered no apology to Gallup nor the citizens his court had hurt. "There was no evidence presented to indicate that the court had at any time violated laws or rules of court in conducting Family Court services," Metroka said to an incredulous Keller. It was as though he had not sat through the earlier arbitration or understood this jury trial, as though Metroka was guided by a Nixonian ideology that whatever the wielder of power did was automatically legal.

Gallup did not see her fight as over and was resigned to battling on. Oddly enough, the judge whom she had once worked under, Julie Mc-Manus, had not been part of the trial. She never re-appeared after her last vanishing act and had finally been retired by the court after months spent collecting disability for a condition Metroka refused to reveal but which was assumed by Gallup to be alcoholism. While Gallup liked McManus's replacement, she was more concerned that Nevada County's mediation department would continue to go rogue and run roughshod over her friends and neighbors' constitutional rights. "Nobody has oversight," she told Keller on the courthouse steps. "I'm not going to feel I'm done with this project until there is some kind of outside oversight . . . I don't think the court should be policing themselves."

By then a spate of scandals nationwide involving family court judges had made the need for oversight quite clear. There was the judge in Wendy Archer's court who had been convicted of nine felonies, but there was also a judge in Pennsylvania who was convicted of sending juveniles to abusive rehabilitation centers that he secretly owned. There was the judge in Tennessee who had defrauded the foster care system by claiming her bailiff's child as her own and the Alabama judge who had taken bribes from an amusement park magnate in exchange for awarding sole custody to the magnate's daughter. There was the Illinois judge caught by a court camera playing solitaire on his laptop instead of listening to the case before him and the Texas judge captured on video savagely beating his handicapped daughter. Each ruled their fiefdom without any real oversight. Each had the power to help or destroy families. None had acted in the "best interests of the child," but the system just assumed that they had.

Gallup returned home that afternoon to a county mildly different than the one she had once worked for. She heard through the grapevine that courthouse mediators were no longer coercing parents to fill out a form that allowed the court to decide custody without them present, and that custody evaluators were now allowed to run criminal background checks in cases where allegations of domestic violence or other issues rose to the standard of "abuse and neglect." But the "emergency room" model remained largely intact, and the constitutional violations that Gallup and the state family bar had warned of years before continue uninterrupted to this day.

A GRANDMOTHER'S FIGHT

Things are different in Indiana, where Dan Brewington, the blogger, was sent to prison, safely tucked away out of sight and out of reach of reporters. While Brewington stews in his cell, his mother, Sue, paces the small living room of her craftsman-style house in a middle-class neighborhood lined with elm trees. Against one wall are legal boxes stacked waist high—the documents from her son's divorce. Lining the other walls are examples of her granddaughters' artwork—untouched since the day that Sue Brewington waved goodbye and said that she'd see them tomorrow. She has not seen them for three years now. Pausing at a series of pencil marks near the front door that documented each girl's growth, she wonders how much taller they will be when she sees them next—if she sees them again.

Sue Brewington is currently suing the family court for violating her due process rights by assigning her former daughter-in-law an interest in the family farm, which was left for her in trust by her late husband but might constitute the bulk of her son's inheritance someday, depending on how long she lives. She worries that, without the ability to borrow against her only real asset, she won't be able to pay the legal bills required to have the title cleared. It's a cruel catch-22. But the effective taking of her property without due process is not the most nagging issue that Sue Brewington has before the court. Like many parents of divorced children, she is trapped in a kind of perfect storm of constitutional issues that prevent her from seeing her granddaughters.

During the sentencing phase of her son's trial, both his judge and psychologist publicly excoriated her for supporting her son's efforts to see his daughters. Before that, the judge refused to approve her as a "visitation supervisor," an adult required to be present during her son's visits with his daughters, even though she was a retired fifth-grade teacher and even though (or maybe because) the court knew that her son could not afford to hire a professional. Once the court denied her son visitation rights, her daughter-in-law was under no obligation to allow Sue access to her granddaughters. That's because of a Supreme Court decision titled *Troxel v. Granville* (2000) in which the court decided that, even though it was in a child's best interest to see their grandparents, the parent's right to raise their children as they saw fit trumped grandparents' interest. In Sue's case, the court had taken a selective approach to the family's constitutional rights. On the one hand, her son's judge's determination of the best interests of the child not only trumped the custody evaluation but the father's right to parent his daughters as he saw fit. Once that right had been denied, however, the court allowed the mother's right to parent her daughters as she saw fit to trump not only the best interests of the children standard but the fact that the children's father wanted his daughters to spend time with their grandmother. The judge had conveniently determined not only that Dan Brewington's parenting would be detrimental while his wife's would not be, an opinion that contradicted the court's custody evaluator who had described Dan as an excellent father and noted that his ex-wife had some troubling psychological issues, but that Dan Brewington deserved no say at all in deciding what was in his daughters' best interest. In other words, the judge had twice disregarded the presumption that parents know what is in the best interests of their children but then used that standard when it served his goals, which appeared to be punishing Dan and his family for speaking out against the court.

THE AUDIT

In January of 2011, the auditor of the nation's most populous state, California, released a comprehensive study of two of its family court systems. The audit had been pushed by a young Assemblyman who had been pressured by a groundswell of increasingly organized and vocal critics in the northern part of the state. As in nearby Nevada County, it appeared that the subjects of the audit, the Sacramento and Marin County courts, were hiring unqualified evaluators, disregarding their own rules, and ignoring litigants' complaints. The cover page of the report contained this admonition: Both Courts Need to Ensure That Family Court Appointees Have Necessary Qualifications, Improve Administrative Policies and Procedures, and Comply With Laws and Rules.

The body painted a portrait of a court system that was not equipped to determine the best interests of the child, indeed a court system that did not seem to care all that much about those interests. What the system was well equipped to do, apparently, was farm out business to its friends, whether qualified or not. Marin County alone had paid out $1,000,000 directly to guardians *ad litem*, the private attorneys appointed by judges to represent children.

The State Auditor made it clear that it was not just self-represented litigants whose rights were being violated. And if one needed more evidence of the court's hostility to oversight, its report included the response from one of the court's presiding judges who dismissed the auditor's findings as trivial and complained that the title of the report was "inflammatory" and "misleading." Echoing Sean Metroka, the Nevada County CEO, the presiding judge asserted that the auditor had presented no evidence and that its report could not be accurate because, well, he said so: "The titles of the two chapters in the report give a similar impression that you found the court to be engaged in widespread disregard for laws, rules, policies and procedures," the judge correctly observed, before adding, "which, of course, is not true."

The judicial branch of our government seems to have become so convinced that they are doing good and so blind to modern reality that they, like doctors who applied leaches to drain blood from patients in the 1800s, have become blind to the real impact of their actions.

Perched only a few blocks from Paul Revere's house and the Freedom Trail, the attorney Gerald Nissenbaum offers some unsolicited advice for no one in particular. "Sometimes," he says, "you just gotta stand up to the judge and say, 'Judge, There's an American flag in this courtroom!'" Those who have followed that advice seem to have fared poorly. For every Emily Gallup who prevails, there seems to be a Mark Byron, Lea Banken, Andrew Karres, and Dan Brewington, to name but a few, all of whom have lost visitation rights with little or no due process.

Fortunately for the courts, the majority give up and the wheels of the mill grind forward. Once deprived of one's basic constitutional rights, there's very little that one can do but accept one's fate as the grist or else strike out—and an entire book could be written on the violence in and around family courts.

THE EXILE

Ulf Carlsson, the former civil servant from Sacramento, one of the court systems criticized in the audit, has become an exile of one of the courts examined by the State Auditor. In the kitchen of his parents' modest home in Landskrona, a coastal village near Malmo, Sweden, he sips coffee with several relatives, including his young cousin Alexandra Borg, the *Sweden's Got Talent!* hopeful whose divorce cost her only a postage stamp. The Swedes cannot grasp what he is telling them about the United States' family courts. How could that be America? They want to know. How could anyone live in such a system? They shake their heads.

The only one who knows is Carlsson's mother, a still spry woman in her mid-70s. She knows because of what the court has taken from her and her husband: a big chunk of their life savings and, more important, her 17-year-old granddaughter. Both Carlsson and his mother found out about his daughter's marriage and recent pregnancy from the Facebook posts of relatives.

Carlsson's mother, who wanted to support her son and her granddaughter at a difficult time, flew to America to attend her son's trial two years ago. Why two adults could not settle these things was confusing, almost unbelievable for her, but she expected the judge to listen and make an equitable decision—to be judicious. She expected the judge to dissolve the marriage and order husband and wife to move forward with their lives. What Carlsson's mother saw was something else. "The judge was there but he wasn't there," she says. "It was like his mind was someplace else. He didn't do anything." She loves America, she says, and the friends she met when her husband was an international shipping executive. But she could never go back there now. "I think," she says, "that in America it [the court system] has become a business. I think it's all about money."

14 | **The Swamp**

We have a society that should encourage people to take care of themselves. But in Massachusetts, when two people split up, the court system ties them together for the rest of their lives.

—Stephen Hitner[25]

I'm confident that, if you gave me the opportunity, I could come up with a family court system that truly acted in the best interests of the child. That would, of course, require a lot of money.

—Joe Kenan, M.D.

I F, AS THE JOURNALIST-ACTIVIST BONNIE RUSSELL'S WEBSITE CONTENDS, everyone older than 11 knows that family court isn't working, why is it still in business? The answer, Russell says with a wry smile, is that family court is actually working very well—for the lawyers, the judges, and the psychologists. The litigants, she says, are just the fuel for the industry's meteoric rise in profits. In Russell's opinion, the greatest—and gravest— misconception about family court is that it's about families rather than the people making money off of them.

THE ECOSYSTEM

Russell claims to have coined the phrase "divorce industry" because family court can only be understood in the wider context of its finan- cial impact and the cottage businesses that feed off of it. Half a century

---

25 "'Til Death Do Us Pay," *Boston Magazine,* July, 2009

ago, divorce had its hangers-on too: private investigators, as well as the photographers and actresses who would stage phony "affairs" in order to provide the cause needed to secure a divorce, and the infamous Reno "divorce ranches" for the women who needed to establish residency in Nevada before they could file. But where family courts once leaked a financial trickle, each now unleashes a dependable tsunami of cash that swirls around the courthouse. If one drew the flowchart, it would resemble a massive fountain. Money would be sucked from the provider spouse and flow into the courtroom, some of it making its way back to the supported spouse. But much, if not most, of the waterfall would be diverted to attorneys, psychologists, custody evaluators, guardians *ad litem*, private investigators, rent-a-judges, expert witnesses, visitation supervisors, and on and on. Part of the money, unfortunately, might flow back to the judge in the form of a re-election campaign contribution, to a law office where he or she decided to become a senior partner, or to an ADR company through which he or she rented his or her services. And a splash or two of money might end up in one of the increasingly common cottage industries: plastic surgeons advertising "revenge surgery," car dealerships that have begun offering divorce specials, tabloids promising the latest gossip on a celebrity, bars offering special nights for "cougars" (divorced women, flush with cash and ready to spend it on young men). Indeed, the divorce industry has created its own version of moving on—not severing the relationship but spending the alimony and child support money as flashily as possible (ergo Linda Hogan's yacht named "Alimoney").

And what, demands the private investigator John Nazarian from the wheel of his $250,000 Bentley, is wrong with *that*? People love to fight. The court is simply providing an arena in which they do, albeit a profitable one for people like him. What could be more American than that? He wants us to know that he thinks Americans are ridiculous for spending so much money on people like him in order to live out our retribution fantasies—but he also wants us to know that he's glad we are this ridiculous.

DROWNING THE MIDDLE CLASS

On another day, Nazarian navigates his new Porsche Panamera through a sea of traffic as he dishes on the big divorce cases in L.A. Jamie and Frank McCourt, the billionaire owners of the L.A. Dodgers, for example. He talks about how a lot of the family court judges downtown are millionaires themselves, how a lot of the psychologists make more than the attorneys, how the big, big money lies over the hills from his home in Glendale, Beverly Hills, Bel Air, the Hollywood Hills, and Malibu. He speaks in breathless, if slightly bemused, terms about how minor's counsel are making hundreds of thousands of dollars protecting the interests of infants who, in his words, "can't say goo goo or ga ga!" He is getting his niece in the supervised visitation racket, sixty bucks an hour to watch kids and spy on the parents. Hire a few people below you, give them half, and pretty soon you're rich. All you gotta do is get in good with the judge . . .

What Nazarian doesn't mention are those living east of the hills, where the average household income ($41,663) is now less than the average cost of a contested divorce ($50,000), or nearly three times the average cost of sending a kid to college for a year. Living east of the hills are the parents who pay most of the fees and the child support and the alimony. Last year, according to a prominent Southwestern family law firm, these parents shelled out more than $100 billion in alimony, child support, legal and professional fees, and other expenses related to their divorces. Or, to think about it another way, the court sucked it out of them and redistributed the money, leaving them with a fraction. It's a staggering amount, more, as Dennis Wasser points out, than flows through all of the other court systems combined. The fees alone are enough to send 5 million students to college or enough to provide a free lunch 365 days a year to all of the children in North America, South America, and all of Africa! It is enough to develop dozens of new life-saving medicines a year. But for its practitioners, this still isn't enough.

In 2007, an elderly man named Marvin Singer was sent to prison for the crime of not paying his ex-wife's attorney $100,000. He had already paid the man $100,000, Singer explained to *The New York Times*, and it was not so much that he wanted to be stubborn, it was that he knew that, once he paid that amount, they would hit him up for even more. In any other court of law, the judge might have ordered his ex-wife's attorneys to finish their case and sort out payment later, perhaps file a lien on his property or garnish his income. In family court, a 71-year-old man is sent to jail indefinitely because he refuses to hand over the fuel that the court demands in order to keep the fighting going.

Singer's take on his ordeal was surprisingly sanguine. "I thought they'd eliminated debtor's prisons in this country," he told a journalist from *The New York Times*.

At least Steve Hitner, the printer who founded Massachusetts Alimony Reform, has finally escaped his own sort of prison. His ex having declined to follow through on her threats to have him sent to prison for non-payment of alimony that he could not afford, Hitner says that he and his ex-wife finally reached a settlement. The year before he lost his house to foreclosure, and he faces the loss of his business as well; but at least, he says, he's a free man—at least according to the Kris Kristofferson's definition in as much as he has nothing left to lose. After the passage of the alimony reform bill, he's received several calls a week from earner spouses who no longer have to pay alimony. Hitner has become a mediator. He says that, by removing the threat of lifetime alimony, the law has brought spouses together to negotiate settlements. People who weren't getting married, for fear of losing their alimony or paying their husband's first wife alimony, are now tying the knot. Alimony now ends at retirement.

In 2012, a task force on child support laws mentioned Hitner's work on alimony reform as it changed the guidelines. Though child support is still linked to the percentage of custody and income, the task force recommended some new limits, including a requirement that judges make sure that employment is actually available before imputing an income to an unemployed spouse. That is, no more judicial opinions that a provider spouse "should" earn a certain sum in contravention of economic reality. These recommendations, if adopted, might immediately reduce the amount of support payments by 10-16%. Hitner says that Massachusetts' new guidelines on alimony and child support, which went into effect in August of that year, are making people better parents because they are spending so much less time arguing over money.

The most surprising byproduct of alimony reform is Hitner's reconciliation with the court that steadfastly refused to modify his alimony payments, threatened to jail him, forced his wife to make alimony payments to his ex, and ultimately bankrupted him. "I never had a problem

with the court," Hitner says. "I had a problem with the *law*. I learned
that the judges . . . It's their job to make sure that people play the game
properly, and make sure the law is followed properly. And there are many
judges who don't do their job the way that they're supposed to because
of bias or whatever. But in general, the judges I've met and the lawyers
I've met are very good people. The resistance from the bar was because
they didn't think we could get anything done . . . For the most part,
they're good people trying to do the best with what they've got."

GIVE US MORE MONEY

Hitner's modest victory in stanching the tide came more than four decades since Ronald Reagan signed no-fault divorce into law and ush-
ered in the era of family courts. This era was supposed to be one of
reconciliation and moving forward. Instead, the divorce rate and duration of proceedings exploded while the dignity and the rights of its citizens withered. For the past several years, California has been wrestling
with the edict from its late Chief Justice that family courts must ensure
everyone equal access to justice and due process. A task force was set up,
but their solution was to encourage more law students to enter family
law and for family court judges to make attorney fee awards earlier during cases. Yet there have still been no public hearings, nor has anyone
forced the legislature and the judiciary to come together to reach an
agreement. The new Chief Justice has refused interviews, claiming that
she is unfamiliar with family law, and so have the state's auditor and the
court's top administrators overseeing the family courts, and for equally
dubious reasons.

That leaves the attorneys to fix a system that, although everyone
agrees is broken, many profit from handsomely. In California, the family
bar has issued their report, a response to the task force that recommended
more attorneys and earlier awards for attorneys' fees. The attorneys say
they agree that litigants' constitutional rights have been routinely violated and, maybe worse, that their dignity has not been respected by the
courts. They say that the emergency room model practiced in Nevada
County, and who knows in how many other courts, is a disaster and
should be discontinued. They say that the court is flooded with *pro pers*
who don't know what they're doing, and therefore often act against

their own interests, while upsetting the litigants who are paying attorneys hundreds of dollars an hour to sit with them in the gallery while they wait their turn. The courts are not only pitting husband against wife and mother against father but lawyered against non-lawyered litigant. The family bar calls out Alternative Dispute Resolution, aka the "rent-a-judge" model, as rife with potential for conflicts of interest that frustrate justice and breed judicial bias, which is probably the greatest threat to any litigant's civil rights. They say that litigants are not allowed to be self-determining.

The family bar acknowledges the problems, but their solution is predictable: more money for the court system. They say that the family courts are chronically underfunded, that they need at least four times as many judges in order to handle all of the custody disputes that are currently on the dockets.

And then the family court insiders lay out their vision of what a "21st century courthouse" looks like:

> Our courtrooms need media/library/learning centers that include practice guides, self-help books, videotapes or digital recordings and other resources for litigants and the bench and bar. They need classrooms that can be used for everything from co-parenting classes to continuing education programs. Our courthouses need childcare facilities, at least minimal food and beverage service, safe handicapped access and nearby parking. They need to be open on some weekends and evenings. We also need to expand the number of settlement conference rooms in our courthouses. Each settlement area needs a computer and printer. The computer should be loaded with a family program such as Attorneys' Briefcase, online access to the internet with shortcuts to the Judicial Council website, suggested language for orders and stipulations, support and arrearage calculation software and a full set of Judicial Council forms. The publishers of much of this software should be asked to donate it. Courthouses need universal wireless access available at a daily rate rather just by monthly or annual

subscription. Courtrooms should be equipped with video-conferencing capability, scanners for transmitting exhibits to remote witnesses, teleconferencing capability, printers at counsel table so attorneys can bring electronic files and quickly print something that the court is missing and sufficient power outlets so that lawyers can plug in laptops or other devices. We need to offer an e-filing option and make that the standard for filing; computers in the courthouses and in public libraries should be e-filing equipped. All of these things would bring our family law courtrooms into the 21st century."

Finally, the lawyers and other court professionals call for development of triage software, mandatory parenting classes, mandatory meetings between court mediators and children, more psychological testing of all parties, mandatory minor's counsel in contested custody cases (in addition to custody evaluators), an in-house collection process to get the court's money back, certain days for *pro pers* and law students to help them fill out their forms (the same law students that, according to the Los Angeles legal services director, are more of a hindrance than a help).

This is what a cutting-edge family court looks like according to those who make their living from it. The goal, as the report suggests, appears to be making the divorce court as much like a business as possible. The writers of the report say, "21st Century family courts should abandon the linear path best exemplified by Lucy Ricardo and Ethel Mertz's experience on the chocolate factory assembly line. Instead, they should adopt the modern 'just-in-time' models pioneered by Wal-Mart and FedEx, with the goal of allowing each case to proceed at its own pace with an experienced bench officer available within a reasonable time when needed." Litigants, in other words, are to be managed like merchandise or like cargo, shepherded through and processed as cheaply and as efficiently as possible—and forced to pay without limits for the privilege.

What might the cost be for all of these "improvements"? It's impossible to know, but easily in the hundreds of billions of dollars. All so that we can continue in the tradition of medieval English chancery courts.

MORE MONEY, MORE PROBLEMS

Bonnie Russell has heard the cries for more funding before, but she's stopped buying them. "The only solution is to get rid of family court," she says matter-of-factly. She says that those who work in the system have become too brainwashed by the echo chamber to understand the absurdity of micro-managing families with computers, subjecting them to expensive psychological tests, and forcing them to hire attorneys for their infants. They have become blind to the obvious solutions. For example, instead of hiring four times as many judges to adjudicate the explosion in custody cases, why not decouple child support from the amount of time awarded to one parent or the other and cap support at the same amount for every child in the country so that it never exceeds the minimum cost of providing basic needs? Instead of segregating *pro pers* from the lawyered and both from the very wealthy, why not simplify the laws to make them more understandable to all? Instead of hiring more minor's counsel and guardians *ad litem* and custody evaluators and mediators, why not recognize that the vast majority of parents can be trusted to act in their children's best interest? Instead of offering a la carte services or means-testing litigants for court services, why not make the law less complex? Instead of demanding the family court judges be experts in domestic violence and human lie detectors, why not allow criminal courts to handle criminal matters? Instead of using support payments to level lifestyles, why not allow exes to move forward in the lifestyle they choose and can afford?

"The judges love to say that they need more money," Russell says. "But they have plenty of money. The problem is what they're spending it on." Perjury, domestic violence, and fraud, for example, should all be decided in a criminal court. Everything else should require nothing more than a form printed in plain English. Blaming the court's dysfunction on a lack of money is just another setup, she says, a way to blame the taxpayers, to blame all of us for not giving more. Here ring echoes of the judge who blamed Wendy Archer for her judge's conflict of interest, the district attorney who prosecuted Dan Brewington, the judge who punished Ulf Carlsson, the custody evaluator who tried to double dip with Deb Singer, and the judge who refused to recuse himself after filing a secret police report against Danielle Malmquist. In the eyes of

Divorce Corp., she says, we (the general public who are the grist for the mill) are the problem because we have not yet learned how to play the game. We have not yet accepted that, as in the chancery court of Dickens' time, once we enter those doors, everything we have suddenly belongs to them.

WITH A LITTLE HELP FROM THEIR FRIENDS

Over the phone, Stephen Hitner is optimistic, even ebullient. Sitting in the gallery of the Massachusetts State House as the roll call was read on alimony reform changed his life. "When I was in that house and it [the reform measure] was passed unanimously, it was the most amazing feeling I've ever had in my life," he says. "That never happens! It was unanimous in both houses!" He is now consulting with alimony reform movements in other states, but progress has been slow. After Massachusetts, Florida was poised as the next state to enact reform. But the bill passed by the Florida Legislature, which would have ended lifetime alimony and imposed a 50/50 presumption on child custody, was vetoed by the governor during the last few days of the legislative session, making it unlikely that lawmakers would have the time to override it. "I have concluded," Governor Rick Scott, a lawyer himself, explained in his veto letter, "that I cannot support this legislation because it applies retroactively and thus tampers with the settled economic expectations of many Floridians who have experienced divorce. The retroactive adjustment of alimony could result in unfair, unanticipated results."

In Texas, another state with an independent streak, the caps on "available resources" for child support were recently raised enough to allow supported spouses to go back to court seeking modifications. According to a local parents rights organization, the measure is sure to increase litigation and fan the flames of more custody battles. The state defended the move, saying that it was necessary for support awards to keep up with inflation. Texas currently allows up to 40% of a single parent's "available resources"—a measure of disposable income—to be ordered paid to the custodial parent as child support.

In certain parts of the United States, the most prominent legislative push has not been to make divorce less acrimonious or to lessen the number of custody battles, but to turn back the clock and make divorce more difficult. Since 1997, legislatures in 24 states (including Florida and Texas) have introduced bills attempting to create so-called "covenant marriages." This new/old type of marriage—and the Biblical insinuation is not accidental—seeks a return to the days of "fault" marriage. Rather than allow either party to seek a divorce on generic grounds like "irreconcilable differences," the couple agrees in advance that the marriage cannot be dissolved except in the event of certain marital crimes, like adultery, alcoholism, and withholding of affection. Covenant marriages would be voluntary, at least in the beginning, so couples would essentially check one of two boxes when getting married: one for no-fault divorce and one for fault.

So far, covenant marriage has only passed in three states—Arizona, Arkansas, and Louisiana—to little effect in each. In no state have the percentages of covenant marriages grown past more than the low single digits. While some old-timers, like Sorrell Trope, would not mind a return to the days of fault, most Americans appear to believe that divorce is hard enough as it is. For their part, the Scandinavians find the notion of keeping a system that further punishes people even more ridiculous.

Sitting in the bar of the posh hotel in Reykjavik, the film director Baltasar Kormakur shakes his head at how Americans have made breaking up so complicated and so punishing. "Why would you want to make divorce more painful?" he asks, more than a little bewildered. "Maybe you should make marriage more difficult."

Cultures change slowly. People become set in their ways and are often hamstrung by the traditions of their ancestors. Some, like the Amish, never leave the past; and others, like the Luddites among us who eschew technological innovation, wish to return to it. Others look for solutions to changes brought on by education, knowledge, technology, and science. The potential solutions to our family court crisis might not be as clear if we did not have the benefit of a natural experiment that has proven successful. But we do. And it's almost free.

15 | Solutions

When the law gets hopelessly bogged down, as is true of our present divorce law, reform is best accomplished by a fresh start from a new premise. That has been the history of the evolution and growth of our legal system.
—Reginald Heber Smith, "Dishonest Divorce,"
Atlantic Monthly, 1947

THE SUPPORT GROUP

Every Monday evening in the community room of the Grass Valley library, Emily Gallup, the former court mediator, hosts a gathering for family court litigants. Their mission: changing how their court operates. The group is called "The Nevada County Family Court Reformers," but the atmosphere in the meeting feels more like it is a support group for people whose lives are now dominated by being dragged back into court by ex-husbands/wives and judges. The gathering forms a large circle, everybody seated in plastic chairs. The collection of long faces, scared and angry expressions in equal measure, evokes Bob Simms' parade of broken dreams.

For example, there is a pretty young woman, a single mother, trying to hold down a job while responding to motion after motion filed by her ex-husband. The other day he verbally assaulted her in full view of the bailiffs, who did nothing, on the courthouse steps. Fighting back tears, she says it's even worse inside the courtroom. The judge publicly ridicules her pleadings, which she is forced to write herself because she cannot afford a lawyer, and refuses to listen to evidence of the horrifying abuse her daughter is suffering during visitation with her ex.

Sitting next to her is an older woman whose husband filed for full custody of their teenage son after she refused to keep taking care of his dog. She had agreed to appear at a hearing without her lawyer because the clerk had promised that nothing would be decided; then she listened in horror as the judge stripped her of her parental rights, ostensibly because she thought her son was not yet responsible enough for a driver's license. "It wasn't even a custody hearing!" she says, her voice shaking.

Across from this woman is a middle-aged lawyer enmeshed in a nasty custody battle with his ex-wife. He says he has been alienated from his daughters. He's also bankrupt, thanks in large part to a series of court-ordered psychological tests that have become progressively more expensive. Then there is the husband and wife fighting for an explanation for their huge minor's counsel bills . . .

Gallup listens patiently to all of the stories, most of which she has heard before. She tries to empathize but, of course, she has her own horror story to tell. Her life has not entirely recovered since the court took aim at her. She tries not to show her nerves to these people, who clearly need hope. She says that she reminds herself that this is not just a support group made up of people whining to each other. She wants it to be a group with a mission, and so Gallup tries to move things in a positive direction; but by the end of the meeting she is visibly exhausted, the perky smile dissolved into a sympathetic frown. Each divorce is its own epic of hurt feelings and love gone wrong, of crimes of the heart and sometimes crimes of a more tangible nature. Two years ago, Gallup was given around 15 minutes to evaluate these sagas before deciding custody arrangements and then convincing both parents to sign off on a temporary agreement that she knew was anything but temporary. It had been a recipe for failure. That things unraveled was not her fault, the litigants sometimes remind her, even as they take aim at her former employer. Sitting amidst the wreckage, one cannot help but feel that the terms "dissolution" and "divorce" are misnomers. If anything, the system described by these folks guarantees that "exes" will remain tied to one another for a very, very long time, maybe until death do them part.

Gallup is aware of the irony. Divorce should be a process of uncoupling that allows the parties to grieve and then start anew. Divorce may be inherently conflictual, but how that conflict is managed will determine the path forward. If the conflict is never resolved, no one really gets to grieve because they're too busy fighting each other. And if no one grieves, no one is able to truly move on. But the solutions that she and the reformers are fighting for are relatively modest—longer mediations and an end to *ex-parte* communications between judges and mediators, for example. If family courts are to be truly reformed, the system will require more fundamental change.

COLLABORATIVE LAW

And family courts continue to create barriers against reform and incentives to produce conflict, especially in cases where one or both sides come to court without a lawyer. The judge might challenge an amicable settlement with a series of pointed questions, like, "Do you understand that you could improve on this if you had a lawyer?" Alternatively, a family court judge can simply reject a dissolution agreement outright as being "unconscionable", "unenforceable", or without explanation, irrespective of the parties' respective wishes. It is up to them to go back to the drawing board, and to spend more time and more money crafting something the judge will bless.

Divorce Corp. insiders like to point out that most divorces are actually settled prior to a formal trial. Here, they say, is irrefutable evidence that the system is working and that the nasty custody disputes and money battles are the rare exception. But while it is true that most divorces settle before trial, those divorces may involve months or years of discovery, depositions, interrogatories, motions, hearings, temporary orders, and most destructively, aggressive litigation to keep the process going—until the money runs out. Settlement is not so much evidence that the parties have been brought to terms peacefully as it is proof that the mental, physical, and financial strain of the process has worn them down to the point where they will sign almost anything. If the parties are represented by attorneys, the judge will probably rubberstamp the agreement, endorsing a second myth: because the attorneys have fought so hard to reach a settlement, because the parties have spent so much of their time and money on the back and forth, it must be a good deal for both, or at least not skewed too far in one direction or the other.

A handful of divorce attorneys in the United States, some who became repulsed by the damage done to families in divorce court and others who simply noticed a unique business niche, have explored alternatives to the antagonistic-unto-pugilistic family court model. If couples were able to work out an amicable split prior to entering the courtroom, they wondered, could such settlements be achieved without a fight? Would it be possible to find a fair solution without the aggressive tactics of the adversarial system? And, perhaps most important, might the family court judge honor their wishes and let them go their separate ways in peace?

"What's truer than the truth?" asks one such attorney, Harvard lecturer David Hoffman, from the deck of his summer home on Cape Cod. He leans back in his chair overlooking the ocean and smiles patiently. "The story," he finally answers. "And every story requires a victim, an abuser, and of course, a rescuer." That rescuer, Hoffman continues, could be a judge or a lawyer. Certainly, that is how divorce attorneys portray themselves and how most judges like to see themselves. But, after 17 years in family law, Hoffman has arrived at the opposite conclusion: courts and lawyers are almost never the rescuers. Rather, the men and women who are supposed to be resolving marital disputes are more often enablers or even villains who, as Hoffman puts it, were not putting out the flames but fanning them. With this in mind, 10 years ago Hoffman founded the Boston Law Collaborative, or BLC for short.

BLC is based on the concept of collaborative law, a derivative of mediation that is designed to remove disputes, like divorce, from the adversarial context of a courthouse. Collaborative law is the brainchild of a Midwestern lawyer named Stuart G. Webb, who also got sick of fueling the flames. Webb hung up his sword and became a Buddhist. Then he figured out a way that he thought divorce could work outside of the adversarial system.

It works like this: Husband and wife sign a participation agreement in which they pledge to work with a variety of professionals to negotiate a settlement. Like mediation, there are no plaintiffs and defendants, or even petitioners and respondents. Husbands and wives are referred to by their first names and sit shoulder to shoulder at a small table.

But unlike mediation, they do have attorneys sitting next to them. The difference is that their attorneys must sign a pledge that they will not represent the clients if a settlement is not reached and the dispute goes to court. Theoretically, this removes the incentive for the lawyers to extend the conflict because, if they don't settle, the divorce-court windfall will go to another lawyer.

Collaborative law is the latest of a number of solutions envisioned by a 1979 article published in the *Yale Law Journal* titled "Bargaining in the Shadow of the Law." The authors wrote, suggesting that, even then, divorce courts were exercising wide discretion over their mandate, "We see the primary function of contemporary divorce law not as imposing order from above, but rather as providing a framework within which divorcing couples can themselves determine their post-dissolution rights and responsibilities." The authors imagined a process called "private ordering," by which husbands and wives were empowered to create their own legally-enforceable agreements. The court would then either be a place of last resort or simply an enforcer of agreements.

The University of Denver has established a Resource Center for Separating and Divorce Families, intended to teach people about alternatives to family court litigation and guide them through an alternative process.[26] The Resource Center incorporates many of the concepts of the Scandinavian model for dissolution and child-sharing, but also offers services that include legal dispute resolution (essentially collaborative divorce assistance), therapeutic counseling for emotional and child-related issues, and financial counseling to help people divide assets and develop fair support arrangements. There are several other such centers being started across the country, but the concept is very new.

This vision of couples coming to their own agreements without the court's involvement has, however, run into several roadblocks. For example, both sides must be convinced that their chances in mediation are better than going to court, a perception that is actively sabotaged by the vast majority of family law firms. But mostly legislatures have resisted

---

26 www.du.edu/rcsdf

allowing litigants to come up with their own solutions. Instead, they have let judges retain absolute control of their fiefdoms. Settlements must be approved by the court, which can still order up psychological evaluations or rework the financial arrangements to more closely resemble the status quo. And even if a couple is fortunate enough to have their settlement approved by the court, there is nothing to prevent either party from coming back at a later date to ask a judge to break it up and start the process all over again.

Further, settlements negotiated outside of the court tend to carry less weight than those decided in it, making it easier for a party with buyer's remorse to drag the other one back into the fight. Maybe the supported spouse ends up making a lot of money in the years after a divorce and the earning spouse decides they are entitled to a piece of it, as happened recently in the divorce of pop star Usher. Or maybe the earning spouse gets remarried and the supported spouse wants part of the new husband or wife's income, as happened to Bob Simms. What can one do to avoid being dragged back into family court *after* reaching a divorce settlement? Not much, as it turns out. Dennis Wasser, the celebrity lawyer, offers a cheeky bit of advice: normally it's best to remarry someone age-appropriate.

But as "Bargaining in the Shadow of the Law" suggests, exes were not supposed to spend the rest of their lives in fear of one another. The idea behind "private ordering" was that two adults were capable of settling their differences, whether through mediation, collaborative divorce, or by themselves. It is worth mentioning that the same year that *Bargaining in the Shadow of the Law* was published, *Kramer versus Kramer*, a film in which two parents are turned against one another by overzealous divorce attorneys in their custody battle for a young son but end up coming to terms after the trial, won the Academy Award. In that film, the lawyers were the bad guys, the judge was ambivalent, and the court an arena, just as Hoffman describes it, where parents and friends were forced to testify against one another. "Basically," Hoffman says, "what the court does is it creates a battleground on which each side hurls the harshest accusations they can come up with because they're desperate to win. What you have is a tinderbox. And virtually anything can ignite that tinderbox. And the lawyers, frankly, are often throwing gasoline on that fire."

THE GOOD DIVORCE

Eva Marie Jonsdottir, the Icelandic television host and patchwork (so-called because she has children by more than one father) mother of five, still remembers when she realized her family was going to survive their divorce. "I was driving," she says, "and my eight-year-old daughter turns to me and she says, 'Mommy, isn't it funny how life doesn't turn out the way you think it will but it's still really good?'" Jonsdottir takes a deep breath while slowly wiping her forehead with the back of her right palm. "I was like, 'Okay, this is going to be okay!'" She laughs. A few miles later, her daughter announced that her mother's next husband should be tall and a non-smoker. Jonsdottir met that man a few weeks later.

Forrest Mosten, the mediator, still believes that a good divorce like Jonsdottir's is possible in the U.S. He points to studies showing that divorced children do as well or better than children from intact homes—as long as the parents are able to cooperate. Since roughly half of marriages don't last, how we divorce determines not only our children's wellbeing but also the health of our future relationships. The ripple effect of a custody battle is impossible to know, but it is surely at least as pervasive as Sorrell Trope has suggested. The same goes for the effects of an unjust court and a dysfunctional system. To some extent, we can inventory the lives lost and ruined. What we will never know is how many chose not to enter into an intimate relationship or have children because the consequences of the failure of that relationship would be too punishing, how many could not face the prospect of lining up to join the parade of broken dreams for the rest of their life, locked in an endless battle over money and maybe alienated from their own children.

While every culture has wrestled with the issue of how to dissolve an unhappy relationship and most, like the United States, devised their systems with the best of intentions, decades of practice have yielded dramatically different thinking. In France, for example, marriage licenses now have a time limit so that divorce is automatic unless the marriage is renewed. At the other extreme, divorce remains illegal in the Philippines, mainly for religious reasons. One can argue endlessly about the motivations and justifications for each system without coming to any resolution, but deciding what is in the best interest of a country is as fruitless an exercise as figuring out what is in the best interests of every child. The only part that's not subjective is the outcome.

ELIMINATE THE BLAME

The United States has been struggling to "fix" its family laws since at least 1947, when the *Atlantic Monthly* noted that 1.2 million divorces had been filed over the previous 12 months, an almost three-fold increase since the end of the war two years earlier and a 6,000% increase over the divorce rate in 1867. Maybe the rise after WWII was the Scandinavian effect—men coming back from long trips overseas to find wives who had become more independent—or maybe the war had convinced both men and women that life was too short and too uncertain to spend it in an unhappy relationship. No one knows. But there is almost universal consensus that that fix has been elusive, that the struggle has been an abject failure.

In 1956, Paul W. Alexander, a respected judge from Toledo, Ohio, who then chaired the American Bar Association's Special Committee on Divorce and Marriage Laws & Family Courts, wrote that the bar had been trying for three-quarters of a century to improve the divorce laws. "In the main," he wrote, "all efforts have been almost complete failures. Most of them failed to take into account the increasingly accepted hypothesis that divorce is effect rather than cause. They started out with the traditional premise that divorce should reward innocence and punish guilt." The court, he said, was using an adversarial proceeding to reward the "good" spouse and punish the "bad" spouse. "In the meantime," he concluded, "the perennial procession of marriage failures, the unbroken parade of broken families, passes through the divorce courts of the land."

Alexander's writings are, sadly, no less relevant nearly six decades later. Substitute "earning" for bad and "supported" for good and the words could be published in a modern law journal. In other words, the family court system has remained a mess because, while the labels have changed, the underlying paternalistic assumptions have not. Maybe there is simply too much money flowing through the system and that current has become too powerful to swim against. Or maybe the paternalistic mindset is too embedded in our culture. But in order to move to a system that allows families to heal and individuals to move on with their lives, it's clear that both must change.

MEANINGFUL REFORM

Must the family courts be abolished, as some have suggested? Reasonable people may come to different conclusions on that question. What is undeniable is that, in order for the family courts to achieve their decades-old goal of healing rather than hurting their clients, they must undertake some big changes. The following reforms, modeled after the Scandinavian system, if implemented on a prospective basis (for all marriages that occur after legislation has been enacted and phased in over a period of years) could help transition to a system that achieves the decades-old goal of healing rather than hurting:

1. True gender neutrality. This means treating fathers and mothers (and husbands and wives) equally under the law. Unless there is a separate written agreement by the parents to the contrary, or a conviction for abuse or neglect by a jury in criminal court, legal and physical custody would be 50/50. Of course, the parents would always have the right to modify, customize, or switch to a different schedule by mutual agreement.

2. The end of alimony as we know it. Alimony, if any, should be governed by optional, private "dependent support agreements" entered into by the parties either before and/or during the marriage. These agreements would specify to whom and for how long alimony should be paid, and how it should be computed. Absent a private written agreement, the state would have no power to order alimony post-divorce.

3. Fixed child support. Child support would be the same modest fixed-dollar amount for every child of a dependent parent in each state, not a percentage of one or the other parent's income. Like other programs that help those in need, this number would be tied to the cost of essentials, it would be paid only if custody was not 50/50 or if child support was specified in an optional dependent support agreement, and it would not change regardless of the degree to which custody deviated from 50/50.

4. Do-It-Yourself divorce. Changing one's status from married to divorced should require no more than filling out a form and waiting six months for a possible reconciliation. A judge would not be allowed to block or delay or change a divorce settlement.

5. Discourage frivolous litigation. Since there will be no need to hire a litigator for routine divorce, child custody, or child support cases, the role of civil litigation in family law will be limited to cases of fraud or the enforcement of contracts. In many parts of the world, the "loser pays" the cost of the litigation. This discourages people from bringing frivolous lawsuits, because they might end up paying both parties' attorneys. Or, if the jury decides that there is no real winner or loser, each side must pay his or her own attorney. This also creates a disincentive to litigate weak cases. And if a party has failed to make support payments, the prospect of having to pay both sides' attorneys will encourage the payer to either catch up on the arrearage or, if they cannot afford to make the payments, to simply admit to the default and work out a payment plan.

REBUTTAL TO THE REBUTTAL

We do not claim to be legislators. These reform proposals will not appeal to everyone. Debate will help to test their soundness and provide helpful refinements. But one thing is undeniable: these tenets have worked extremely well for many years for about 25 million people in a highly developed, highly educated, economically prosperous part of the world where gender equality is a prized ideal, and where, alternatively, a traditional provider/dependent relationship (with negotiated support obligations) can be freely practiced if a couple so wishes.

We anticipate certain responses to the 5 tenets listed above, and have some additional thoughts.

1. 50/50 child sharing works in Scandinavia, and it works for many parents in America; but it may not be for everyone. Fine. If an individual would not be comfortable with a 50/50 arrangement, then that individual should choose a mate who shares those views and would be willing to work out a dependent support agreement that fits the desired arrangement. Hopefully most people will recognize

the value of including both parents equally in a child's life, but where that is not desirable or practicable for both parties, an alternative arrangement can be structured. If, over time, that alternative arrangement no longer works for both parties, the parties must mutually agree to modify it.

If couples discuss these important issues before they get married or have children, they will know what to expect. Why hide the implications and obligations of marriage and child rearing in voluminous, unintelligible law books that are understood only by family law lawyers and judges? By making the parties discuss their relative roles and expectations ahead of time, we might get better parents, and we can keep our government out of the business of imposing an outdated, cookie cutter, dependent/provider relationship on all marriages. Our societal norms have changed, and the dependent/provider model should no longer be the premise underpinning the family laws.

By eliminating the government's role in selecting a "primary custodial parent", we eliminate the need for custody evaluations, custody evaluators, and custody battles. If parents cannot come up with their own 50/50 sharing schedule, they could consult a mediator, or a psychologist, or choose an approved sharing template; and if the parents fail to agree to a custody schedule voluntarily, a 50/50 schedule would be assigned to them by a social worker, subject to later modification by mutual agreement. Substantial failure to abide by a schedule (excluding unavoidable circumstances or minor timing issues) would be treated as emotional child abuse and subject to a criminal jury trial and criminal penalties. Allegations of neglect, or physical or sexual child abuse would be handled by the criminal justice system, not a family court.

2. Alimony is no longer appropriate for the majority of modern relationships. The traditional provider/dependent relationship is now the exception rather than the rule. If a couple wishes to adopt a traditional relationship, fine. They can enter into a dependent support agreement appropriate for however long they wish to have a provider/dependent relationship. But to allow our government to

impose dependency where there is none, and to allow lawyers to charge for expensive legal discovery investigations in every divorce case, when it may be appropriate in only a minority of such cases, is a disservice to the American people and a waste of resources.

3. The majority of our society no longer views child rearing as a full time occupation, nor the exclusive domain of one sex or the other. Today, both parents work in over 80% of married households. Child support is for children; not a reward for the parent who finagles custody away from the other parent. Again, couples can elect to adopt a more traditional plan if they so desire, but our government should not impose it on them. By decoupling the size of child support payments from the time-sharing schedule and from the size of the parents' incomes, we eliminate custody battles that are motivated by money or that endlessly pursue changes in support levels based on changes in income. Placing a child in the middle of a tug-of-war over custody and money is abusive, and our government should get out of that business.

By removing the financial motivation to acquire more custody time, we eliminate the incentive to make false accusations of abuse or neglect. As a result, true allegations of abuse or neglect will be heard, and an appropriate criminal investigation and prosecution can proceed without suspicion of false motives. Those accused of these crimes will be afforded the appropriate constitutional safeguards as with any other crime.[27]

Some critics might argue that children are entitled to the lifestyle of their parents, and that child support needs to be a percentage of income. Why? Married parents are free to teach their children the meaning and value of hard work and the pride associated with earning what they receive. Married parents are not required to hand over a percentage of their income to their children each week. If married parents wish to spoil their children with lavish gifts and luxuries (so help them) they are free to do so; but there is no law

---

27 The fate of children that result from rape or incest is a very difficult subject, and not within the scope of this book.

entitling the children of married parents to a certain lifestyle. Why then should divorced or separated parents be forced by our government to provide a lifestyle that in many instances may be far too comfortable and potentially demotivating than what the same parents would have provided while married? Food, clothing, and shelter: of course, they are necessary. If a parent wishes to be more generous, no law will stop them. But lets stop breeding a sense of entitlement into U.S. children, or into adults who view children, as Gerald Nissenbaum puts it, as "little bags of money".

Some critics might ask how poor people will be able to make the same sized child support payment as middle class or wealthy people. People living below the poverty level struggle with all types of payments, and today our government provides a modest safety net. Child support for single parents living below the poverty line would obviously need to come from the government safety net, as it already does. But a statewide, fixed child support amount would need to be so modest in size that all people living above the poverty line could afford it. Does this mean that dependent parents will not be able to buy Ferraris, or finance reality TV shows with their child support payments? Right, unless, of course, they negotiate these items into a dependent support agreement. But beware! As the old saying goes, "If you marry for money, the hours are long." The new addendum will be, "and there's no retirement plan."

4. Critics might ask, "How do you divide the assets?" You do so with an accountant or a mediator or trusted advisor, not a litigator. There are many ways to divide assets without litigation. Business partnerships often utilize buy-sell agreements and valuation formulas that eliminate the need for expensive investigations and valuations. Allegations of fraud that cannot be settled through mediation would be handled in civil court and require a full presentation of evidence before an impartial jury.

Certain critics might fear that making divorce too easy will promote the breakdown of families. That has not happened in Scandinavia. The divorce rate in Scandinavia is essentially the same as in the U.S. even though it is far easier to get divorced in Scandinavia.

For those who would prefer covenant marriage, however, it would be available. A marriage license could, optionally, be accompanied by an agreement to first take certain steps, such as participating in counseling or mediation, or subject oneself to a private hearing over "fault", prior to filing for a divorce. A few states currently offer covenant marriage as an option, but only a very small percentage of couples pursue this alternative. The vast majority of Americans do not believe that people should be stuck in a bad marriage (nor subject their children to the acrimony of a bad marriage), nor do they believe that divorce should be painful or expensive. Let's change the laws to reflect what most people believe rather than remain mired in beliefs that were appropriate in a different era.

5. Without subjective alimony or child support variables to battle over, there simply will be little to fight over or win in court. Under the current family law system, the temptation to over-litigate and/ or take a scorched earth approach is far too great, and far too harmful to the children caught in the middle of these battles.

The family law reforms that were enacted in the 1960s, 70s, and 80s were intended to provide protections to dependents during a transition from patriarchy to gender equality. Many have fought hard to achieve gender equality, and we are closer than ever before to achieving this goal. Some can debate whether gender equality is nature's way. On a historical scale, it's a rare sociological experiment. Like with racial equality, gender equality is still progressing; but showing encouraging signs. People respond well to fairness.

Many of the family laws that were enacted in the last 50 years conflict with these modern principals. These laws should be revised or terminated. Unfortunately, the laws have bred an industry that is so deeply entrenched in our government's power base, and so profitable, that it will be difficult to change the laws to better serve our current social norms. And so we are stuck in a family law time warp. Couples blame each other for the acrimony these laws create. The lawyers and judges tell the couples that they are to blame for the acrimony, and that the current system has good intentions and stands for the ideals of our people. But, despite what these individuals think or say, the current system is not good for the resolution of family law matters. The general public needs to know that they and their ex-spouses are not to blame for the horrendous outcomes so common in family court.

We acknowledge that the majority of lawyers and judges are good people who do not want to take advantage of the American public. Many of them are highly competent, but either greatly overworked or asked to perform impossible jobs. Even most family law professionals who profit from the current system do not have bad intentions; however, the culture and beliefs common within their profession cause them to become numb or blind to the adverse effects of their actions on normal, good people.

It will be difficult to motivate the entrenched professionals and legislators to dismantle a $50 billion industry. But change needs to occur, and that means calling attention to the problems. That is why we made the movie Divorce Corp., and why we have written this book. The next step is to offer solutions. The tenets proposed in this chapter can be a starting point. True reform must work for all those caught in the system. We believe the 5 tenets above will work for the vast majority of people, while not imposing hardship on those who elect to pursue more traditional alternatives. We have devoted a section of our web site, divorcecorp.com, to these and other reform initiatives. We hope that those who have an interest will visit the site and, if motivated, will help with these initiatives.

With such changes, we are confident that the turmoil that feeds our divorce and custody battles will eventually burn itself out, as it has in Scandinavia. The tinderbox will empty and the fire will disappear for lack of fuel. People will be able to transition more quickly and with less long-term damage to their relationships. Ex-spouses will be able to communicate about their children with less tension and suspicion. There will be far fewer custody battles, far less alienation, and far fewer false accusations. Extended families may be able to attend birthday parties, holiday dinners, graduations, and weddings together without acrimony or resentment. Most importantly, the children will be viewed as co-creations to be proud of, rather than as financial assets to coax away from the other side. The Scandinavian people are not perfect, but at least when it comes to marriage and divorce they have set an example that we should not ignore. We like to be leaders in America. We like to do things our own way, and we sometimes set a good example for the world. But the adversarial courts of equity that we inherited from the British no longer work for family matters. Together we can, and should, change that for the common good.

Acknowledgments

I am very fortunate to have engaged James Scurlock in this endeavor. James conducted many of the interviews used in the movie, Divorce Corp. James is known for directing the movie, *Maxed Out*, as well as for authoring the companion book, *Maxed Out*. He also authored the highly successful book *King Larry*. Without James, this book would not have been nearly as engaging or interesting. James' ability to capture the human perspective made this book far more relatable than I could have managed. Divorce can be a depressing topic, and the intricacies of family law are nearly impossible to understand. Fortunately, James' ability to weave the emotional considerations together with the facts greatly enhanced this work, and his perceptive insights helped bridge many of the concepts into a coherent story. I hope to work together with James on future projects, and anticipate more great things from him.

Philip Sternberg has been an inspiration, for both the movie and the book. Philip may not intend to be a perfectionist, but if he is not one, then they do not exist. His relentless pursuit of high quality work product has kept me on track for much longer than my own impatience would have allowed. While he was dubious about the subject matter when I first suggested the topic of divorce, he quickly recognized the power of the tragic stories that were all too common for those who have been through the family court system. As a veteran of the entertainment business, he saw that this topic could be developed into an engaging movie and an informative book.

Blake Harjes, the primary editor of the movie, also provided great insight and research on the subjects of divorce and child custody. Being merely a first-time director, I naively thought than an editor was someone who was good at making cuts and splices. I did not realize how much Blake would eventually contribute to the telling of the story and unveiling the facts behind it, much of which was also used in the book.

Michael McIrvin provided an excellent copy edit for this book. Not only did he fix some poor grammar and loose references, he questioned some of the concepts and conclusions in ways that helped improve the meaning.

I want to thank David Hoffman, Doug Kepanis, Forrest Mosten and Katherine Porter for reading the manuscript at an early stage. The joke goes, "Why do 99% of the lawyers ruin it for the rest of them?" Well, it's not politically correct to say that anyone is in the 1% any more; so let's just say that these folks are on the good side of the practice of law. They have all recognized a role for compassion and humanity in the practice of law and have chosen approaches that are far more holistic than that practiced by a majority of their colleagues. Thank you for your vision!

Meagan Piker has been incredibly helpful in taking an early look at the manuscript and in helping facilitate many of the communications and interactions that are absolutely necessary to accomplish the writing and marketing of a book.

I'd like to thank Andrew Firmin, Alexey Novoradosky, Amber Dozier, Woody Thompson, and Alison Kane for helping to sort out the intricacies of book publishing and distribution, especially in today's e-world, and for helping me stay focused. The publishing industry is changing rapidly. Hopefully the Amazon/Apple oligopoly will give way to other, more competitive forms of distribution and the hard work that these people did in getting this book completed and distributed will be less time consuming in the future.

And then there is an extremely long list of people who have helped in many direct and indirect ways. If I were to attempt to name them all, I would undoubtedly forget a few and forever feel sorry. Therefore, I will only mention a few. But no doubt, I do appreciate the impact that so many people had on me and on this endeavor. I appreciate the support that my children Kristina, Andrew, and Daniel (now all very successful adults) have shown toward the creation of the movie and the book. I am pleased to say that although they lived through some of the acrimony that the family courts bring out in parents, they managed to stay above the fray, and are actually able to discuss various topics in the movie and book with me without getting dragged back to a less happy time. Three cheers for the benefits of settling the divorce, at least, out of court! And special thanks to Daniel for keeping his minor's counsel under control – if you can manage a lawyer whose holding a blank check, Dan, you can manage anyone ☺. I also want to thank my many friends, especially Hanna Mauritzson, for understanding how time consuming making a movie and writing a book can be. If one can find happiness without the interference of a dysfunctional government, why get them involved? I also want to thank many of my friends who have been married and divorced, and shared some of their painful stories with me, especially Gordon Wangers, Peter Ellman, Dave Zeiger, Dwight Dubois, and Michael Scally. And for my single friends, like Chris McClure and Bryan Touhey, who have said that Divorce Corp has scared the daylights out of them, well, hopefully we'll get some decent legislation passed and you will be able to consider marriage sometime before you get too old to say "I do". And for my married friends: congratulations. You beat the odds!

Lastly to the victims depicted in our movie and book, my heart goes out to you. The system wronged you. Evil and greedy people with power took advantage of you. I don't know if I could have survived what you have been through. You are all very brave for telling your stories to the public. Hopefully this exposure will help uncover injustice and oust some of the tyrants of family court. I hope that we can join together with others in the reform movement going forward and bring about meaningful change.